Contents

KU-647-380

CD track list

an

ople

N EDITION

by Bivon

by Terry Doyle

BBC Active, an imprint of Educational Publishers LLP, part of the Pearson Education Group
Edinburgh Gate, Harlow
Essex CM20 2JE
England

First published 1980. Revised edition published 1995. New edition published 2006. Reprinted 2006, 2007
© BBC Worldwide Ltd. 2006

ISBN 978-0-563-51974-4

Cover designed by Gary Day-Ellison
Cover photograph: © culliganphoto/ Alamy
Designer: Giles Davies
TV producer: Terry Doyle
Audio producer (first edition): Alan Wilding
Audio producer (new edition): Martin Williamson, Prolingua Productions
Project manager (first edition): Phoenix Publishing Services
Editorial consultant: Sue Purcell
Project editor (new edition): Melanie Kramers
Senior production controller (new edition): Man Fai Lau

Photo credits
Corbis European Living (vol. 117) page 130 both, Wade Eakle/ Lonely Planet Images page 15 left; Nikolai Ignatiev/ Network pages 35 top, 49, 78 bottom, 156 and 163, Bourcat/Rapho/ Network page 73, Witold Krassowski/ Network page 53, Paul Lowe/ Network page 115, Dod Miller/ Network page 87 right; Novosti (London) pages 21 bottom, 22 right, 44 bottom, 60, 64, 86 all, 96 all; Photodisc/ World Landmarks and Travel page 147, Russia and Eastern Images pages 29 centre right, 97 and 105 top; SCRSS Photo Library pages 23 bottom, 37 top, 79 left, 80 top, 101 all, 102 all, Chris Cambray/ SCRSS pages 28 right and 106 left, Ray Mitchell/ SCRSS pages 110 and 137 David Toase/ SCRSS page 164. The remaining photographs were supplied by the authors, Terry Doyle and Mary Sprent. Every effort has been made to trace all copyright holders, but the publisher would like to apologise should there have been any errors or omissions.

Printed and bound in China   CTPSC/03
The Publisher's policy is to use paper manufactured from sustainable forests.

Also available: CD pack (two audio CDs) ISBN 978-0-563-51975-1

About the authors

Terry Culhane, former lecturer at the University of Essex, was Language Advisor for the BBC television series *Russian Language and People*, and wrote the original book to accompany the series. The course gives learners an elementary knowledge of Russian and of Russia, with an emphasis on information gathering from realistic and authentic sources. Terry Culhane is also the author of many articles and papers on language teaching methodology and language testing.

Dr Roy Bivon was Lecturer in charge of Russian Language at the University of East Anglia and later at the University of Essex. For many years he ran a summer course for students of Russian and was involved in Adult Education. He was co-author, with Terry Culhane, of the 1995 edition of *Russian Language and People*, and has written a number of books on Russian Grammar and Linguistics, including a beginners' course for university students, *The Russian Verb* and *Element Order in Russian*. He travels regularly to Russia, both in his work for RLUS, an educational charity that arranges language courses in Russia for undergraduates, and for his own travel language company.

Introduction

The present course is the second update of *Russian Language and People*. The first update of the original (1980) course was published in 1995, after the fall of the Soviet Union and the movement from communism to a free-market economy. Many things have changed in the last twenty-five years, and we have tried to reflect this in the course. Since the publication of the second edition in 1995, the Russian economy has stabilised, and this has helped us to provide more accurate information for the visitor to Russia.

The course is designed to provide a self-taught introduction to the Russian language and Russian society. Based mainly on skills of *understanding* rather than *speaking*, it is also ideal for use in classes.

We have had three aims in mind in writing the course. Firstly, we hope to provide a stimulus for future study, by giving you some insight into Russia and a painless and enjoyable introduction to the language. Secondly, we hope to provide something of immediate practical use to the learner who wishes to visit Russia for business or pleasure, by using authentic materials in the course, and by using many language exercises based on the sort of situations that you might typically find in a Russian environment. Timetables, newspapers, menus, signs, maps, have all been used to this end. Thirdly, we want the course to be accessible to the average person who does not have a particular 'gift for languages'. The course is largely based on skills of understanding, and many of the exercises, even in the later units of the course, are accessible to any student with a knowledge of the alphabet and a minimal amount of grammar.

The two CDs, which have been re-edited and supplemented by additional recorded material, are an integral part of the course, and contain material for use in each lesson. Exercises recorded on the CDs are marked 💿.

The course has 20 units, each of which is divided into sections, as follows:

ALPHABET (UNITS 1–5)

The alphabet is taught a few letters at a time, using simple words recorded on the CDs, many of which are similar to English words, and all of which are in current use in everyday Russian. You will later be taught to recognise Russian script and Russian handwriting.

LIFE IN RUSSIA

Each unit has a section devoted to some aspect of Russian life, and there are language exercises based on this, preparing you for linguistic survival in these situations.

LANGUAGE INFORMATION

These sections contain grammatical and other information about language, expressed in a concise way. If you wish to study without the help of grammar feel free to skip these sections.

LOOKING AT WORDS

Word-building is an important and fascinating aspect of the learning of Russian, and a great help in understanding Russian vocabulary. It is introduced gradually.

A SITUATION TO REMEMBER

A typical 'situation setting' containing useful phrases which acts as an aide-memoire for the learner. This can be used for basic oral practice as well as revision purposes. It contains some role-play and other situations which could be used in the classroom to develop speaking skills.

WHAT YOU KNOW

A summary of the main points covered in the unit.

KEY WORDS

Contains the most useful vocabulary in each unit. The words which occur here also appear in the vocabulary at the back of the book.

Units 5, 10, 15 and 20 are mainly concerned with the revision of the preceding four units, and contain exercises for revision purposes.

At the back of the book are the following reference sections:

- A transliteration and pronunciation guide
- A summary of the grammar contained in the course
- Scripts of all recorded material not printed in the units
- An answer key to the exercises
- A complete Russian-English vocabulary, containing all the words used in the course, together with the number of the unit in which they occur.

● TIPS FOR THE STUDENT

1 Go at your own pace.

2 Don't be afraid of pausing the CD and going back over an exercise, or stopping in between items in an exercise if you need more time.

3 Listen carefully to the recorded material and try and base your pronunciation on what you hear, rather than what you think it should be from your reading of the words.

4 Don't expect to understand every word or grammatical form that you meet. If, for example, you ask your way to somewhere, the reply you receive is likely to contain words and expressions that you do not understand in their entirety. This reply, however, will contain some key words and expressions, the understanding of which will enable you to get to your destination. It is the object of this course to teach you simple ways of expressing yourself in Russian, and provide you with enough gist understanding of language to decode more complex spoken and written Russian by selecting the essential, relevant items.

5 Don't be put off if you don't completely understand a grammatical explanation. You may find that it falls into place later. In any case, you'll find that you are able to do exercises later in the course without necessarily understanding absolutely everything that has gone before.

6 In some of the early units examples of written Russian are given. Writing exercises are provided in Units 11–16 for learners who wish to start writing Russian.

7 When revising, think in terms of what to say or do in a given situation. Use the *Situation to remember* section to help you with your oral practice and do not be afraid of saying things out loud – in private, of course! Make use of the checklists in Units 5, 10, 15 and 20.

We sincerely hope that you will enjoy the experience of learning Russian with *Russian Language and People*.

Getting started

NOMER ODIN

нómер одúн

Asking questions

Saying *yes please* and *no thank you*

Saying *hello* and *goodbye*

● The Russian alphabet

Introduction

The Russian alphabet is called Cyrillic after the Greek missionary St Cyril, who, along with his brother St Methodius, was said to have invented it in the late 9th century in order to write down the Gospels for the peoples around the area we now know as Moravia, in the Czech Republic.

Some letters are derived from Latin letters, others from Greek and some from Hebrew. Apart from Russian, versions of the Cyrillic alphabet are used for some other Slavonic languages, including Bulgarian, Serbian, and Ukrainian. Slavonic languages such as Polish and Czech use the Roman alphabet.

Once you have mastered the sound of a Russian letter, it usually stays the same, and in this respect Russian is much more 'logical' than English.

We shall introduce the letters a few at a time over the first five units. When there is a word which contains letters you have not met, we shall print it in small capitals. The stressed syllable will be indicated with an accent – SPASÍBO (meaning *thank you*). From Unit 5 onwards we shall write everything in Russian characters.

Alphabet 1

There is a group of letters which look and sound very much like their English counterparts. Together they form a word – **KOMÉTA**, which means what you would expect it to. All the sounds of these letters are very close to English, but the **E** is pronounced 'ye' and the **T** is pronounced with the tongue touching the back of the teeth, with the teeth slightly apart.

С П Р И Н В

The new letters have sounds very much like English sounds, but they look a little different.

С sounds like English 's'.
П sounds like English 'p'. This comes from the Greek letter 'pi', often used in mathematical formulae.
Р sounds like a Scottish 'r'. Please be careful: in English we often do not pronounce the letter 'r'; in Russian it is *always* pronounced.
И is pronounced 'ee'.
Н is like English 'n'.
В is like English 'v'.

All the letters explained in this unit are picked out in bold in the following list:

а б **в** г д **е** ё ж з **и** й к л м **н** о **п р с т** у ф х ц ч ш щ ъ ы ь э ю я

The words chosen below are the sort of words you might already know because of their similarity to English. All of them are common words in everyday use in Russia. They are recorded on your CD.

Notice that we have put stress marks (´) on the words. The part of the word under the stress is pronounced more strongly than the rest of the word, and Russian stress is heavier than English. It may also occur on a different part of the word than you might expect from the English, as in words 5, 7, 11, 12, 15, 16. Note this as you go along. Try to get the stress right from the very start.

1 комéта ☐		8 óпера ☐		15 ресторáн ☐	
2 аппарáт ☐		9 спорт ☐		16 оркéстр ☐	
3 самовáр ☐		10 парк ☐		17 áвиа ☐	
4 кácca ☐		11 таксú ☐		18 мáрка ☐	
5 теáтр ☐		12 пианúст ☐		19 нет ☐	
6 áтом ☐		13 винó ☐		20 стоп ☐	
7 метрó ☐		14 Москвá ☐		21 пáспорт ☐	

- **АППАРА́Т** is any kind of apparatus, also commonly used to mean *a camera*, short for FOTO**АППАРА́Т.**

- **САМОВА́Р** is a device traditionally used by Russians to heat water to make tea. Russians used to drink tea from a prettily decorated **СТАКА́Н** (*glass*), but now commonly use china mugs.

- **КА́ССА** is where you buy a ticket for the theatre or pay for your entrance into a museum or art gallery.
- **ТЕА́ТР** is a theatre. Notice that the **Е** and **А** are pronounced separately, and the **Р** is rolled.
- **МОСКВА́** *Moscow* will probably be the first word you see in big letters when you fly into Moscow. Note where the stress is, resulting in the **О** being pronounced almost as an 'a'.
- **О́ПЕРА**, **СПОРТ**, **ПАРК** are all good examples of rolled 'r' in Russian.

- **А́ВИА** means *airmail*. You will see it printed on envelopes.

- **МА́РКА** is a stamp. Russians love collecting them.
- **ПА́СПОРТ** can be a passport for travelling abroad, as well as a document that Russians carry at all times to prove who they are. Once again, don't forget to pronounce the 'r'.

You will probably have noticed that most Russian capital letters are either very similar to the small letters: **Вв, Пп**, or as you'd expect them to be written: **Аа, Ее**.

. . . .

⚙ EXERCISE 1

Look at the list of words numbered 1–21 on the previous page.

First time round listen to the recording and repeat the word.

Second time round, you say the word after you hear the number and check it with the CD. If you are satisfied with your attempt, put a tick in the box. If not, try again.

. . . .

EXERCISE 2

1 What would you do here?

2 What would you put in this?

3 What happens here?

4 What's the name of this metro station on the main street in St Petersburg?

5 What would you wait for here?

6 What would you make with this?

● Language information

A, an, the

There is no word for *a* in Russian, and no word for *the*. This makes things simpler!

Éто **теáтр** means *This is **a** theatre* or *This is **the** theatre*.
Уа **пианúст** means *I am **a** pianist* or *I am **the** pianist*.
Он таксúст means *He is **a** taxi driver* or *He is **the** taxi driver*.

Verb *to be*

You will also notice that you do not use the verb *to be* in the present tense. Even simpler! You are literally saying: *This theatre, I pianist, He taxi driver*.

What is, Who is

Sнто éто? means *What is this?*
Кто éто? means *Who is this?* and *Who is it?*

⊙ EXERCISE 3

Listen to the CD and look at the pictures below.
You will be asked Sнто éто? *What is this?* or Кто éто? *Who is this?* You reply Éто ...
The correct answer will then be given.
The pictures are numbered to help you.
Tick the box when you are satisfied with your answer.
If you are not sure what to do, play the recording through. For the first one you will hear **нóмер** odín, *number one*, Sнто éто? You reply Éто **таксú**, and you hear the correct answer Éто **таксú**.

1 ☐   4 ☐   7 ☐   10 ☐
2 ☐   5 ☐   8 ☐
3 ☐   6 ☐   9 ☐

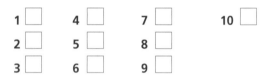

Asking questions

You can change a statement into a question by making your voice go up on the word you are questioning. Compare a statement:

Э́то **ма́ма**.

with a question: Э́то **ма́ма**?

⊙ EXERCISE 4

Listen to the CD.
Now you should try to ask questions with э́то and give replies.
Make sure that in the question your voice goes up on the word you are questioning. Repeat the question and reply in the gaps provided.

Saying *yes, no, not*

DA means *yes*, **нет** means *no*. The word **не** means *not*. Notice that Russian has the **т** on the Russian for *no*, and no **т** on the Russian for *not*. All you have to do is to add **не** to an ordinary sentence to make it negative:

Э́то **па́па**. *This is dad.*
Э́то **не па́па**, Э́то **ма́ма**.
This is not dad, this is mum.

⊙ EXERCISE 5

Look at the pictures in Exercise 3 and listen to the CD. This exercise requires negative answers.
You will be asked Э́то ...? (*Is this a ...?*)
You should answer **Нет**, Э́то **не ...**
(*No, it's not a ...*) Э́то ... (*It's a ...*)
You will then be given the correct answer.
Thus the first one would be as follows:
но́мер ODÍN, number one, Э́то **па́па**?
You should reply **Нет**, Э́то **не па́па**, Э́то **такси́**.

⊙ EXERCISE 6

Replay Exercise 5.
In each example the wrong object or person is identified in the first part.
You should find the object or person identified and place the number in the box. Thus, in the first example you would hear **но́мер** ODÍN, number one, Э́то **па́па**?
You find the picture of **па́па** and put the number in the box. This is done for you. Notice that the examples are intentionally unrealistic!

1 [7]	4 ☐	7 ☐	10 ☐
2 ☐	5 ☐	8 ☐	
3 ☐	6 ☐	9 ☐	

EXERCISE 7

Here is a jumbled list of the words indicated by the pictures.
Place the number of the appropriate picture in the box at the side of each word. The first one is done for you.
We have left the stress marks off the words. See if you can put them in without looking at the original list.

1	оркéстр	[10]	6	парк	☐
2	вино	☐	7	мама	☐
3	папа	☐	8	метро	☐
4	такси	☐	9	пианист	☐
5	ресторан	☐	10	театр	☐

Going by taxi

⊙**EXERCISE 8**

Here is a recording of a short conversation between a taxi driver and some people who have just called him to their flat. You won't understand all the conversation, but this doesn't matter. Listen for the words for:

hello	ZDRÁSTVUYTE
please	POZHÁLSTA
thank you	SPASÍBO
good	KHOROSHÓ
goodbye	DO SVIDÁNIYA

Where are the people going to?

● Looking at words

Peter the Great founded St Petersburg in 1703 as 'a window on the West'. Since that time the Russian language has borrowed many words from Western European languages. This process was continued during the time of Catherine the Great (1729–1796), when it was considered sophisticated by Russian courtiers to speak French. In recent times English has become the most commonly used foreign language and many English words are now used in Russian. Many advertisements now occur in a mixture of English and Russian.

EXERCISE 9

Look at the following pictures. Answer the question which follows each picture. Don't expect to understand every word.

2   What would you drink here?

3   This is an advert for a bank. What is its name?

4   This is a poster for a Mozart and Beethoven concert. What is the conductor's name?

5   What would you find if you followed the arrow to the left?

1   What would you go to see here?

A situation to remember

Identifying things

Here is a short conversation in which one person asks the other what an object is.

A: ZDRÁSTVUYTE!
B: ZDRÁSTVUYTE!
A: SHTO ÉTO?
B: ÉTO **винó**.
A: SPASÍBO. DO SVIDÁNIYA!
B: DO SVIDÁNIYA!

Now you ask your partner about:

1 a restaurant
2 a theatre
3 Moscow
4 the underground
5 a stamp
Play both parts, if necessary.

You can then vary the conversation by asking:

– ÉTO **винó**? and getting a reply:
– **Нет**, ÉTO **не винó**, ÉTO **пи́во** (*beer*).

● Playing with words

A number of the words you have met are concealed in the square below. See if you can find them and fill in the blanks on the right. You can move in any direction, sometimes changing direction in the middle of a word, and the last letter of a word starts the next word. You may use the same letter more than once. Start in the top left-hand corner.

С	И	Н	Е	Р
П	Н	Е	Т	Е
О	Т	А	С	И
Р	Е	К	Р	Т
Т	С	И	П	О

1 С _ _ _ _
2 Т _ _ _ _
3 Р _ _ _ _ _ _
4 Н _ _
5 Т _ _ _ _

WHAT YOU KNOW

Saying *hello, goodbye, please* and *thank you*

hello	ZDRÁSTVUYTE
please	POZHÁLSTA
thank you	SPASÍBO
goodbye	DO SVIDÁNIYA

Identifying things and people

What is this (it)?	SHTO ÉTO?
Who is this (it)?	**Кто** ÉTO?
Is this (it) dad?	ÉTO **па́па**?

Understanding the replies

This (It) is dad.	ÉTO **па́па**.

Agreeing and disagreeing

yes	DA
no	**нет**
This (It) is dad.	ÉTO **па́па**.
This (It) isn't dad.	ÉTO **не па́па**.

KEY VOCABULARY

винó	wine
пи́во	beer
кто	who
ма́ма	mother, mum
Москва́	Moscow
нет	no
он	he
па́па	father, dad
ресторáн	restaurant
теáтр	theatre

DA	yes
DO SVIDÁNIYA	goodbye
ÉTO	this, it
KHOROSHÓ	good
POZHÁLSTA	please
SHTO	what
SPASÍBO	thank you
YA	I
ZDRÁSTVUYTE	hello

Where is? How is?

NOMER DVA

Asking where
something is

Meeting somebody
for the first time

Asking someone
their name and
how they are

● Alphabet 2

Here are the new letters for this unit:

З Д Л У Й

The letters you have met so far are picked out in the
following list:

а б в **г** **д** **е** ё ж **з** и **й** к **л** м н о п р с т **у** ф
х ц ч ш щ ъ ы ь э ю я

So by the end of this unit you will already know half the
letters!

All of the letters have sounds similar to English sounds.

З is similar to the English 'z'.
Д is similar to the English 'd'.
Л is the Russian version of the English 'l': listen carefully
to the way it is pronounced in words 3–6 on the next page.
У is very like 'oo' in *mood*.
Й is like 'y' in *boy*.

Don't forget the stress! It is sometimes a good idea to exaggerate
the stress when pronouncing Russian. It is stronger than in
English and tends to affect the pronunciation of the unstressed
vowels in a word. Thus the 'o' in the first syllable of **КОМЕ́ТА**,
the first word you learned in Unit 1, is pronounced almost like an
'a', whereas **МЕТРО́** sounds a bit like *mitro*.

Always try and get your pronunciation as close as possible to that
on the CD, and make a habit of practising listening and repeating
a little without the aid of the book to attune your ears to the stress
patterns of Russian.

Here are some words containing the letters from Units 1 and 2.

1 вода́ ☐	9 пе́пси ☐	17 апте́ка ☐
2 во́дка ☐	10 пра́вда ☐	18 Марс ☐
3 лимона́д ☐	11 крокоди́л ☐	19 кио́ск ☐
4 литр ☐	12 Кавка́з ☐	20 Толсто́й ☐
5 кило́ ☐	13 зоопа́рк ☐	21 Война́ и мир ☐
6 киломе́тр ☐	14 дом ☐	22 росси́йский ☐
7 университе́т ☐	15 да́та ☐	23 Украи́на ☐
8 Ко́ка Ко́ла ☐	16 квас ☐	24 здра́вствуйте ☐

- **ВОДА́** (*water*) and **ВО́ДКА** look very much alike, but do not mistake one for the other! The two words have the same root, **ВОД-**, and **-КА** here denotes something small that is endearing! It is important to work out what different parts of a word mean: you can often guess the meaning of a word you have never heard before.
- **КО́КА КО́ЛА** and its 'rival' **ПЕ́ПСИ** are about as popular in Russia as they are elsewhere in the world.
- **ПРА́ВДА** means *truth*. Before the fall of **КОММУНИ́ЗМ**, it was the name of the main daily newspaper, the circulation of which dropped considerably with the onset of **КАПИТАЛИ́ЗМ**. **Пра́вда?** is also used as a question meaning *Is that so?* or *Really?*
- **КРОКОДИ́Л** – you should be able to guess the meaning of this word.

Mt. Elbrus, The Caucasus

- **КАВКА́З**, the Caucasus, is the range of mountains to the south of Russia. Its highest point is Mount Elbrus, at 5633m. Probably the most spectacular in the range is Mount Kazbek.
- **ДОМ** literally means *house* or *home*, and in this sense **ДО́МА** can be used to mean *at home*. It is also used to refer to a large block or apartment building.
- **КВАС** is a traditional Russian drink made of fermented black bread. It is very slightly alcoholic.
- **АПТЕ́КА** is a chemist's. Compare the English *apothecary*.

- **МАРС** is not only the planet, but also the name of the chocolate bar.
- **ТОЛСТО́Й** is the famous Russian author of **ВОЙНА́ И МИР**, *War and Peace*.
- **РОССИ́ЙСКИЙ** has come to mean *belonging to the country of Russia*. The usual word for Russian is **ру́сский**, and *in Russian* is **по-ру́сски** – note the small letters. If you want to ask what a word is in Russian, you say: **Как по-ру́сски ...** (*What is the Russian for ...*).
- **УКРАИ́НА**, Ukraine, one of Russia's largest neighbours.
- **ЗДРА́ВСТВУЙТЕ** is Russian for *hello*. If you have difficulty pronouncing all the letters, then so do the Russians! They often shorten it to ZDRÁSTYE.

☉EXERCISE 1

Look at the list of words numbered 1–24 on the previous page.

First time round listen to the recording and repeat the word.

Second time round, you say the word after you hear the number and check it with the CD. If you are satisfied with your attempt, put a tick in the box. If not, repeat your attempt.

☉EXERCISE 2

Now we're going to mix up the words.

Look at the list of words numbered 1–24 on the previous page.

Find the number of the word that has just been read.

Place it in the appropriate box below.

Example

You hear **но́мер оди́н**, *number one*, **университе́т**, you find **университе́т** in the list and place 7 in the box next to number one.

1	7	6	
2		7	
3		8	
4		9	
5		10	

EXERCISE 3

Here are some of the words written in the Roman alphabet. Identify them by their original numbers, using the boxes provided. The first one is done for you.

1	LIMONÁD	3	6	KAVKÁZ	
2	KILÓ		7	ZOOPÁRK	
3	PÉPSI		8	VÓDKA	
4	PRÁVDA		9	VODÁ	
5	KROKODÍL		10	KILOMÉTR	

● Language information

ОН, ОНА, ОНО, ОНИ

You will have noticed that nouns have different endings. Nouns like **лимона́д**, **Кавка́з**, **крокоди́л** may be referred to by **ОН** (*he, it*). Those ending in **-А** (**пра́вда**, **во́дка**, **Москва́**) are usually referred to by **ОНА́** (*she, it*). **Па́па**, and other nouns referring to males, would be **ОН**. Nouns ending in **-О** or **-Е** (**вино́**, **кило́**) are referred to by **ОНО́** (*it*). Plural nouns are always referred to by **ОНИ́** (*they*).

EXERCISE 4

Look at the picture below.

The question each time is *Where is ...?* (GDE ...?)

The answer is **Вот он**, **Вот она́** or **Вот оно́**. You choose which of these it is, underline it, then write the number on the correct object in the picture. The first one is done for you.

1	Gde оркéстр?	<u>Вот он.</u>	Вот онá.	Вот онó.
2	Gde пáпа?	Вот он.	Вот онá.	Вот онó.
3	Gde мáма?	Вот он.	Вот онá.	Вот онó.
4	Gde пианúст?	Вот он.	Вот онá.	Вот онó.
5	Gde стол?	Вот он.	Вот онá.	Вот онó.
6	Gde вóдка?	Вот он.	Вот онá.	Вот онó.
7	Gde водá?	Вот он.	Вот онá.	Вот онó.
8	Gde винó?	Вот он.	Вот онá.	Вот онó.
9	Gde пúво?	Вот он.	Вот онá.	Вот онó.

. . . .

☺EXERCISE 5

On your recording is a series of questions asking you where objects are.

Supply the answers **Вот он**, **Вот онá** or **Вот онó**.

A space is provided on the recording for your answer and then the correct answer is given.

The boxes below are for you to tick your answers, if you are satisfied with your response. If not, try again.

1	☐	6	☐
2	☐	7	☐
3	☐	8	☐
4	☐	9	☐
5	☐	10	☐

. . . .

In, on, at

The nouns you have met up to now have been in the *nominative case*, which is the case you will find in a dictionary.

If you want to answer the question GDE STUDÉNT? with the response that he is in or at the university, **университéт**, you might reply **Он <u>в университéте</u>**.

Look at the picture in Exercise 4 above. You will see **Мáма и пáпа <u>в ресторáне</u>**. You will see **стол**, *a table*, and various things **<u>на столé</u>** (*on the table*). This is the *prepositional case*, sometimes called the *locative case* because it is used after **в** (*in*) and **на** (*on*) when we want to indicate where something is located.

The prepositional case normally ends in **-е**:

ресторáн	в ресторáн**е**
аптéка	в аптéк**е**

Some nouns, especially foreign ones, e.g. **таксú**, **кинó** (*cinema*), **метрó**, do not change at all.

таксú	в таксú
кинó	в кинó
метрó	на метрó

As you might expect, the prepositional is often used with places. Note that **на** occurs with some words where you might expect **в**. Sometimes you will see **и** as the ending of the prepositional case.

. . . .

EXERCISE 6

See if you can make out the following.

Торóнто в Канáде
Стадиóн «Динáмо» в Москвé
Ивáн в Лóндоне
Мадрúд в Испáнии
Нúна на Кавкáзе
Кúев в Украúне

. . . .

● Looking at words

Russian will often change the ending to indicate that a person is female:

СТУДÉНТ   *a male student*
СТУДÉНТКА *a female student*

Sometimes Russian will adopt a foreign word and then change it, as in the case of **СТУДÉНТ**. This sometimes leads to some strange words. **СПОРТСМÉН** means a sportsman, in the sense of someone who participates in sport. The meaning of **СПОРТСМÉНКА** should be obvious. **РЕКОРДСМÉНКА** is a little less obvious: it means a female record holder.

A situation to remember (1)

Introducing someone

You are introducing Viktor to your parents.

YOU:	**Мáма**, ÉTO **Вúктор**.
MAMA:	ZDRÁSTVUYTE, ÓCHEN' **рáда**.
	Hello, very pleased to meet you.
VIKTOR:	ZDRÁSTVUYTE, ÓCHEN' **рад**.
YOU:	**Пáпа**, ÉTO **Вúктор**.
PAPA:	ZDRÁSTVUYTE, ÓCHEN' **рад**.
VIKTOR:	ZDRÁSTVUYTE, ÓCHEN' **рад**.

You might want to ask your friend (or someone else!) some questions. Here are some which involve the word **как** (*how*):

☉ EXERCISE 7

On your recording you will hear another 'meeting' dialogue. Listen carefully for the expressions in the table at the bottom of this page, and underline as many as you can in the table and in the dialogue in *A situation to remember (1)*.

EXERCISE 8

Read through the following conversations and then make up some of your own.

Как вас зовýт?	Как делá, Нúна?
MENYÁ зовýт	NICHEVÓ.
Владúмир.	А как дóма?
А как вас зовýт?	PLÓKHO.
Áнна Петрóвна.	
Как делá, Вúктор?	Как дóма?
SPASÍBO, KHOROSHÓ.	KHOROSHÓ.
А как мáма?	А как Антóн?
NICHEVÓ.	NICHEVÓ, SPASÍBO.

Как does not have to be part of a question. It may sometimes be used as part of an exclamation, as follows:

Как PRIYÁTNO ZDES'!   *How pleasant it is here!*
Как ZDES' KHOROSHÓ! *How good it is here!*

Question		Answer	
Как вас зовýт?	*What is your name?* (lit. how do they call you?)	Вúктор.	*Viktor.*
		MENYÁ зовýт Вúктор.	*My name is Viktor.*
Как делá?	*How are things?*	SPASÍBO, KHOROSHÓ.	*Fine, thank you.*
Как дóма?	*How are things at home?*	*or* NICHEVÓ.	*OK.*
Как мáма?	*How's your mum?*		
И пáпа?	*And your dad?*	*or* PLÓKHO.	*Terrible (Lit. bad)*

Notice how it can take many more words in English to express an idea!

If you have the chance, practise this conversation with someone else. If you are on your own, remember the situation and the expressions you would use in it. There are some suggestions in the Key at the back of the book.

You meet your neighbour **Ива́н** in the park (**в па́рке**).
What do you say when you first meet?
He asks you how your mother (VÁSHA MÁMA) is.
You thank him, say she is well and ask after **Ли́за**, his sister (**сестра́**).
You ask if she is at home, and he says no, she is in **Ки́ев**. She is a student at the university. You say how nice it is in the park, and your friend agrees.

● Playing with words

Word square 1

Here is another word square, slightly larger than the last one, and containing more words. The rules are the same as before. See how many words you can find, starting at the top left-hand corner. The last letter of a word starts the next one and letters may be used more than once. If you find you're at a 'dead-end', try a different route.

Word square 2

You may have noticed that there are a few words for drink in this lesson. Everyone knows the Russian word **ВО́ДКА**. The Russian for *beer* is **ПИ́ВО**. See how many more you can find hidden in the square below. This time all the words are in straight lines; they may be in any direction and may start anywhere. There are one or two you will have to guess, but they are very like English words, so it is not too difficult.

К	А	К	А	О	П	Л
О	Л	В	О	Т	У	И
Р	И	А	Л	О	С	М
С	К	С	П	И	В	О
Е	С	В	И	Н	О	Н
В	И	Н	Т	О	Д	А
Л	В	О	Д	К	А	Д

К	Н	Е	Т	А	Р
А	Р	А	П	А	К
В	О	Т	П	М	И
К	Т	О	Р	А	Н
А	О	С	Е	П	О
З	О	Е	Р	Е	М

1 _ _ _ _ _ _
2 _ _ _ _ _ _ _
3 _ _ _ _
4 _ _ _ _ _
5 _ _ _ _ _ _
6 _ _ _ _ _
7 _ _ _ _ _ _ _ _
8 _ _ _ _ _

19

WHAT YOU KNOW

Asking where something is

GDE ...?	ТЕА́ТР	ОН
	КА́ССА	ОНА́
	МЕТРО́	ОНО́

Saying where something is

ВОТ	ОН	НА СТОЛЕ́
	ОНА́	В ПА́РКЕ
	ОНО́	В РЕСТОРА́НЕ

Asking after someone's health

| КАК | ДЕЛА́? |
| | МА́МА? |

Asking/Giving one's name

| КАК | ВАС ЗОВУ́Т? |

MENYÁ ЗОВУ́Т ...

Saying how nice it is

| КАК | PRIYÁTNO! |
| | KHOROSHÓ! |

KEY VOCABULARY

апте́ка	chemist
вода́	water
во́дка	vodka
да́та	date
дом	house
до́ма	at home
здра́вствуйте	hello
зоопа́рк	zoo
кило́	kilo
киломе́тр	kilometre
кино́	cinema
кио́ск	kiosk
литр	litre
метро́	metro
пра́вда	truth, is it true?
рад	pleased
росси́йский	Russian
стол	table
такси́	taxi
ÓCHEN'	very
NICHEVÓ	OK
PLÓKHO	terrible, bad

20

Asking the way

Finding out when a place is open

Finding your way around

NÓMER TRI

● Alphabet 3

There are five new letters in this unit:

Х Ю Б Ф Ь

The letters you have met so far are picked out in the following list:

а **б** в г д е ё ж з и й к л м н о п р с т **ф**
х ц ч ш щ ъ ы **ь** э **ю** я

Х is pronounced like 'ch' in Scottish *loch*. It is the first
    letter in **хоккéй** (*ice-hockey*).

Ю is like 'yew'.

Б sounds like the English 'b'.

Ф sounds like the English 'f'.

Ь is called 'soft sign'. It does not have a sound of its own,
    but 'softens' the sound before it. Listen carefully and see
    if you can hear what happens when it occurs.

1 футбóл ☐		10 бюрó ☐		19 Динáмо ☐		
2 клуб ☐		11 фóто ☐		20 стадиóн ☐		
3 вход ☐		12 Кремль ☐		21 Спартáк ☐		
4 костю́м ☐		13 фильм ☐		22 Торпéдо ☐		
5 меню́ ☐		14 ю́мор ☐		23 Локомоти́в ☐		
6 перехóд ☐		15 автóбус ☐		24 ремóнт ☐		
7 телефóн ☐		16 буфéт ☐		25 администрáтор ☐		
8 бульóн ☐		17 узбéк ☐		26 хоккéй ☐		
9 кафé ☐		18 кли́мат ☐		27 кинó ☐		

- Russians are very fond of **ФУТБÓЛ**. There are several football grounds in Moscow, some shared by two or more teams. **Стадиóн «Динáмо»** (*Dynamo Stadium*) is a big sports complex. Apart from **ДИНÁМО**, common names for football teams include: **ЛОКОМОТИ́В**, the railway workers' team, **ЗЕНИ́Т**, **СПАРТÁК** and **ТОРПÉДО**. Many large cities will have teams with these names, often associated with particular trades or professions. Notice that all the words in this paragraph have the stress where you might least expect it. For example, **СТАДИÓН** as opposed to the English st*a*dium, **ДИНÁМО** for D*y*namo.

- **КРЕМЛЬ**, the Kremlin. The word means *fortress,* and you can see them in many ancient Russian towns. The Moscow Kremlin is the seat of the Russian government, and the site of some beautiful churches and cathedrals. Listen out for the soft **Л** at the end of the word.

- **БУФÉТ** is a *buffet* or *snack bar* in a hotel. It also means a *sideboard*. If you want a bar, then the Russians have borrowed our word: **БАР**.

- **УЗБÉК** is a native of **Узбекистáн**. This was a republic of the Soviet Union and is now an independent country.

- **РЕМÓНТ** is a borrowed word from French and means *repair*. **На ремóнте** outside a shop or public building means that it is closed for repairs.

- **АДМИНИСТРÁТОР** is the manager of a hotel, restaurant or other large institution.

- **ХОККÉЙ**, *ice-hockey,* is also an extremely popular sport. The teams often have the same names as football teams. Other winter sports that are very popular are **катáние на конькáх**, *skating*, and **катáние на** LÝZHAKH, *skiing*. During winter months many Russians go cross-country skiing on the outskirts of Moscow and other cities.

● **КИНО́**, *cinema*, is extremely popular in Russia. Many of the films shown nowadays are dubbed films from America and Europe, also available on video and DVD, but home-produced films also pull in the crowds. The Russian cinema industry now earns a lot of its money by providing facilities for Western film companies.

Most of the words listed above will easily be recognised by their similarity to English. **БЮРО́** (*office*) and **БУЛЬО́Н** (*clear soup*) are examples of words borrowed from French. You will also often hear **О́ФИС** instead of **БЮРО́**.

EXERCISE 1

Look at the list of words numbered 1–27 on the previous page. First time round listen to the recording and repeat the word. Second time round, you say the word after you hear the number and check it with the CD. If you are satisfied with your attempt, put a tick in the box. If not, repeat your attempt.

EXERCISE 2

Now we shall mix up the words.
Look at the list of words at the beginning of the unit.
Find the number of the word that has just been read.
Place it in the appropriate box below.
The first one is done for you.

Example

You hear **но́мер оди́н**, number one, **фо́то**, you find **фо́то** in the list and place 11 in the box next to number 1. The first one is done for you.

1 `11`   4 ☐   7 ☐   10 ☐

2 ☐   5 ☐   8 ☐

3 ☐   6 ☐   9 ☐

EXERCISE 3

Here are some of the words written in the Roman alphabet. Identify them by their original numbers, using the boxes provided. The first one is done for you.

1 AVTOBUS   `15`   6 KHOKKEY   ☐

2 PEREKHOD   ☐   7 UZBEK   ☐

3 STADION   ☐   8 BYURO   ☐

4 BULYON   ☐   9 YUMOR   ☐

5 TELEFON   ☐   10 TORPEDO   ☐

Try to mark the stress without referring to the list at the beginning of the unit. Then check your answers.

● Language information

Directions

In the last unit the question GDE? was asked and you had to provide the answer **Вот он** or **Вот она́**, etc. You may also be given much more complicated replies. Knowing what to expect is important, and helps you to pick out the key bits of the answer. Words to watch out for are:

нале́во	*on the left*
напра́во	*on the right*
PRYÁMO	*straight ahead*
далеко́	*far*
недалеко́	*near*

EXERCISE 4

Look at the sign showing where to find things in a park. Which are to the right and which to the left? Mark → for **напра́во** and ← for **нале́во**.

1	авто́бус	☐	5 туале́т	☐
2	кино́	☐	6 кафе́	☐
3	ка́сса	☐	7 буфе́т	☐
4	телефо́н	☐	8 рестора́н	☐

Try inventing a few sentences of the type: **авто́бус нале́во, телефо́н напра́во**.

⊚ EXERCISE 5

Now listen to the recording. People are giving directions. Sometimes there is one direction indicated, sometimes two or more. If the first direction is to the right, put an arrow pointing to the right; if to the left, put an arrow pointing to the left. If the direction is straight on, put an arrow pointing straight upwards. If the place is a long way, put ✓ in the box under **далеко́?** Don't expect to understand every word, but pick out the key points. The first one is done for you.

		→	←	↑		далеко́?
1	метро́	→	←	↑		
2	кино́					
3	стадио́н					
4	рестора́н					
5	такси́					

EXERCISE 6

At the top of the next page is a plan of a park. All the paths have been laid out in a squared pattern. We will give you directions using these squares, telling you which direction you have to follow. We will then ask you where you are, and you have to pick out the answer from the list on the left and put its number in the box provided. We have done the first one for you. Start at the same point (**ВХОД**) each time.

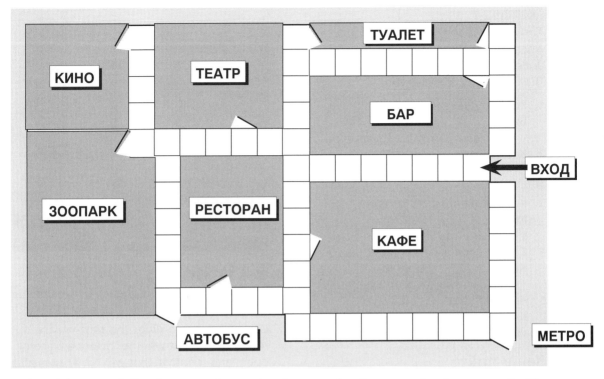

1 В кафе́	6 В теа́тре
2 В ба́ре	7 В кино́
3 В зоопа́рке	8 В авто́бусе
4 В рестора́не	9 В метро́
5 В туале́те	

1	PRYÁMO 8	нале́во 5	напра́во 3	GDE VY? ☑
2	нале́во 6	напра́во 8	напра́во 11	GDE VY? ☐
3	напра́во 4	нале́во 8	напра́во 1	GDE VY? ☐
4	PRYÁMO 8	напра́во 1	нале́во 6	GDE VY? ☐
5	нале́во 6	напра́во 8	напра́во 3	GDE VY? ☐

When

The Russian for *when* is KOGDÁ. The reply may contain one of the following words:

SEVÓDNYA	*today*
за́втра	*tomorrow*
SEYCHÁS	*now*
VSEGDÁ	*always*

Open, closed

When you want to say the restaurant is open, you say **рестора́н** OTKRÝT. To say it is closed, say **рестора́н** ZAKRÝT. If you want to say the same thing about **кафе́** you would need to add **-о**, or with **апте́ка** you would need to add **-а**. Watch out for this as you proceed in the course.

EXERCISE 7

Answer the following questions, explaining
when various places are open.
Underline the correct time word.
The first one is done for you.

1 KOGDÁ **буфéт** OTKR´YT? *(always)*
  Буфéт _____ OTKR´YT.
  VSEGDÁ/**зáвтра**/SEVÓDNYA/SEYCHÁS
2 KOGDÁ **стадиóн** OTKR´YT? *(tomorrow)*
  Стадиóн _____ OTKR´YT.
  VSEGDÁ/**зáвтра**/SEVÓDNYA/**сейчáс**
3 KOGDÁ **кинó** OTKR´YTO? *(today)*
  Кинó _____ OTKR´YTO.
  VSEGDÁ/**зáвтра**/SEVÓDNYA/SEYCHÁS
4 KOGDÁ **кáсса** OTKR´YTA? *(now)*
  Кáсса _____ OTKR´YTA.
  VSEGDÁ/**зáвтра**/SEVÓDNYA/SEYCHÁS
5 KOGDÁ **клуб** OTKR´YT? *(always)*
  Клуб _____ OTKR´YT.
  VSEGDÁ/**зáвтра**/SEVÓDNYA/SEYCHÁS

Being polite

Notice that when people want to be polite
to one another they will say **извинúте**
or **простúте** (*excuse me*) and usually add
POZHÁLSTA (*please*).

● Looking at words

напрáво, налéво

Notice that **налéво** and **напрáво** have
на- (*towards*) in common.

-ход

Many words end in **-ход**, all connected
with moving around on foot. **Вход** is
an entrance (literally *going in*). The sign
ВХОД В МЕТРÓ tells you where to enter
the underground. **Перехóд** is a crossing;
пере- at the beginning of a word means
across. You'll see this sign on the street. In
theory you're not supposed to cross the
road except where there's a sign, but most
Russians ignore this rule! **Перехóд** also
indicates that there is an underpass under a
busy road. On the underground follow this
sign if you want to change lines.

● Listening

☉ EXERCISE 8

Listen to the recording. This time we are
trying to find out whether or not a place is
open, and if not when it will be. Answer the
questions in English.

1 Is the restaurant open?
2 When is the cinema open?
3 When is the cafe open?
4 Why is the buffet closed?
5 What do they have in the cafe?

A situation to remember (1)
Finding your way in Russia

If you have a partner, devise a conversation
with him/her. If you are on your own, you'll
have to play both roles.
You have stopped a passer-by in the street.
Ask the way to GUM, the big department
store in Red Square, politely, of course!
The directions are left, right and right again.
Ask if it is open.
Ask if it's far. (It isn't.)
End the conversation politely.

Now devise some more conversations asking
your way – in Moscow to BOLSHÓI TEÁTR, or
in St Petersburg to the Hermitage museum
(ERMITÁZH) or the main street (NÉVSKY
PROSPÉKT).

A situation to remember (2)

Directing a Russian in Britain

Use what you have learnt so far to work out directions in your own environment. Imagine, for example, a Russian friend is visiting you in Britain. She is going to your local town centre for the first time by herself. She asks you the way to the cinema, the chemist's, the park, the university. Give her as detailed directions as possible and don't forget to tell her if it is a long way.

● Playing with words

Alphabet game

Here is another alphabet game. Fill in the blanks below to make up words, using each letter once only. Initial letters are given in bold.

к е а ю р д о о о о о о б **б** в л ф ф ф
у х т т

1 Ф _ _ _ _ _
2 К _ _ _
3 Ф _ _ _
4 Б _ _ _
5 В _ _ _

Jumbled words

Here are some jumbled words. See if you can decipher them. Use the boxes provided for your answers.

1 ЮМЕН
2 НМДИОА
3 ЕХДПРОЕ
4 НФОТЛЕЕ
5 ИРЕЕНИУСВТТ

WHAT YOU KNOW

Asking the way
GDE **метро́**?
Метро́ напра́во/нале́во/PRYÁMO.

Is it far?
ÉTO **далеко́**?
Да, далеко́/Нет, недалеко́.

Being polite
Извини́те, POZHÁLSTA.
Прости́те, POZHÁLSTA.

Is it open?
Ресторан OTKRÝT?
Нет, ZAKRÝT.

When?
KOGDÁ **ресторан** OTKRÝT?
SEVÓDNYA/**За́втра**/SEYCHÁS.

KEY VOCABULARY

вход	entrance
далеко́	far
за́втра	tomorrow
извини́те	excuse me
Кремль	Kremlin
нале́во	to the left
напра́во	to the right
недалеко́	not far, near
перехо́д	crossing
стадио́н	stadium
футбо́л	football
хокке́й	ice-hockey
KOGDÁ	when
OTKRÝT	open
PRYÁMO	straight ahead
SEVÓDNYA	today
SEYCHÁS	now
VSEGDÁ	always
ZAKRÝT	closed

Asking permission

NOMER CHETYRE

● Alphabet 4

Here are the new letters for this unit:

Э Г Я Ы Ё

The letters you have met so far are picked out in the following list:

а б в г д е ё ж з и й к л м н о п р с т у ф х ц ч ш щ ъ ы ь э ю я

Most of the new letters are quite unlike any English letters.

Э is like the English 'e' in *extra*. Russian uses this letter rarely and usually only in foreign words. Don't confuse it with 'e', which is pronounced *ye*.

Г is like English 'g' in *god*.

Я is 'ya' as in *kayak*.

Ы is a bit like the 'i' sound in *fixture*, but made further back in the throat.

Ё is like the 'yo' sound in *yacht*. It is always stressed. The two dots are usually missed out in normal Russian print.

You have now seen all the Russian vowels. Russian has twice as many as English, four of them starting with a 'y' sound:

English	a	e	i	o	u
Russian	а	э	ы	о	у
	я	е	и	ё	ю

1 го́род	☐	9 газе́та	☐	17 грибы́	☐
2 телегра́мма	☐	10 Росси́я	☐	18 О́льга	☐
3 год	☐	11 ГУМ	☐	19 май	☐
4 тури́сты	☐	12 экспре́сс	☐	20 неде́ля	☐
5 Аэрофло́т	☐	13 эне́ргия	☐	21 ряд	☐
6 самолёт	☐	14 програ́мма	☐	22 бланк	☐
7 экску́рсия	☐	15 вы́ход	☐	23 МГУ	☐
8 изве́стия	☐	16 выходи́ть	☐	24 ме́сто	☐

- **АЭРОФЛО́Т** is the major Russian airline, operating many flights abroad and internally in Russia. It is a two-part word: **флот** is the Russian word for *fleet*. Notice that the **А** and **Э** in Aeroflot are pronounced separately.
- **ИЗВЕ́СТИЯ** is the word for *news*. It is also the name of a Russian newspaper.
- **ГАЗЕ́ТА**, *a newspaper*, can easily be recognised from the English *gazette*. **Литерату́рная газе́та** is the main literary newspaper, which contains articles on sociological problems, theatre, cinema, television and foreign affairs, as well as on literature.
- **РОССИ́Я** is not only the name of the country but also of a large cinema in central Moscow.

- **ГУМ (Госуда́рственный Универса́льный Магази́н)** – *The State Universal Store*. This is perhaps the most famous Russian shop, situated on one side of Red Square. It was built at the end of the 19th century as a vast shopping arcade. It is now a private company and many famous Western shops have rented space in GUM.

- **МГУ** If you mix the letters of **ГУМ** you have **МГУ**, *Moscow State University*, pronounced **эм-гэ-у́** (EM-GE-Ú). It is situated on the highest point in Moscow and the view from there is a must for most tourists. It is the most prestigious Russian university and there is great competition to get a place to study there. You may need a pass (**про́пуск**) to enter the buildings.
- **ПРОГРА́ММА** is a theatre or football programme, and it is also used to indicate a TV or radio channel.

Most of the words in the list are like English, and you should recognise them. Be careful, though: **бланк** means *a form*, blank until you fill it in! Ones you will not be able to guess are **го́род** (*town, city*), **самолёт** (*plane*) and **год** (*year*). **Го́род** and a related form are seen as the second part of the names of a number of Russian towns and cities: **Но́вгород** and **Ленингра́д**, the previous name for **Санкт-Петербу́рг**. **Год** is often shortened to **г.**, and you will see 2006 **г.** or **в ма́е** 2006 **г.** (*in May, 2006*).

- -

💿 EXERCISE 1

Look at the list of words numbered 1–24 on the previous page.

First time round listen to the recording and repeat the word.

Second time round, you say the word after you hear the number and check it with the CD. If you are satisfied with your attempt, put a tick in the box. If not, repeat your attempt.

- -

💿 EXERCISE 2

Now we're going to mix up the words. Look at the list of words numbered 1–24 on the previous page.

Find the number of the word that has just been read.

Place it in the appropriate box below.

Example

You hear **но́мер оди́н**, *number one*, **вы́ход**, you find **вы́ход** in the list and place 15 in the box next to number 1. The first one is done for you.

1	15	4	☐	7	☐	10	☐
2	☐	5	☐	8	☐		
3	☐	6	☐	9	☐		

- -

- **ГРИБЫ́**, *mushrooms,* are one of the Russians' favourite foods. There is a huge variety in the woods and forests, and regular expeditions are organised to collect them. The mushrooms are salted, dried, bottled, boiled, fried or stewed. Perhaps the best place to enjoy them is in a Russian home.

- **НЕДЕ́ЛЯ**, *a week.* Russians start their week on **понеде́льник**(Monday).

- **РЯД** is a row. You will see it on a theatre or cinema ticket (**биле́т**). Apart from the date and time of the performance you also need to know if you are in the stalls (**партѐр**) or the balcony (**балко́н**). You may be lucky and be in a box (lózha) or out of luck and be in the Gods (**я́рус**). Watch out for **МЕ́СТО**: on a theatre ticket it gives you your seat number and is found next to your **ряд**. Otherwise **ме́сто** simply means *a place*.

EXERCISE 3

Here are some of the words written in the Roman alphabet. Identify them by their original numbers, using the boxes provided. The first one is done for you. Put in the stress marks and check your answers from the original list.

1	GRIBY	*17*	6	ROSSIYA	☐
2	IZVESTIYA	☐	7	TELEGRAMMA	☐
3	VYKHOD	☐	8	SAMOLYOT	☐
4	RYAD	☐	9	ENERGIYA	☐
5	VYKHODIT'	☐	10	AEROFLOT	☐

● Life in Russia

It is important to know what you can and cannot do in Russia, a country very different from our own. Smoking, for example, is forbidden in all public buildings and on public transport. The word *to smoke* is **кури́ть**: the most common notice is: **НЕ КУРИ́ТЬ!**

If you need to smoke, you will usually find a smoking room: look for the sign **кури́тельная ко́мната** (*smoking room*). It is usually by the toilets. On a train, you can smoke at the open section where two carriages join.

If you are unsure about whether something is permitted, you should use the word MÓZHNO. Make your voice go up when you ask:

MÓZHNO **кури́ть**? *Can I smoke?*
MÓZHNO **фотографи́ровать**? *Can I take photographs?*
or just simply say MÓZHNO?
Listen for the answer.
MÓZHNO or MÓZHNO, POZHÁLSTA means that it is allowed; **нельзя́**, or **нет, нельзя́** means that it is not, that it is forbidden.

EXERCISE 4

The man in the drawing is arranging some notices forbidding things. See if you can guess what they mean. The first one is done for you.

1 по газо́нам не ходи́ть!
   Don't walk on the grass!

2 вхо́да нет! _____

3 не фотографи́ровать!

   _____

4 нет вы́хода! _____

5 здесь не ку́рят! _____

6 перехо́да нет! _____

7 не кури́ть! _____

● Language information

MÓZHNO

As we have pointed out earlier, some Russian words are especially useful in expressing a lot of information. One of these words is MÓZHNO. You may use it as a way of asking permission, or asking for the loan of something, as in the examples below.

Бланк MÓZHNO?	*May I have a form?*
Газéту MÓZHNO?	*May I read your newspaper?*
Телефóн MÓZHNO?	*May I use your telephone?*
Нúну MÓZHNO?	*May I speak to Nina?*
Винó MÓZHNO?	*May I have some wine?*

Russian simply misses out the verbs (*have, read, use, speak*), as it is obvious from the context.

Notice that **газéта**, *newspaper*, changes to **газéту** and **нинá** to **нину**. **Бланк**, **телефóн** and **винó** do not change. You are using the *accusative case*.

Granting permission often includes the word POZHÁLSTA (*please*), which is used in many more situations than its English counterpart (see Unit 6).

EXERCISE 5

Here is a sample conversation:

A: **Газéту** MÓZHNO?
B: POZHÁLSTA. **Вот онá**.
A: **Спасúбо**.

Here are some pictures of some objects. Using the conversation as a model, ask if you can have it, then reconstruct the rest of the conversation for yourself. Look back at the *Language information* in Unit 2 to make sure you know when to use **Вот он, онá, онó** or **онú**.

1 билéт

2 вóдка

3 грибы́

4 мáрка

5 стакáн

6 телефóн

Plural

You may have noticed that some of the words in this unit end in **-ы** (**грибы́**, **тури́сты**). You add **ы** for the plural just like you add *s* in English to make a word plural. **Грибы́**, for example, means *mushroom*s and **тури́сты** means *tourist*s. You can easily work out when you see **тури́ст** that it means one tourist, and that **гриб** means one mushroom.

Words ending in **-а** also have **-ы** in the plural, e.g. **газе́та** – **газе́ты** (*newspaper*s). **И** is used instead of **ы** after **к** and a few other letters: **студе́нтка** – **студе́нтки** (*female students*). The ending **и** is also found in **они́** (see Unit 2). Sometimes, with 'borrowed' or 'imported' words, the result looks strange. **Бу́тсы**, taken from the English, means *football boots*. The singular is hardly ever used.

● Looking at words

In Unit 3 you met the words **вход** (*entrance*) and **перехо́д** (*crossing*). There is another similar word in this unit: **вы́ход** (*exit*). Be careful with this one, as it means exactly the opposite of **вход**, and you don't want to confuse one with the other! You may also have noticed **выходи́ть** (*to exit*). This gives you a three-part word: **вы-** (*out*), **ход** (*go*) and **-ить**, which tells you that it is a verb, that an action is involved. Most words ending in **-ать** or **-ить** are verbs, meaning *to do* something: e.g. **фотографи́ровать** (*to photograph*).

● Listening

On the telephone

⊚ EXERCISE 6

On your recording is a telephone conversation. A man is trying to make a date with a woman (Olga). Listen to the conversation and see if you can answer the questions in English or Russian.

1 Who does the man speak to first?
2 Does she know him?
3 What is the man's name?
4 What does he want Olga to do?
5 What is her reply?
6 When do they intend to go to the theatre?

A situation to remember

You ring someone up on the phone and arrange to go to the theatre. Devise a conversation with a partner. Here are some prompts:

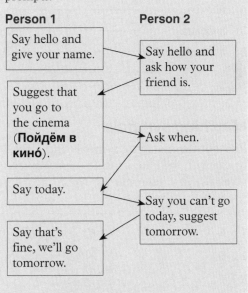

Person 1

> Say hello and give your name.

> Suggest that you go to the cinema (**Пойдём в кино́**).

> Say today.

> Say that's fine, we'll go tomorrow.

Person 2

> Say hello and ask how your friend is.

> Ask when.

> Say you can't go today, suggest tomorrow.

Next time round, suggest that you go to the theatre, to GUM, to a cafe or to a restaurant.

● Playing with words

Jumbled words 1

Here, in jumbled form, are some of the words introduced in this lesson. Work out what they are, using the boxes provided. There is a hidden word in one of the vertical columns. What is it?

1 ырбиг

2 гмраомарп

3 нгяэире

4 торфоалэ

5 хывдо

Hidden word:

Jumbled words 2

Here is another game like the last one.

1 азгтае

2 усотвба

3 сскэрепс

4 исрясо

5 кярскиэус

6 ятвзисие

Hidden word:

Matching symbols

Pick out the matching symbols and form words with the letters inside them. You are given the first letter in each word.

1 С _ _ _ _ _ _

2 Б _ _ _ _ _

3 Р _ _ _ _ _

4 В _ _ _ _ _

5 Н _ _ _ _ _ _

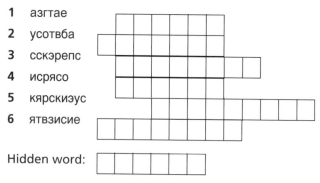

WHAT YOU KNOW

Asking permission
Мóжно фотографи́ровать?
Да, мóжно.
Газéту мóжно?
Нет, нельзя́.

Plurals
тури́ст – тури́сты
газéта – газéты

KEY VOCABULARY

билéт	ticket
вы́ход	exit
выходи́ть	to exit
газéта	newspaper
год	year
гóрод	town
грибы́	mushrooms
извéстия	news
кури́ть	to smoke
мéсто	place, seat (in theatre)
мóжно	possible
недéля	week
нельзя́	impossible
прогрáмма	programme
Росси́я	Russia
ряд	row
тури́ст	tourist

Revision

NOMER PYAT

● Alphabet 5

There are six new letters in this unit, and they are all quite unlike any English letters:

Ж Ч Ш Щ Ц Ъ

Now you have seen the whole alphabet:

**а б в г д е ё ж з и й к л м н о п р с т у ф
х ц ч ш щ ъ ы ь э ю я**

Notice the order of the alphabet. The order from **и** (i) to **у** (u) is very similar to the order of the Roman alphabet, and most of the 'exotic' letters occur towards the end.

Ж is pronounced much like the 's' in *measure*.
Ч is similar to 'ch' in *Charles*.
Ш resembles 'sh' in *shush*.
Щ is like the 'shch' in *fresh cheese*.
Ц is pronounced like the last two letters in *cats*.
Ъ the hard sign, the rarest letter in the Russian alphabet, only occurs in the middle of words and does not have a sound of its own.

35

1 Че́хов	☐	11 москви́ч	☐	20 щи	☐
2 ча́йка	☐	12 эта́ж	☐	21 ша́пка	☐
3 маши́на	☐	13 мо́жно	☐	22 же́нщина	☐
4 электри́чество	☐	14 хорошо́	☐	23 цирк	☐
5 информа́ция	☐	15 шоссе́	☐	24 по́чта	☐
6 бифште́кс	☐	16 цветы́	☐	25 центр	☐
7 шашлы́к	☐	17 ве́чер	☐	26 конце́рт	☐
8 демонстра́ция	☐	18 ночь	☐	27 подъе́зд	☐
9 матч	☐	19 Кра́сная			
10 Большо́й теа́тр	☐	пло́щадь	☐		

- **ЧЕ́ХОВ.** Анто́н Па́влович Че́хов (Chekhov) wrote a large number of mainly humorous short stories and a few famous plays, revealing the changes in society at the end of 19th-century Russia. He died in 1904, aged 44.
- **ЧА́ЙКА** is a seagull and the name of a play by Chekhov. It also used to be a very grand Russian car (**маши́на**), used by communist party members under the old regime. Other Russian makes of car are **Москви́ч** (*Muscovite*), **Во́лга** and **Жигули́**. The **Жигули́** is made in a factory built by Fiat. We know the export version in this country as **Ла́да**. Russians nowadays prefer to drive imported cars, if they can afford them.
- **БИФШТЕ́КС** is usually used to describe a hamburger or rissole of some sort. You will also see the word **га́мбургер**! Russians often use the letter **г** to replace an English **h**. Another good example is the Shakespeare play **ГА́МЛЕТ**. **ЩИ** is the traditional Russian *cabbage soup*. (For more information about food see Unit 9.)
- **ШАШЛЫ́К**, or more often referred to in the plural **шашлыки́** (notice the shift in stress) are barbecued pieces of meat on a spit, larger than kebabs, often served with spring onions. Get them at a **шашлы́чная**, a specialist restaurant, and look out for them on most restaurant menus, especially those specialising in Georgian or Armenian cuisine.

Bolshoi Theatre

- **БОЛЬШО́Й ТЕА́ТР** is the most famous theatre in Russia, with its own ballet and opera companies. **Большо́й** means *big*. Of course, nowadays there are bigger theatres, but none with the same atmosphere as the Bolshoi. The theatre also has a huge stage, big enough even to accommodate people on horseback.
- **ЭТА́Ж** has been borrowed from French and means a *floor* or *storey* in a building. Most Russians live in flats and you will need to know which **эта́ж** they live on to find their flat.
- **ШОССЕ́** is another French borrowing: it is a *highway*, leading out of one town towards another. Russians pronounce

ЦИРК ☺ представления для детей ☺ В/О-СОЮЗГОСЦИРК·

the 'e' as if it was spelt with **Э**. This makes it sound foreign to a Russian. Listen out for it on the CD.

- **ВЕ́ЧЕР** means *evening* and **НОЧЬ** means *night*. You wish someone **до́брый ве́чер** (*good evening*) when you go to see them in the evening and **споко́йной но́чи** (*good night*) when they are going to bed.

- **КРА́СНАЯ ПЛО́ЩАДЬ** was called Red Square long before the advent of communism. **Кра́сный** used to have the meaning *beautiful*. Today **краси́вый** is the usual word for *beautiful*.
- **ША́ПКА** is a traditional Russian cap or hat made out of fur, with or without ear-flaps to keep out the cold.
- **ЖЕ́НЩИНА**, *woman*. The sign you see on ladies' toilets is **Ж**, occasionally **Д** (the word **да́ма** means *lady*). Men's toilets are marked **М** (the word **мужчи́на** means *man*).

- **ЦИРК**: Russians love the circus. The Moscow State Circus is the most famous in the world. It has two permanent buildings: **Ста́рый цирк**, the old building on the inner ring road, and the new building, **Но́вый цирк**, near **МГУ**.
- **ПО́ЧТА**, a *post office*, is where you buy **ма́рки** (*stamps*) and **откры́тки** (*postcards*). Notice the similarity between **откры́тки** and **откры́т** (*open*). **ПО́ЧТА** is also written on letterboxes, as in the example in the photograph.

- **КОНЦЕ́РТ**, besides *concert*, means *concerto*.
- **ПОДЪЕ́ЗД** is the entrance to a block of flats. You will often find that the entrance that you require is not from the street, but from a **двор** (*courtyard*). If you are lost, ask one of the old women (**ба́бушки**) who are usually to be found sitting on the benches. You may see a few old men, but women of this age tend to outnumber men, many of whom died during the second world war.

37

🎧 EXERCISE 1

Look at the list of words numbered 1–27 on page 36.

First time round listen and repeat.

Second time round you say the word after you hear the number and check it with the recording.

If you are satisfied with your attempt, put a tick in the box. If not, repeat your attempt.

🎧 EXERCISE 2

Now we shall mix up the words. Look at the list of words, find the number of the word that has just been read in the list on page 36 and place the number in the box below.

Example

You hear **но́мер оди́н**, number one, **электри́чество**. You find **электри́чество** in the list and place 4 in the box next to number 1. The first one is done for you.

1	4	4		7		10	
2		5		8			
3		6		9			

EXERCISE 3

Here are some of the words written in the Roman alphabet. Identify them by their original numbers, using the boxes provided. The first one is done for you.

1	TSVETÝ	16	6	SHCHI	
2	BIFSHTEKS		7	ZHENSHCHINA	
3	SHOSSE		8	VECHER	
4	SHAPKA		9	TSENTR	
5	ETAZH		10	SHASHLYK	

When you have put in all your numbers see if you can mark all the stresses in the correct position from memory. Check your answers from the list.

🎧 EXERCISE 4

On your CD is a conversation about what is going on in various places in Moscow. Each time one person asks the question Что идёт в …? The other person looks in the newspaper and provides the answer. You have to make sentences by joining up the words below.

В па́рке	идёт	о́пера
В кино́	идёт	конце́рт
В Большо́м теа́тре	идёт	ле́кция
В университе́те	идёт	фильм

● Language information

Alphabet

You have now met the whole of the Russian alphabet, so we shall not use any more transliterations. You may have noticed that very often one letter in Russian can take several letters in English.

Some names for well-known Russians now have a standard spelling in English. **Чайко́вский** is spelt Tchaikovsky (and not Chaykovsky, which is a more accurate transliteration).

The Cyrillic alphabet has definite advantages when it comes to the representation of Slavonic sounds. The Polish language does not use it, and it has sz for **ш**, cz for **ч**, and szcz for **щ**! The Russian word **щипцы́** (*tongs, forceps*) in Polish is *szczypce* (eight letters).

● Looking at words

-ЦИЯ

The meaning of **информа́ция** should be obvious. The ending **-ция** on this word as well as on the end of the words **демонстра́ция** and **конститу́ция** corresponds to the English *-tion*. The ending **-ство** in **электри́чество** (*electricity*) corresponds to the English *-ity*. **-ство** can have a variety of translations in English: *-ity*, *-cy* or *-ism*.

EXERCISE 5

Here are some examples of words ending in -ство or -ция, where foreign words are 'Russified'. See if you can guess what they mean.

1 аге́нтство _____

2 пира́тство _____

3 хулига́нство _____

4 администра́ция _____

5 мобилиза́ция _____

6 концентра́ция _____

7 конфедера́ция _____

8 револю́ция _____

Prefixes

The most frequent initial letter in Russian is **п**. This is because most prefixes begin with this letter. See the Grammar section for further information.

пере-	перехо́д	*crossing*
про-	про́пуск	*pass*
по-	пойдём	*let's go*
под-	подъе́зд	*entrance*
при-	приходи́ть	*to arrive*

● Revision

⊙ EXERCISE 6

Listen to the CD.
You will hear **Э́то рестора́н** (*This is a restaurant*) and then **Вот Ви́ктор** (*Here is Viktor*). You have to say that *He is in the restaurant* – **Он в рестора́не**. You will be given the correct answer on the CD.

EXERCISE 7

Underline the correct alternative. The first one is done for you.

1	Москва́	<u>в Росси́и</u> в А́нглии в Аме́рике
2	Кра́сная пло́щадь	в Ло́ндоне на стадио́не в це́нтре Москвы́
3	Э́то вы́ход. Здесь нельзя́	переходи́ть выходи́ть входи́ть
4	Э́то вход. Здесь мо́жно	входи́ть выходи́ть кури́ть
5	Э́то вы́ход. Здесь нет	перехо́да вы́хода вхо́да
6	На стадио́не сейча́с идёт	матч конце́рт крокоди́л

EXERCISE 8

Here is a drawing with some signs on it. Match the Russian words to the drawing by placing the appropriate number in the box.

авто́бусы	4	не кури́ть		
туале́т(м)		такси́		
ка́сса		Ни́на		
вы́ход		туале́т(ж)		
метро́		телефо́н-автома́т		

● Playing with words

Here are two sets of jumbled words. This time the hidden words may be vertical or diagonal, and will answer the question **что идёт в теа́тре?** Put in all the stresses.

Jumbled words 1

1 оомнж

2 чптао

3 вхеоч

4 ицрк

5 жнаимуч

6 Что идёт в теа́тре?

Jumbled words 2

1 кйача

2 сеошс

3 фцмярииноа

4 ртнце

5 щанижен

6 ршхооо

7 чтма

8 Что идёт в теа́тре?

40

LANGUAGE REVIEW

You now know all the alphabet. Here are some important words and phrases that we have transliterated until now. The unit where they first occurred is given in brackets. Write in the English translation.

До свида́ния! (1) _____
закры́т (3) _____
Здра́вствуйте! (1) _____
Когда́ (3) _____
Кто э́то? (1) _____
мо́жно (4) _____
ничего́ (2) _____
откры́т (3) _____
пожа́луйста (1) _____
пря́мо (3) _____
сего́дня (3) _____
сейча́с (3) _____
спаси́бо (1) _____
Что э́то? (1) _____

Note that **ничего́** and **сего́дня** are spelt with a **г** but pronounced with a 'v': NICHE_VÓ_, SE_V_ÓDNYA.

Questions and answers

You should know how to ask the following questions and understand the answers. If you need to remind yourself of how to say any of these things, the unit where we first practised the phrases is given on the right.

KEY VOCABULARY

Большо́й теа́тр	Bolshoi Theatre
же́нщина	woman
конце́рт	concert
Кра́сная пло́щадь	Red Square
маши́на	car
москви́ч	Muscovite
по́чта	post office
туале́т	toilet
хорошо́	good
цветы́	flowers
центр	centre
цирк	circus
ча́йка	seagull
Че́хов	Chekhov
ша́пка	hat
шашлы́к	kebab
шоссе́	highway
щи	cabbage soup
электри́чество	electricity
эта́ж	floor, storey

Question	Answer	Unit
What is this?/Who is this?	This is ...	1
Where is it?	Here it is.	2
	It is in the restaurant/on the table.	2
	It is straight ahead/on the left/on the right.	3
	It is a long way away/nearby.	3
When is it open/closed?	today/tomorrow/now	3
Can I smoke?	You can/can't ...	4
Can I have the paper?		

номер шесть

6

Travelling around town

Travelling around

How Russians go shopping

Numbers

● Life in Russia

Travelling around a town

There are four types of public transport in most large Russian towns:

bus	автобус
trolleybus	троллейбус
tram	трамвай
minibus	маршрутка

Moscow, St Petersburg and a few other large cities in Russia also have an underground (**метро**). A **маршрутка** (short for **маршрутное такси**) follows a fixed route (**маршрут**) but will stop anywhere for you. They are a very useful (and cheap) way of getting from one of Moscow's airports to the nearest underground station.

42

It doesn't matter how far you want to travel, there is a standard fare covering any distance in a town. If you go by metro, this standard fare allows you to change lines (**де́лать переса́дку**) as often as you want.

If you are being given directions, listen out for the phrases:

by bus	на авто́бусе
by trolleybus	на тролле́йбусе
by tram	на трамва́е
by minibus	на маршру́тке
by underground	на метро́

You will need to know where the nearest stop (**остано́вка**) is, or how to find the underground station (**ста́нция метро́**).

To find your way to Red Square, ask:
Как мне пройти́ на Кра́сную пло́щадь?
How can I get to Red Square?

A typical answer might be:
Иди́те *(go)* пря́мо и пото́м *(then)* нале́во.

You should recognise the direction words from Unit 3.

Another direction word you might hear is **напро́тив** *(opposite)*.

If you are a long way from Red Square, ask instead:
Как мне прое́хать на Кра́сную пло́щадь?

This is the answer that you night hear:
Лу́чше *(it is better)* на авто́бусе. Там напро́тив остано́вка.

EXERCISE 1
Using the sample questions and answers given above, work with a partner and ask your way to the following places:

в Москве́
1 **в Большо́й теа́тр**
2 **в Третьяко́вскую галере́ю** (the Tretyakov Gallery, the biggest collection of Russian art in Moscow)
3 **на Арба́т** (one of the main streets in Moscow)

в Санкт-Петербу́рге
4 **в Мари́инский теа́тр** (this is the theatre in St Petersburg that used to be known as the Kirov)
5 **на Не́вский проспе́кт** (one of the main streets in St Petersburg)
6 **в Эрмита́ж** (the Hermitage museum: the finest collection of Western art in Russia)

If you want to travel by bus, trolleybus or tram, you will need to buy a ticket (**тало́н**). You can sometimes pay the conductor, if there is one. You can also buy tickets at a kiosk (**кио́ск**) or cash desk (**ка́сса**) or from the driver (**води́тель**) at a stop. Be warned, it will cost you more to buy on board! When you get on, you need to punch your ticket at one of the machines (**компо́стер**), one for each journey. If you don't do this, you may get fined by an inspector (**контролёр**). On a **маршру́тка** the driver will collect the money.

Public transport tends to be very crowded: you will be amazed at how many people can get into a Russian bus! You may need to be forceful in elbowing your way on and off. As you are getting near your stop, position yourself near the exit. If the person in front doesn't appear to be getting off, ask him or her: **Вы сейча́с выхо́дите?** Listen out for the answer **Да, выхожу́**: this means they are getting off. Alternatively they will try to move aside to let you past. It may be a very tight squeeze. If *you* get asked the question, don't forget to move out of the way if you are not getting off, or you may find yourself getting off, even if you don't want to!

The first Russian underground was started in Moscow in 1935 and the early stations are very grand affairs with lots of marble, mosaics, statues, etc. The stations on the circle line in Moscow (**кольцева́я ли́ния**) are fine examples of this style. The first underground line in St Petersburg was opened in 1955 and is much simpler. Many central stations have doors in the wall that open when the train arrives. It is very deep and you can't usually see the top of the escalator (**эскала́тор**) from the bottom.

The underground is the fastest and most efficient way of travelling round a big Russian city. Trains are very frequent, every two minutes or even less in the rush hour. You will usually find buses, trolleybuses or trams at the underground stations to take you on further. The underground closes between midnight and 1am.

To use the underground, you need to buy a card from the **ка́сса.** In Moscow you can buy tickets for more than one journey at the same time – the more you pay for in advance the cheaper it becomes. In St Petersburg you can buy a token (**жето́н**) for a single journey or a card for several journeys. Put your card or the **жето́н** into a machine and go through the barrier when you see the green light or the word **ИДИ́ТЕ**. If you go through when it's the red light, or the word **СТО́ЙТЕ** is showing, you'll be grabbed by a set of mechanical arms!

Moscow underground

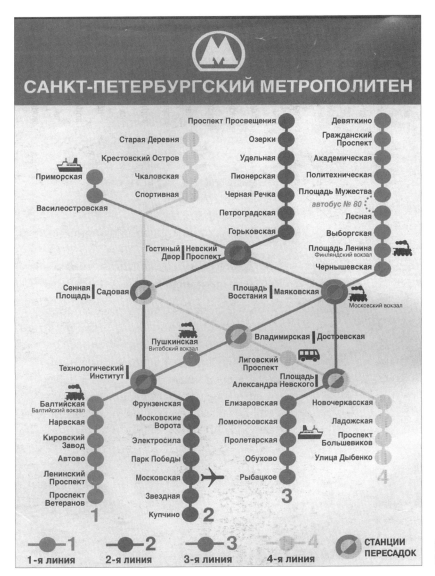

St Petersburg metro map

There are maps of the underground network in each station and on each platform you will see a list of stations for the current line, with interchanges indicated. The station names on the platform are not as clear as in London; you will have to listen out for the recorded announcements given at each station. The phrase **сле́дующая ста́нция** means *the next station is.* The other message you will hear at every station is **Осторо́жно, две́ри закрыва́ются!** (*Careful, the doors are closing.*)

Metro token

If you are in Russia for a long time, it might be worth buying a season ticket (**проездно́й биле́т**). You can also buy a **еди́ный биле́т**, which gives you access to all forms of transport for a month.

Shopping

Service in Russian shops varies from the very rude to the extremely helpful. To attract a woman shop assistant's attention, say: **Де́вушка!** You would also use it to a waitress in a restaurant. Don't confuse it with the word **де́вочка**, who is a girl far too young to be working in a shop! A **де́вушка** may be insulted if you call her a **де́вочка**!

Here are the sort of expressions you might need in a shop.

If you were trying to buy a metro map (**план метро́**), you might have the following conversation:

– Де́вушка, у вас есть (*do you have*) план метро́?
– Есть.

If you can see the metro map, but want to look at it before you buy, the conversation might start as follows:

– Де́вушка, покажи́те план метро́!
– Вот он, пожа́луйста.

The assistant will usually tell you how much it costs (**ско́лько сто́ит**). Don't worry at this stage if you can't understand the answer, just ask her to write it down for you:

– Напиши́те, пожа́луйста.

Of course, most transactions will not be as complicated as this. Here is someone buying something in a bar (**бар**):

A: Де́вушка, у вас есть чай?
B: Нет, э́то бар.
A: А что у вас есть?
B: У нас конья́к, пи́во, шампа́нское и вино́.
A: Да́йте (*Give*), пожа́луйста, вино́ и пи́во.
B: Вот, пожа́луйста, вино́ и пи́во.

You will notice that many prices in top class restaurants and of expensive imported goods are priced in **у.е.** pronounced *oo ye*, the initial letters of **усло́вные едини́цы** (*conditional units*). 1 **у.е.** equals a dollar or a euro. The number of roubles to an **у.е.** will be stated and you will be expected to pay in roubles.

● Language information

Numbers 1–10

The Russian numbers from 1–10 are:			
оди́н	1	шесть	6
два	2	семь	7
три	3	во́семь	8
четы́ре	4	де́вять	9
пять	5	де́сять	10

When Russians count they start **раз**, **два**, **три** instead of using **оди́н**, **два**, **три**. **Раз** literally means *once*, **два ра́за** *twice*, etc.

раз   два

три   четы́ре

Notice that **два** starts with the same letter as *duet*, *double* and *duo*, and **три** is like English.

Make sure that you distinguish the number 9 (**де́вять**) from 10 (**де́сять**). **Де́сять** is related to the English de*cimal*.

⊙ EXERCISE 2

Five short conversations are recorded on your CD. Each one involves a young woman (**де́вушка**) at a kiosk and a customer. He asks for an item and she asks him how many (**ско́лько**) he wants. You have to put the quantity he asks for in the box. The first one is done for you.

биле́ты ☐

пи́во ☐

откры́тки ☐

ма́рки [6]

жето́ны ☐

Russian numerals might at first sight appear daunting, but they are not as difficult as they might first appear. If you know the numbers up to nine, with a little bit of help you can work out numbers all the way up to 1000.

Numbers 11–19

. . . .

EXERCISE 3
Look at the following list of numbers and see if you can identify them. They are the numbers from 11–19, but not in order. Fill in the blanks.

восемна́дцать	1__
двена́дцать	1__
девятна́дцать	1__
оди́ннадцать	1__
пятна́дцать	1__
семна́дцать	1__
трина́дцать	1__
четы́рнадцать	1__
шестна́дцать	1__

. . . .

Numbers 20–90

. . . .

EXERCISE 4
Now try to work out the numbers from 20–90. You should be able to recognise the numbers **два** through to **де́вять** in the first part of all but the last number. The numbers are not in order.

во́семьдесят	__0
два́дцать	__0
девяно́сто	__0
пятьдеся́т	__0
се́мьдесят	__0
три́дцать	__0
шестьдеся́т	__0
со́рок	__0

. . . .

Numbers 100–900

. . . .

EXERCISE 5
Finally, try the numbers from 100–900. As usual they are all jumbled up. The one that you may not guess is left until the end. What does it mean?

две́сти	__00
пятьсо́т	__00
семьсо́т	__00
три́ста	__00
восемьсо́т	__00
четы́реста	__00
девятьсо́т	__00
шестьсо́т	__00
сто	__00

. . . .

Going to a place

Russian uses the same words for *to* (**в**, **на**) as it does for *in, on, at*. The only difference is the ending on the noun. If the noun ends in **-е** or **-и** (prepositional case), the meaning will be *in, on, at*. We have looked at this construction in Unit 2. If the noun does not change, or ends in **-у** instead of **-а**, the meaning is *to*. This is another use of the accusative case, which we first met in Unit 4.

. . . .

EXERCISE 6
Look at the phrases with **в** or **на**, then check the ending of the following word. Write down in, on, at, to in the box to indicate the meaning of **в** or **на**. The first one is done for you.

1 в Москве́	*in*		**6** в кварти́ру		
2 в Эрмита́же			**7** на конце́рте		
3 в ГУМ			**8** в Ло́ндон		
4 на Арба́т			**9** на пло́щадь		
5 во дворе́			**10** в Росси́и		

. . . .

Asking for things

If you want to look at an article in a shop, you use the phrase:

Покажи́те, пожа́луйста (*Show me, please*)
or
Да́йте, пожа́луйста (*Give me, please*).

This is followed by the accusative case (the object of the verb):

– Покажи́те, пожа́луйста, журна́л и кни́гу.
– Вот, пожа́луйста, журна́л и вот кни́га.

If you are certain that you want to buy them, say simply:

– Да́йте, пожа́луйста, журна́л и кни́гу.

EXERCISE 7

Now you make up some conversations asking for the following articles. Use either **Покажи́те, пожа́луйста** or **Да́йте, пожа́луйста**.

1 во́дка и вино́
2 ма́рка и откры́тка
3 кни́га и газе́та
4 стака́н и ча́шка (cup)
5 самова́р и чай

Пожа́луйста

Пожа́луйста has got a variety of meanings. It can mean *please*:

Покажи́те, пожа́луйста *Show me, please*
Извини́те, пожа́луйста *Excuse me, please*

Besides meaning *please*, **пожа́луйста** means *don't mention it* when used in response to **спаси́бо**.

It is also used as a polite word when handing things over, as in the phrase **вот пожа́луйста**. You have already seen it in the responses by the shop assistant and the waitress when handing over the metro map and the drinks. When not on its own, **пожа́луйста** usually occurs as the second item in a sentence.

У меня́, у тебя́, у вас, у нас

У меня́, **у тебя́**, **у вас**, **у нас** can mean: *I have, you have* (informal), *you have* (formal or plural), *we have*. In this meaning they are sometimes followed by **есть**, often for emphasis.

У меня́ есть кварти́ра в Москве́.
I've got a flat in Moscow.
У тебя́ (вас) есть кварти́ра в Санкт-Петербу́рге.
You've got a flat in St Petersburg.
У нас всё есть! *We've got everything!*

They are also used in the sense of *in our place, in our country*, etc.

у нас до́ма   *in our house*
у нас в А́нглии   *with us in England*
у нас в Москве́   *with us in Moscow*
This is very similar to the French *'chez'*.

У вас есть ...? (*Have you got ...?/Do you have ...?*) is the usual way of asking for something in a shop.

● Looking at words

Russian numbers

If you have done Exercises 3, 4 and 5, you will realise that you can easily recognise Russian numbers after ten.

The numbers from eleven to twenty all end in **-надцать**. This is a distorted form of **на де́сять** (*on ten*) and is the equivalent of the English *-teen*.

Most of the numbers from twenty to ninety end in **-де́сят** or an abbreviated form, **-дцать**. The only exceptions are **девяно́сто** (*ninety*), which starts with a shortened form of **де́вять**, and **со́рок** (*forty*). This is an oddity and we are told that it comes from Russians' love of hunting and that it originally meant a bundle of forty sable furs.

The hundreds all end in a form of the word for a hundred (**сто**). The word for a thousand is **ты́сяча**. In fast speech it will sound more like **ты́ща**.

● Listening

Hotels have a service desk (**Бюро́ обслу́живания**) where the staff will provide advice and information on booking cars, restaurants, theatre tickets and flights, as well as arranging tourist excursions. The guides often speak English well but will, no doubt, be pleased if you can speak to them in Russian.

⊚ EXERCISE 8

This is a conversation between a woman in a **бюро́ обслу́живания** and a tourist. Answer the following questions in English or Russian.

1 What does the guest want?
2 Why can't he get it?
3 What does he suggest as an alternative?
4 What is the reply?
5 How many tickets does he finally order?

A situation to remember

Shopping in Russia

Here is a typical situation in a Russian shop. Devise a conversation with a partner.

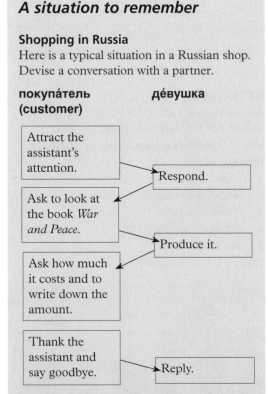

покупа́тель (customer)   де́вушка

- Attract the assistant's attention.
- Respond.
- Ask to look at the book *War and Peace*.
- Produce it.
- Ask how much it costs and to write down the amount.
- Thank the assistant and say goodbye.
- Reply.

Now try to buy a samovar, vodka and some flowers.

Doing your sums

Practise counting from 1–10 in Russian.

Ask a friend the answer to some simple sums in Russian:

два плюс два, пять ми́нус три, три плюс семь, де́вять ми́нус во́семь, четы́ре плюс два

● Playing with words

Кроссворд

Here is a Russian crossword. You have met almost all the words. The clues for the ones you have not met are marked with ★. You should be able to guess them fairly easily, by solving adjacent clues.

Across

1   семь, во́семь ____
5   No
6   I
8   раз, два, ____ , четы́ре
10 Opposite of **нет**
11 Swan Lake, for instance
13 In, into in some places
14 A fur one to keep out the cold
17 Storey, floor
19 A telephone might be this, though not automatically
21 Cabbage soup
22 He, it
23 A telephone has one, and so does a room in a hotel
25 Eating place
26 Where you live
27 Former Soviet press agency*
29 Port on the Black Sea, famous for its steps*
30 Halt!
31 Every footballer has them
32 She

Down

1   Young lady
2   The thing to say when you point at something
3   Three
4   Where to go for a meal or just a drink
7   **Кино́, кафе́, метро́** may each be replaced by this but not by 32 across
9   A kind of pop music*
12 This for peace in a power station
13 You
15 **Марс, Юпи́тер**, for example*
16 You catch this when you cannot afford а **такси́**
17 This
18 Moscow football club
20 Joke or anecdote*
24 When a woman is pleased
27 That, not quite **э́тот**
28 * **щи** and **бульо́н** are examples of a Russian one

Put things in their place

Complete the following, using the crossword as a reference. Look up the word on the left and put it *in* or *on* the word on the right. Don't forget to change the ending of the word on the right to make it into the prepositional case. The first one is done for you.

1 down **Де́вушка** в 29 across **Оде́ссе**

14 across _____ на 1 down _____

31 across _____ в 16 down _____

32 across _____ в 23 across _____

Find the clue

Look at the clues below, find their numbers in the list of clues in the crossword and print the number of the clue in Russian. The first one is done for you.

I	номер шесть
Young lady	но́мер _____
раз, два, _____, четы́ре	но́мер _____
The thing to say when you point at something	но́мер _____
A kind of pop music	но́мер _____
No!	но́мер _____
Three	но́мер _____
Opposite of нет	но́мер _____

Which numbers between 1 and 10 are missing?

но́мер _____   но́мер _____

WHAT YOU KNOW

How to get to places
Как мне пройти́/прое́хать на Кра́сную пло́щадь?
Иди́те напра́во, нале́во, пря́мо.

Лу́чше на авто́бусе/на тролле́йбусе/на трамва́е/на метро́.
Там напро́тив остано́вка.

Asking for things in shops
У вас есть план метро́?
Есть.

Покажи́те (Да́йте), пожа́луйста, план метро́.
Вот он.

Having things
У меня́ есть план метро́.
У тебя́ есть проездно́й биле́т.
У нас есть тало́ны.
У вас есть жето́ны.

Numbers
оди́н, два, три, четы́ре, пять, шесть, семь, во́семь, де́вять, де́сять, сто, ты́сяча

KEY VOCABULARY

авто́бус	bus
Да́йте пожа́луйста ...?	Give (me), please
де́вушка	girl (form of address in shop)
жето́н	token (on underground)
Как мне прое́хать ...	How do I get to (by vehicle)
Как мне пройти́ ...	How do I get to (on foot)
конья́к	brandy
лу́чше	better
метро́	metro, underground
напро́тив	opposite
остано́вка	stop
план	map
Покажи́те, пожа́луйста ...	Show me, please
ста́нция	station
тало́н	ticket (on bus)
трамва́й	tram
тролле́йбус	trolley bus
У вас есть ...?	Have you got ...?
чай	tea
четы́ре	four
шампа́нское	champagne

но́мер семь

Being introduced to people

Russian names

How to address close friends and children

Different nationalities

● Life in Russia

Russian names

If you have read a Russian novel in translation, you will probably at some stage have been confused, because the same person can have a bewildering variety of names. All Russians have three names. A man might be called **Ива́н Петро́вич Па́влов**, his sister **Ната́лья Петро́вна Па́влова**.

Russian surnames typically end in:

-ов for a man, **-ова** for a woman (see the above example)
-ин for a man, **-ина** for a woman (e.g. **Воро́нин**, man, **Воро́нина**, woman)
-ский for a man, **-ская** for a woman (e.g. **Ма́йский**, man, **Ма́йская**, woman)

In addition to a surname (**фами́лия**) and first name (**и́мя**), each Russian has a *patronymic* (**о́тчество**) derived, as its name implies, from the name of one's father (**оте́ц**) by adding **-ович** or **-евич** for a man and **-овна** or **-евна** for a woman.

Father	Son	Daughter
Ива́н	Ива́нович	Ива́новна
Серге́й	Серге́евич	Серге́евна
Алекса́ндр	Алекса́ндрович	Алекса́ндровна
Алексе́й	Алексе́евич	Алексе́евна
Пётр	Петро́вич	Петро́вна

Russian does not have any equivalent of Mr, Mrs, Miss, Ms. The combination of the first name and patronymic (**имя и óтчество**) is used instead. Schoolchildren address their teachers in this way. Politicians are also often referred to by their **имя-óтчество**. Their surnames are often omitted.

• •

EXERCISE 1

The following are the **имя-óтчество** of some of the leaders of the Soviet Union or Russia. Can you supply their surnames? The first one is done for you.

1   Влади́мир Ильи́ч   <u>Ле́нин</u>

2   Ио́сиф Виссарио́нович   _____

3   Ники́та Серге́евич   _____

4   Михаи́л Серге́евич   _____

5   Бори́с Никола́евич   _____

6   Влади́мир Влади́мирович   _____

• •

EXERCISE 2

Here is a family tree for the Ivanov family.

Ивано́вы

Бори́с Ива́нович = Людми́ла Алекса́ндровна

| 1 | = Ната́лья Васи́льевна

Па́вел Петро́вич = | 2 |

| 3 | = Тама́ра Макси́мовна

| 4 | = Óльга Серге́евна

Ви́ктор Ива́нович = | 5 |

54

Complete the Ivanov family tree. Look for the name of the father and match it with the patronymic below. Put the number in the right box. The first one is done for you.

Алексе́й Бори́сович | 1 |

Ива́н Никола́евич | |

Ни́на Алексе́евна | |

Áнна Ива́новна | |

Серге́й Па́влович | |

• •

Russian first names usually have two different forms, the standard one used together with the **óтчество** and a so-called *diminutive* one. This is used immediately you are on informal terms with someone. When talking to foreigners, Russians often just refer to themselves by the diminutive form of their first name. You are then spared the problem of remembering their name and patronymic.

Examples of diminutive forms are:

Male	Diminutive
Алексе́й	Алёша
Бори́с	Бо́ря
Ви́ктор	Ви́тя
Влади́мир	Воло́дя
Ива́н	Ва́ня
Михаи́л	Ми́ша
Пётр	Пе́тя
Серге́й	Серёжа
Юрий	Юра
Алекса́ндр	Са́ша
Евге́ний	Же́ня

Female	Diminutive
Óльга	Óля
Áнна	Áня
Гали́на	Га́ля
Ири́на	И́ра
Ната́лья	Ната́ша
Еле́на	Ле́на
Алекса́ндра	Са́ша
Евге́ния	Же́ня

Note that Са́ша and Же́ня can be either a man or a woman.

English also has shortened forms of first names (James = Jim, Jimmy, etc.). In English the use of a shortened form depends on the individual. In Russian it is normal to use the diminutive form, once you have decided you are on informal terms with someone.

If you were introduced to **Ива́н Петро́вич Ле́вин**, your new teacher, you would call him **Ива́н Петро́вич**. On the other hand, if he turned out to be a fellow student and not your teacher, you would call him **Ва́ня**. Young people usually use the diminutive form straight away when meeting people of the same age and status. You always use diminutive forms when talking to children.

Russian first names can have a whole range of forms indicating endearment, affection, and occasionally, contempt. The endearment forms often end in **-ечка**, **-очка**, **-енька**, **-ушка** or **-юшка**. Many names have more than one form. **Ива́н,** for example, has at least five 'endearment' forms (**Ваню́ша**, **Ва́нечка**, **Ваню́шечка**, **Ваню́шка** and **Ива́нушка**) but only one 'contempt' form (**Ва́нька**). It is advisable to stick to the basic diminutive form, or you might end up suggesting a close relationship that you do not intend!

ты or вы

Russian has two words meaning *you*: **ты** and **вы**. This has a parallel with many other European languages (compare French *tu/vous*, German *du/Sie*).

You always use **вы** if you are talking to a group of people. Talking to one person, a Russian would use **ты**, if using the diminutive form of the first name. If a Russian uses **и́мя-о́тчество** when talking to a person, he or she would normally use the **вы** form. **Вы** is always used to people of an older generation or to superiors at work, **ты** is used to friends and is always used to children. Alternatively you can ask

Мо́жно на ты? *Can I use* **ты**? A Russian may suggest **Дава́йте на ты!** (*Let's use* **ты** *to one another.*)

You should listen to how a Russian addresses you and reply with the same word **ты** or **вы** as the Russian used to you. If in doubt, use **вы**.

● Language information

Forms with ты and вы

A number of words have got different forms, depending on whether you are using **ты** or **вы**:

ты form	вы form	
здра́вствуй[1]	здра́вствуйте	*hello*
извини́	извини́те	*excuse me*
скажи́	скажи́те	*tell me*
Как ты пожива́ешь?	Как вы пожива́ете?	*How are you?*
Как тебя́ зову́т?	Как вас зову́т?[2]	*What's your name?*
Ско́лько тебе́ лет?	Ско́лько вам лет?[3]	*How old are you?*

1 As an alternative to **здра́вствуй** in informal language, you can say **Приве́т!**
2 **Как тебя́ зову́т?** means literally *How do they call you?* Your reply should start off with the phrase **Меня́ зову́т ...** (*They call me ...*)
3 The answer is **Мне ... лет.** (*I am ... years old.*)

A useful word when getting to know people is **Познако́мьтесь!** It is said by someone when introducing two strangers. It means literally *Get acquainted.* It has only one (**вы**) form, as two people are being addressed.

Look at the following telephone conversations. The first one is formal, the second one informal. The versions are not meant as exact translations, but as an indication of what is likely in formal and informal situations.

Formal

- Здра́вствуйте, Ви́ктор Ива́нович!
- Говори́т Ивано́в. Как вы пожива́ете?
- Бори́с Миха́йлович, как дела́ у вас в Санкт-Петербу́рге?

Informal

- Здра́вствуй, Ви́тя! Как пожива́ешь? Э́то Бо́ря.
- Бо́ря, приве́т! Как там у тебя́ в Санкт-Петербу́рге?

. . . .

EXERCISE 3

You are staying with a Russian family. They decide to have a party.
The following people come in through the door. Greet each of them by underlining either **здра́вствуй** or **здра́вствуйте**.

⊙ EXERCISE 4

On your recording an older person is talking to a small child.
Listen to the conversation. Then answer the questions.

1 What is the child's name?
2 How old is she?
3 What is she playing with?
4 How many has she got?
5 What does her father do?
6 What does her mother do?

Are they on **ты** or **вы** terms?

. . . .

Adjectives

Adjective endings change depending on the noun which follows.

'**Он**' nouns (masculine) have adjectives ending in:

-ый: вку́сн**ый** чай (*tasty tea*)
-ий after **к** or **ш**: Не́вск**ий** проспе́кт; хоро́ш**ий** студе́нт
-о́й if the ending is stressed: Больш**о́й** теа́тр

'**Она́**' nouns (feminine) have adjectives ending in -**ая**: Кра́сн**ая** пло́щадь

'**Оно́**' nouns (neuter) have endings in **-ое**: кра́сн**ое** вино́

If the noun is plural, the ending is **-ые**: краси́в**ые** же́нщины (*beautiful women*); **-ие** after **к** and **ш**: ру́сск**ие** же́нщины (*Russian women*); хоро́ш**ие** студе́нты (*good students*)

EXERCISE 5

Look at the following and join them up to make sentences. The first one is done for you. **Страна́** means country, **столи́ца** means capital city.

1	Росси́я	ру́сский	футболи́сты
2	Оли́мпус	англи́йский	порт
3	Де́вушка, у вас есть	америка́нская	шампа́нское
4	Москва́	япо́нский	столи́ца
5	На столе́	росси́йская	газе́та
6	Дина́мовцы	кра́сное	царь
7	Нью-Йорк Таймс	украи́нский	вино́
8	Бори́с Годуно́в	францу́зское	фотоаппара́т
9	Оде́сса	больша́я	го́род
10	Ма́нчестер	хоро́шие	страна́

● Looking at words

Many of the adjectives in this unit are to do with nationalities – **ру́сский**, **брита́нский**, **америка́нский**, etc. Notice that nationality words start with a small letter. Only names of countries start with a capital, e.g. **Аме́рика**. Look at these examples:

Country	Adjective	Male	Female
А́нглия *England*	англи́йский	англича́нин	англича́нка
Аме́рика *America*	америка́нский	америка́нец	америка́нка
Герма́ния *Germany*	неме́цкий	не́мец	не́мка
Ирла́ндия *Ireland*	ирла́ндский	ирла́ндец	ирла́ндка
Кана́да *Canada*	кана́дский	кана́дец	кана́дка
По́льша *Poland*	по́льский	поля́к	по́лька
Росси́я *Russia*	ру́сский	ру́сский	ру́сская
Уэльс *Wales*	валли́йский	валли́ец	валли́йка
Украи́на *Ukraine*	украи́нский	украи́нец	украи́нка
Фра́нция *France*	францу́зский	францу́з	францу́женка
Шотла́ндия *Scotland*	шотла́ндский	шотла́ндец	шотла́ндка

Only **Герма́ния**, *Germany*, has a nationality word (**не́мец**, *a German*) from a different source. This comes from the word **немо́й**, *dumb*, and was originally applied to all foreigners who could not speak Russian. **Аме́рика** refers to the whole continent. The USA is **США** in Russian, short for **Соединённые Шта́ты Аме́рики**.

Alongside **ру́сский** there is a second adjective, **росси́йский**, mentioned in Unit 2. The country's full title is **Росси́йская федера́ция**. However, note that **ру́сский** and **ру́сская** are always used for citizens of the country: this is the only nationality to use an adjective for the citizen of a country.

EXERCISE 6

Look at the map and insert the number of the country in the correct place on the map. The first one is done for you.

1	Россия	5	Украина
2	Áнглия	6	Пóльша
3	США	7	Канáда
4	Гермáния	8	Фрáнция

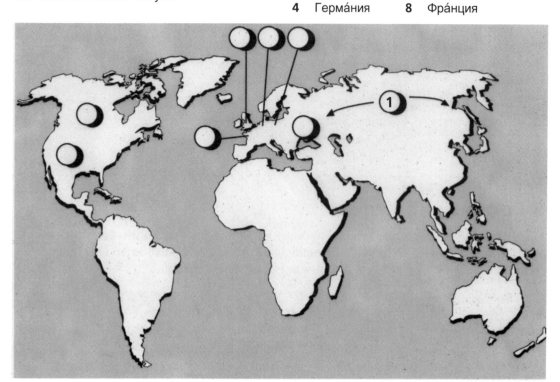

A situation to remember

Getting to know each other

You are staying at a Russian's flat. Your host decides to have a party.

Each of the characters from Exercise 3 comes through the door. They say 'hello' and give their name.

You give yours, say that you are pleased to meet them (**Óчень приятно!**). Ask them how they are.

Use **ты** or **вы**, taking your cue from the Russian.

Talking on the telephone

Useful key phrases when talking on the phone are:

Аллó *or* **Слýшаю вас** *hello*
Вы не тудá попáли *or* **Не тот нóмер** *wrong number*
Перезвонúте *try again*

 Now turn once more to your recording. A man is trying to make a call from a phone box (**телефóн-автомáт**).

He gets the wrong number at the first attempt.

Listen out for the key phrases given above. Re-enact the conversation, if possible, with the help of a friend.

Reading handwriting

Decipher the illustrated written forms and print them underneath the photographs.

WHAT YOU KNOW

Asking someone's name
Как тебя/вас зовут?

and giving your name
Меня зовут Борис/Наташа

Describing things
Кра́сный	авто́бус
Кра́сная	ма́рка
Кра́сное	вино́
Кра́сные	авто́бусы

ты or вы
здра́вствуй – здра́вствуйте
скажи́ – скажи́те
извини́ – извини́те

Making polite requests
Скажи́те, пожа́луйста

KEY VOCABULARY

алло́	hello (on the phone)
англи́йский	English
англича́нин	Englishman
англича́нка	Englishwoman
вы	you (formal)
и́мя	first name
Как вы пожива́ете/ ты пожива́ешь?	How are you?
Как тебя́/вас зову́т?	What is your name?
оте́ц	father
о́тчество	patronymic
Познако́мьтесь	Can I introduce ...?
приве́т	hello
ру́сский	Russian, Russian man
ру́сская	Russian woman
скажи́/скажи́те	tell (me)
слу́шаю	hello (on the phone)
столи́ца	capital city
ты	you (informal)
фами́лия	surname
хоро́ший	good

Russian weather and Russian television

Russian weather

Time zones

What's on television

Likes and dislikes

● Life in Russia

The Russian climate

Russia is the biggest country in the world, stretching almost half way round it.

There are eleven time zones from one side to the other. Moscow is roughly on the same latitude as Edinburgh, and St Petersburg is on the same latitude as the Shetland Islands, the southern tip of Greenland and the most northerly point of Newfoundland. Moscow is usually thought of as being very cold. In fact it has a continental climate, cold in winter and hot in summer.

As you travel eastward on any latitude the average temperature goes down, and the coldest area is around **Верхоя́нск**, where the average winter temperature is below minus 50 degrees Celsius in January. The subsoil remains frozen all the year round in over 45 per cent of Russia, making difficult the exploitation of the vast mineral resources. The fact that the major rivers in Siberian Russia flow from south to north creates difficult conditions in spring and makes it impossible fully to exploit the rivers as sources of hydro-electricity.

Russians like talking about the weather (**пого́да**): they complain as much as the British do! If you want to say you are hot or cold, use the following phrases:

Мне хо́лодно *I'm cold.*   Мне тепло́ *I'm warm.*
Мне жа́рко *I'm hot.*   Мне о́чень хо́лодно means *I am very cold.*

Literally these phrases mean *it is cold/warm/hot to me*. If you simply want to state that the weather is cold, warm or hot, use the same words without **мне**.

You have met most Russian numbers in Unit 6. If you need the intervening ones, simply combine the numbers **оди́н** to **де́вять** with **два́дцать**, **три́дцать**, etc. as you would in English:

два́дцать оди́н *21*   три́дцать два *32*   со́рок три *43*   пятьдеся́т четы́ре *54*

EXERCISE 1

Here are some temperatures from a weather forecast for October.
Read the temperatures and write them in (гра́дус means *degree*).
State if you feel hot, warm or cold. The first one is done for you.

1 В Москве́ плюс оди́н гра́дус.   Мне хо́лодно. _____   +1 ___

2 В Му́рманске ми́нус два гра́дуса.   _____   ____

3 В Волгогра́де плюс семь гра́дусов.   _____   ____

4 Во Владивосто́ке плюс шестна́дцать гра́дусов.   _____   ____

5 В Верхоя́нске ми́нус два́дцать два гра́дуса.   _____   ____

6 В Краснода́ре плюс два́дцать три гра́дуса.   _____   ____

Telling the time

The 24-hour clock is widely used for official purposes: e.g. in railway and air timetables and for television and radio programmes.

EXERCISE 2

Here are some times written out in full. Write them in numbers.
The first one is done for you.
Ско́лько сейча́с вре́мени? *What time is it?*

1   Восемна́дцать часо́в два́дцать мину́т   *18.20*

2   Два́дцать оди́н час пять мину́т   _____

3   Два́дцать два часа́ де́сять мину́т   _____

4   Девятна́дцать часо́в пятна́дцать мину́т   _____

5   Двена́дцать часо́в два́дцать две мину́ты   _____

6   Пятна́дцать часо́в два́дцать пять мину́т   _____

7   Семна́дцать часо́в три мину́ты   _____

8   Трина́дцать часо́в три́дцать пять мину́т   _____

9   Два часа́ со́рок де́вять мину́т   _____

10 Де́сять часо́в пятьдеся́т пять мину́т   _____

Note that after numbers 2–4 and 22–24 **часа́** is used. After **оди́н** the form **час** is used. In every other case the form is **часо́в**.

Moscow time is three hours ahead of London and two hours ahead of the rest of Western Europe. Look at the time zone map below. The time in west European Russia is called Moscow time (**моско́вское вре́мя**), even if you are in St Petersburg!

EXERCISE 3

You are given **моско́вское вре́мя**, Moscow time. You are then asked what time it is in another town.
Write down the correct time.
The first one is done for you.

1 Моско́вское вре́мя 12 часо́в.
  А в Ло́ндоне ско́лько сейча́с вре́мени?
  <u>9 часо́в</u>

2 Моско́вское вре́мя 11 часо́в.
  А в Новосиби́рске ско́лько сейча́с
  вре́мени?   __ час__

3 Моско́вское вре́мя 4 часа́.
  А в Пари́же ско́лько сейча́с вре́мени?
  __ час__

4 Моско́вское вре́мя 17 часо́в.
  А в Ирку́тске ско́лько сейча́с вре́мени?
  __ час__

5 Моско́вское вре́мя 15 часо́в.
  А в Му́рманске ско́лько сейча́с
  вре́мени?   __ час__

6 Моско́вское вре́мя 7 часо́в.
  А в Волгогра́де ско́лько сейча́с
  вре́мени?   __ час__

7 Моско́вское вре́мя 3 часа́.
  А в О́мске ско́лько сейча́с вре́мени?
  __ час__

8 Моско́вское вре́мя 12 часо́в.
  А в Магада́не ско́лько сейча́с вре́мени?
  __ час__

9 Моско́вское вре́мя 21 час.
  А во Владивосто́ке ско́лько сейча́с
  вре́мени?   __ час__

Russian television

Russians have a variety of channels to watch, some of them local to the city where they live. They can also subscribe to national and international satellite channels.

The main national channels are **Пе́рвый кана́л** (*Channel One*), **Росси́я**, also known as **РТР**, short for **Росси́йское телеви́дение и ра́дио** (*Russian Television and Radio*) and **НТВ** short for **Незави́симое телеви́дение** (*Independent Television*). All are owned or controlled by the State, and though there is no official media censorship they rarely criticise the government. All channels are at least part-financed by **рекла́ма** *advertising*.

On the right you will see the programmes for a typical evening on **Пе́рвый кана́л**. There are two news broadcasts, one simply called **но́вости** *news*, derived from the word **но́вый**, *new* (compare to the English word *novel*). The main news of the night, at 9pm, is called **Вре́мя** *Time*.

Russians love their sport, and **прямо́й эфи́р** *live coverage* of football matches and other events is often shown. Game shows also feature heavily in the TV schedules, including formats that are familiar to us. Can you work out the name of the game show on Channel One?

Soaps are also popular, both Russian produced and imported. The South American '**Хозя́йка судьбы́**' *Mistress of Fate* is watched by large numbers of Russians every day. Can you spot episode 33 in the listings? The word **се́рия** is related to the English *series*. Russians also watch lots of films, many of them foreign. There are two showing after the main news – can you work out their English titles? **Ма́льчик** means *boy*.

ПРОГРАММА

14.00	Футбол. Чемпионат России. 'Динамо' – 'Спартак' прямой эфир
16.00	Гала-концерт
18.00	Новости
18.30	Сериал 'Хозяйка судьбы' 33-я серия
19.50	'Кто хочет стать миллионером?'
21.00	Время
21.30	Премьера. Хью Грант в комедии 'Мой мальчик'
23.00	Триллер 'Мистер Фрост'

. . . .

EXERCISE 4

Look at the TV programmes for Channel One and answer the following questions in English. **Что идёт в** means *What is on at...?* Place the time in the left-hand box and the programme title in the right-hand one. The first one is done for you.

1 Что идёт в восемна́дцать часо́в?

18.00	News

2 Что идёт в два́дцать оди́н час?

3 Что идёт в девятна́дцать часо́в пятдеся́т мину́т?

4 Что идёт в два́дцать три часа́?

5 Что идёт в четы́рнадцать часо́в?

6 Что идёт в шестна́дцать часо́в?

7 Что идёт в восемна́дцать часо́в три́дцать мину́т?

63

Now listen to your recording. Programmes for the afternoon and evening are being announced. The announcement finishes with «**Передаём после́дние изве́стия**» – *Here is the latest news.*
Answer the following questions:

1   When should football fans tune in? Who is playing?
2   When can you watch Sophia Loren?
3   What concert is on at 6.15pm?
4   When is this evening's soap opera on? (Listen out for a programme in many parts.)
5   If you want to find out about murders and robberies in Russia, when should you tune in?
6   When can you watch this evening's film premiere with Pierce Brosnan?
7   When are the two evening news broadcasts?

Ostankino TV tower, Moscow

● Language information

Present tense of verbs

Just like French, German, Spanish or Italian, Russian verbs change their forms, depending on who is performing the action.

игра́ть *to play*			
я (I)	игра́**ю**	мы (we)	игра́**ем**
ты (you)	игра́**ешь**	вы (you)	игра́**ете**
он (he)	игра́**ет**	они́ (they)	игра́**ют**
она́ (she)			

говори́ть *to say*			
я (I)	говорю́	мы (we)	говори́м
ты (you)	говори́шь	вы (you)	говори́те
он (he)	говори́т	они́ (they)	говоря́т
она́ (she)			

The dictionary form of verbs usually ends in **-ть**: this is the equivalent of the 'to' form in English. From now on this is the form we will use in the vocabulary lists in this book. Verbs ending in **-ать** or **-ять** have forms like **игра́ть**, those ending in **-ить** like **говори́ть**. Common verbs ending in **-еть** also usually have endings like **говори́ть**.

Я игра́ю в футбо́л, а Ми́ша игра́ет в хокке́й.
I play football and Misha plays ice-hockey.

Ты говори́шь по-ру́сски?
Do you speak Russian?

Она́ чита́ет рома́н «Война́ и мир».
She is reading the novel 'War and Peace'.

Мы не ку́рим.
We don't smoke.

Вы лю́бите смотре́ть телеви́зор?
Do you like watching television?

Они́ гуля́ют в па́рке.
They are walking in the park.

As you can see from the above translations, English has more than one present tense. Russian is much simpler: there is only one! You can deny things very easily in Russian: just add **не** to the verb. The best answer to a question, if you are not sure of something, is **Не зна́ю** (*I don't know*).

EXERCISE 6

Here is a matching exercise. Join the words together to make complete sentences. The first one is done for you.

1	Я	говоря́т по-ру́сски
2	Она́	игра́ю в футбо́л
3	Вы	лю́бит игра́ть на гита́ре
4	Они́	гуля́ете в па́рке
5	Он	смо́тришь телеви́зор
6	Ты	не зна́ем
7	Мы	говори́т по-англи́йски

По

A very common word in Russian is **по**. It can mean *along*: **по коридо́ру** (*along the corridor*); **по у́лице** (*along the street*). You will also see it with a number of communication words: **по телеви́зору** (*on television*); **по ра́дио** (*on the radio*); **по телефо́ну** (*on the telephone*). Note the endings:

add **у** to '**он**' (masculine) nouns
change **а** to **е** on '**она́**' (feminine) nouns.

This is the *dative case*.

По is also used to make new words, often hyphenated. *You speak Russian* is **Вы говори́те по-ру́сски**. *In English* is **по-англи́йски**. Look at the table on page 57 in Unit 7 and work out how to say *in French*, *in German* or even *in Ukrainian*! If you have an opinion you will need to know **по-мо́ему** (*in my opinion*), **по-тво́ему** or **по-ва́шему** (*in your opinion*).

Sometimes it becomes part of a new word: **почему́?** (*why?*) to which the answer is **потому́ что** (*because*).

EXERCISE 7

Here are a number of questions asking 'why' and a number of answers beginning with the word 'because'. Match up question and answer. The first one is done for you.

	Question	Answer
1	Почему́ рестора́н закры́т?	Потому́ что хорошо́ игра́ю.
2	Почему́ вы гуля́ете в па́рке?	Потому́ что она́ краси́вая.
3	Почему́ вы лю́бите те́ннис?	Потому́ что он о́чень краси́вый го́род.
4	Почему́ вы лю́бите Ни́ну?	Потому́ что там хорошо́.
5	Почему́ вам хо́лодно?	Потому́ что идёт ремо́нт.
6	Почему́ вы лю́бите Санкт-Петербу́рг?	Потому́ что сего́дня ми́нус два́дцать гра́дусов.

● Talking about words

Я тебя люблю

Liking/loving

There are two ways of saying *I like* or *I love* in Russian: **я люблю** or **мне нравится**. **Мне нравится** means that I like something specific and is never as passionate as *I love*. *You like* is **Вам (Тебе) нравится**. **Люблю** is more general and can mean *I like* or *I love*, depending on the passion in your voice. You should be careful about how you say **Люблю тебя** to a Russian! **Люблю** comes from **любить** and has forms like **говорить**. Note the extra **л** in the 'I' form only.

Look at the following examples:

Я люблю му́зыку	Вам нра́вится конце́рт?
Я люблю теа́тр	Вам нра́вится пье́са? *(play)*
Он лю́бит спорт	Мне нра́вится матч
Вы лю́бите те́ннис?	Вам нра́вится переда́ча?
Вы лю́бите кино́?	Мне нра́вится э́тот фильм.

Notice that if you want to say 'very much' you simply add the word **о́чень** (*very*), e.g. **Я о́чень люблю теа́тр** (*I like the theatre very much*).

Вам нра́вится Москва́? Да, о́чень.
Я о́чень люблю Ло́ндон.
Вам нра́вится э́та де́вушка? Не о́чень.

You can also use both forms to say that you like *doing* something, in which case the pattern looks like this:

Я люблю чита́ть.
Мне нра́вится смотре́ть телеви́зор.

If you want to say that you don't like doing something, simply add **не**: **я не люблю** or **мне не нра́вится**.

игра́ть *to play*

If you play a game in Russian, add the word **в**:

Он игра́ет в футбо́л.
Мы игра́ем в те́ннис.

If you play a musical instrument, use **на** and the **е** form of the noun (prepositional case):

Ми́ша игра́ет на гита́ре, а Са́ша игра́ет на балала́йке.

● Looking at words

New words

Russian has been changing rapidly since the collapse of the old Soviet Union. New borrowings from English and other Western European languages are flooding into the language.

Here are some new words that are now regularly used in Russian:
шо́ппинг
се́рвис
креди́т
а́удео
ви́део

If you are interested in computers, you shouldn't find the vocabulary too hard to understand:
компью́тер
Ви́ндос (*remember, Russian has no 'w'*)
софт
файл
интернет
сайт
се́рвер
при́нтер

EXERCISE 8

Every week Russians receive free newspapers, either delivered to their home or handed out in the street or at metro stations. Here are some words taken from adverts in a newspaper which describes itself as **Газе́та росси́йского бизнесме́на**. See if you can work out what they mean.

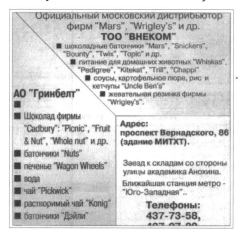

1	видеока́мера	7	при́нтер
2	дистрибью́тор	8	радиа́тор
3	инве́стор	9	сейф
4	йогу́рт	10	суперма́ркет
5	колле́дж	11	ча́ртер
6	компью́тер	12	шоп-тур

● Listening

What you do in your spare time

☞ EXERCISE 9

Listen to the recording. Four people are talking about leisure and work. Their names are **Са́ша**, **Ви́ктор**, **А́нна** and **Ни́на**. Listen particularly for the information asked for in the questions below, and answer the questions.

1 What is Nina's occupation?
2 What does Anna like doing?
3 What does Sasha do in his spare time?
4 Which TV programmes do they all like?
5 Which does Victor like very much?

● Playing with words

Reading handwriting

Russians sometimes use handwriting-style typefaces in advertisements. Here are a few from a free newspaper.

Try to work out what the adverts mean. Have a go at writing out the slogans, copying the Russian handwriting.

Decipher the illustrated written forms, and print the words beneath the photographs.

Word square

Here is a word square with some Russian words, borrowed from English. There are ten in all for you to find.

ф	д	о	к	м	к
а	и	д	с	а	о
к	л	и	е	н	т
с	е	с	р	г	т
т	р	к	о	о	е
р	п	н	к	о	д
о	ф	и	с	ш	ж

WHAT YOU KNOW

Temperature
Мне хо́лодно/тепло́/жа́рко.

Present tense of verbs

игра́ть to play	
игра́ю	игра́ем
игра́ешь	игра́ете
игра́ет	игра́ют

говори́ть to say	
говорю́	говори́м
говори́шь	говори́те
говори́т	говоря́т

По
по у́лице, по коридо́ру
по телеви́зору, по ра́дио, по телефо́ну

Я говорю́ по-ру́сски/по-англи́йски.

по-мо́ему/по-тво́ему/по-ва́шему
Почему́ рестора́н закры́т?
Потому́ что идёт ремо́нт.

Like/love
Я (о́чень) люблю́ спорт.
Мне (о́чень) нра́вится футбо́л.

Play
Я игра́ю в футбо́л.
Я игра́ю на балала́йке.

KEY VOCABULARY

вре́мя	time
говори́ть	to say
гуля́ть	to walk
жа́рко	hot
знать	to know
игра́ть (в футбо́л)	to play (football)
(на балала́йке)	(the balalaika)
идёт	is on
изве́стия	news
люби́ть	to like, to love
но́вости	news
(мне) нра́вится	(I) like
переда́ча	broadcast
по	along, on (TV, radio ...)
по-англи́йски	in English
по-ва́шему	in your opinion
по-мо́ему	in my opinion
по-ру́сски	in Russian
по-тво́ему	in your opinion
потому́ что	because
почему́?	why?
Ско́лько сейча́с вре́мени?	What's the time?
смотре́ть (телеви́зор)	to watch (television)
тепло́	warm
хо́лодно	cold
час	hour, o'clock
чита́ть	to read

9

но́мер де́вять

What Russians like to eat and drink

Eating out in a Russian restaurant

Asking for what you want in a restaurant

What to expect when you are invited out for a meal

Russian cooking

● Life in Russia

Eating out

Russia offers great and varied opportunities for eating out. You'll find the usual pizza places and fast-food outlets, as well as Chinese and Japanese restaurants. For something more authentic, look for restaurants specialising in Georgian or Uzbek cuisine. Restaurants serving typically Russian food often have a buffet, which, as well as being good value, let you sample lots of different dishes. Russians call the buffet **шве́дский стол** *smorgasbord*, (literally, *Swedish table*). Two popular chains are **Ёлки-па́лки** (roughly, *Blow me down!*) and **Дрова́** (*Firewood*).

Typical Georgian dishes include **саци́ви**, chicken in a creamy walnut sauce, **ло́био** *beans* (cooked in a variety of ways) and **шашлы́к,** pieces of meat or fish on a skewer, cooked over charcoal. In an Uzbek restaurant try **плов**, a rice-based dish similar to pilaff or pilau.

Restaurants in Russia rarely have menus outside, which makes it hard to predict prices. Don't be embarrassed to go in and ask: **Покажи́те меню́**. If it's all in Russian, try asking **По-англи́йски,**

69

пожа́луйста. If you don't like what you see, just say **Спаси́бо** and leave. Below are some exchanges that might take place. Notice the different ways your question could be answered.

Question	Answer
Здесь свобо́дно?	Свобо́дно. (*free*)
	Нет, за́нято. (*occupied*)
Мо́жно?	Мо́жно.
	Сади́тесь, пожа́луйста.
	Please take a seat.

You might just hear **пожа́луйста** to show it is all right to sit down.

Don't forget, **Мо́жно?** is a very useful way of asking if you can do something (see Unit 4).

> Что вы хоти́те?

> Мне, пожа́луйста, икру́ и шампа́нское.

The waitress asks you what you want. You give the first part of your order – caviar and champagne.

> И пото́м?

> У вас есть борщ? И суда́к?

> Есть

She assumes that you want something to follow. You ask for beetroot soup and zander, after checking they are on the menu.

> Хорошо́. Да́йте, пожа́луйста, борщ и судака́.

She brings you the first part of your meal and wishes you 'bon appetit'.

> Вот, пожа́луйста, икра́ и шампа́нское. Прия́тного аппети́та!

> Спаси́бо.

> Пожа́луйста.

> Свобо́дно?

> Пожа́луйста. Сади́тесь.

> Де́вушка!

> Слу́шаю вас!

You enter the restaurant and look for a free table

You call over the waitress

> Да́йте, пожа́луйста, меню́.

> Вот, пожа́луйста, меню́.

You ask for the menu, which the waitress produces

> Де́вушка, да́йте мне, пожа́луйста, счёт.

> Вот он.

You ask for the bill.

Useful words and phrases in a restaurant are:

свобо́дно	*free*
де́вушка	(used to address a waitress)
Слу́шаю вас.	(said by waiter/ waitress when ready to take your order)
пото́м	*next*
Да́йте, пожа́луйста...	*Can I please have ...*
or Мне, пожа́луйста...	
Сади́тесь, пожа́луйста.	*Please sit down.*
Да́йте, пожа́луйста, счёт.	*Can I have the bill, please?*
Прия́тного аппети́та!	*Enjoy your meal / 'Bon appetit'.*

If you choose a traditional Russian restaurant, this is the sort of menu that you might expect. Notice that there are no stress marks on the vowels – which is normal practice in written Russian. See if you can work out which syllable is stressed in each word.

МЕНЮ

закуски
1. салат из помидоров
2. салат мясной
3. рыбное ассорти
4. икра красная
5. салат «Цесарь»
6. грибы со сметаной
7. солёные огурцы

первые блюда
8. щи
9. борщ украинский
10. бульон
11. суп грибной

вторые блюда
12. судак жареный
13. шашлык из осетрины
14. лосось с красной икрой
15. бефстроганов
16. филе из говядины
17. пельмени
18. курица с картошкой
19. свинина с рисом

сладкое
20. торт «Наполеон»
21. профитроли «Принцесса»
22. фруктовый салат
23. мороженое

напитки
24. водка «Столичная»
25. коньяк
26. шампанское
27. вино грузинское, красное
28. вино французское, белое
29. виски
30. джинтоник

31. чай с лимоном
32. кофе «Эспрессо»
33. кофе «Капуччино»
34. сок
35. минеральная вода
36. Фанта
37. лимонад

A **меню́** in a Russian restaurant is divided into the following sections:

заку́ски	hors d'oeuvre, starters
пе́рвые блю́да	soups (literally first dishes)
вторы́е блю́да	main course (literally second dishes)
сла́дкое	dessert
напи́тки	drinks

You will notice from the menu above that many dishes have names that are recognisable from their (mainly) French equivalents. **Борщ** and **щи**, two types of soup, are both meat-based and contain lots of vegetables. They are usually served with **смета́на** sour cream. The essential ingredient of **щи** is cabbage, and that of **борщ** is beetroot. **Суда́к** zander is a popular freshwater fish related to the perch. **Пельме́ни** are Siberian dumplings, which are stuffed with meat or vegetables. Some other words that you may see on a menu are:

помидо́ры	tomatoes
мя́со/мясно́й	meat
ры́ба/ры́бный	fish
икра́	caviar
огурцы́	cucumbers
солёный	salted
осетри́на	sturgeon
лосо́сь	salmon
говя́дина	beef
свини́на	pork
ку́рица	chicken
карто́шка	potatoes
торт	gateau
моро́женое	ice-cream
грузи́нское вино́	Georgian wine
сок	juice

EXERCISE 1

You are a waiter in a Moscow hotel, and a group of four business people (**бизнесме́ны**) arrive from Britain. You are taking their order.

Here is a list of what they choose. From the menu on page 71 put the number of each item in the box next to their choice.

Ms Benson

lemonade ☐

meat salad ☐

beetroot soup ☐

dumplings ☐

profiteroles ☐

French wine ☐

Mr Brown

vodka ☐

caviar ☐

cabbage soup ☐

fillet steak ☐

gateau ☐

brandy ☐

Mr Smith

mineral water ☐

mushroom soup ☐

kebabs ☐

fruit salad ☐

cappuccino ☐

Georgian wine ☐

Mr Hart

juice ☐

salted cucumbers ☐

zander ☐

ice-cream ☐

lemon tea ☐

champagne ☐

🎧 EXERCISE 2

Listen to your CD. It contains the dialogue from page 70, but each time something else is added.

Listen carefully and see if you can understand what is being said. The questions will help you understand the recording.

1 Does the man like the restaurant?
2 What time do they serve dinner?
3 What type of food does he look for on the menu?
4 What is missing from the menu?
5 What does he order to finish off with?
6 What does he think of Russian champagne?
7 What does he think of the bill?

EXERCISE 3

Look at the picture below and match the food to the words below by putting the correct numbers in the boxes.

чёрная икра́ ☐		сала́т ☐
шампа́нское ☐		шашлы́к ☐
ку́рица ☐		ко́фе ☐
фру́кты ☐		моро́женое ☐
ры́ба ☐		грибы́ ☐
вода́ ☐		во́дка ☐

Eating in

Of course, you will want to try genuine Russian cooking, and the best place to do this is in a Russian home. If you are lucky enough to be invited for a meal or to be staying in a Russian home, you will experience the generous hospitality for which Russians are famous.

Russian meals are as follows:

За́втрак. This is the equivalent of breakfast but is far more substantial than in Britain. Here are some dishes you might be given for breakfast:

кефи́р	*a kind of yoghurt*
сыр	*cheese*
тво́рог	*curd cheese*
блины́ со смета́ной	*pancakes with sour cream*
яйцо́	*egg*
яи́чница	*a fried egg dish, often with ham* (ветчина́)
сок	
чай, ко́фе	

Обе́д is a large meal served in the middle of the day; **у́жин** is served in the evening. **Обе́д** or **у́жин** will usually start with **заку́ски** (*snacks* or *hors-d'oeuvre*) often washed down with glasses of vodka, brandy or juice. There is often a large variety of these **заку́ски**, which can be the most substantial part of the meal.

Заку́ски

Ры́ба (*fish*)
креве́тки (*prawns*), **форе́ль** (*trout*), **осетри́на** (*sturgeon*)
Икра́ (*caviar*), **кра́сная** (red) from Pacific salmon, or **чёрная** (black) from sturgeon if your hosts can afford it.

Мя́со (*meat*)
Колбаса́ (*continental sausage*), or **ветчина́**

Сала́т (*salad*)
Помидо́ры, **огурцы́** often in dill or salted (**солёные**).

Both are often accompanied by **смета́на** (*sour cream*), a bowl of which usually remains on the table for use with the soup course.

Супы́ (*soup*)

Russians love to eat hearty soups full of vegetables. Perhaps the most famous are **щи** (*cabbage soup*) and **борщ** (*beetroot soup*). **Суп-лапша́** (*noodle soup*) and **бульо́н** (*clear soup*) are also popular. Soup is usually served during **обе́д** rather than **у́жин**.

Вторы́е блю́да will contain meat or fish dishes and may be followed by **сла́дкие**, often a very sweet gateau (**торт**) or ice-cream (**моро́женое**).

Russians love conversation, and **обе́д** or **у́жин** in a Russian household can often take a lot longer to consume than in most other countries. So if you are invited out for a meal by Russian friends, make sure you're not rushing off anywhere afterwards!

On certain special occasions, Russians will prepare a big meal. They may drink quite a lot during this feast, and accompany each drink with a **тост**. A general toast would be **За ва́ше здоро́вье!** *Your health!* Besides **во́дка**, **пи́во** and **вино́**, they will often drink **шампа́нское**. **Сухо́е** is *dry*, **полусухо́е** *medium-dry* and **сла́дкое** *sweet*.

The word for *ready* is **гото́в**; thus you might hear **У́жин/обе́д гото́в**. In a domestic situation you might hear the expression **Ку́шайте** or **Ку́шайте на здоро́вье!** (literally *eat for the good of your health*). **Ку́шать** is an old word for *eat*, and is an expression that you will certainly hear but should not try and use, as it is limited in its use. **Ку́шайте!** is an encouragement to eat, almost like the English *Tuck in!*

Russians tend to eat more freshwater species of fish than we do. **Суда́к**, **щу́ка** (*pike*) and **лосо́сь** are all popular dishes, and **осетри́на** is a great delicacy. Fish is sometimes sold live in the markets and some Russian recipes will give special instructions on how the fish should be treated before it is killed, to give it the best taste.

If you have enjoyed your meal, besides saying **Большо́е спаси́бо** you might tell your host how tasty the meal was – **О́чень вку́сно!**

Whether in a restaurant or in a Russian home you will always find **хлеб** (*bread*) on the table. Bread and salt (**соль**) are a traditional symbol of hospitality. There is a wide variety of bread, but the ones that appear most frequently are **бе́лый хлеб** and **чёрный хлеб**.

Чёрный хлеб is usually prepared with rye flour, wheat germ and molasses and traditionally made by the sourdough method. It is much heavier than white bread, though much tastier and, of course, more typically Russian. Some Russians will not serve black bread to non-Russians,

as many foreigners do not like it, and city-dwellers often consider it to be a 'peasant' food. If you want butter with your bread (it is normally served without), you simply ask for **хлеб с ма́слом**.

Russians are very fond of **моро́женое**. Alongside traditional Russian ice-cream you'll find the usual brands, produced under licence in Russia.

. . . .

☉ EXERCISE 4
Listen to the CD. You are in a Russian home and your Russian host is asking you to take your place at the table.
See how many of the **заку́ски** you can recognise. What is the main course?

. . . .

● Language information

Want

я	хочу́	мы	хоти́м
ты	хо́чешь	вы	хоти́те
он, она́	хо́чет	они́	хотя́т

You can ask people if they want something with the word **Хоти́те?** Reply with **(не) хочу́**. Try to make your voice go up on the **и** of **хоти́те**.

Хоти́те вино́?	*Do you want some wine?*
Хоти́те осетри́ну?	*Do you want some sturgeon?*
Хочу́ or Не хочу́.	*I do* or *I don't.*

To ask if you are hungry or thirsty you say:

| Хоти́те есть? | *Are you hungry?* |
| Хоти́те пить? | *Are you thirsty?* |

You reply simply:

Хочу́	*Yes, I am.*
or	
Не хочу́	*No, I'm not.*

The sentences mean literally *Do you want to eat? Do you want to drink?*

You will often hear Russians changing the word order to give the sentence a bit more emphasis: **Есть хотите?** They also frequently miss out the words **я, вы**, etc.

Requests

If you want to be more direct, you can request someone to give you something. It may be food or drink or any object:

Дáйте мне, пожáлуйста, сметáну.
Give me the sour cream, please.
Мне, пожáлуйста, кýрицу.
I would like the chicken, please.

Russians often say **пожáлуйста** when they hand the object over.

EXERCISE 5

Below is a list of things that you would like. Identify the object by placing the number of the Russian word in the circles in the picture.

Дайте, пожалуйста,

1	грибы́	**6**	кýрицу
2	счёт	**7**	хлеб
3	газéту	**8**	самовáр
4	билéт	**9**	пи́во
5	цветы́		

Дáйте, пожáлуйста.

Пожáлуйста.

With

С лимóном, со сметáной, с грибáми
are all examples of **с** meaning *with*. **С** is followed by the *instrumental case*. This ends in:

masculine and neuter	-ОМ	чай с лимóн**ом** *tea with lemon*
feminine	-ОЙ	огурцы́ со сметáн**ой** *cucumbers with sour cream*
plural	-АМИ	свини́на с грибá**ми** *pork with mushrooms*

● Looking at words

Having breakfast, dinner, supper

Зáвтрак, **обéд** and **ýжин** can all be turned into verbs by simply adding **-ать**.

зáвтракать	*to have breakfast*
обéдать	*to have dinner*
ýжинать	*to have supper*

They also sometimes appear with **по-** at the beginning of the verbal form. **Хоти́те позáвтракать?** means *Would you like a little breakfast?* Again notice the economy of Russian.

A situation to remember

Ordering food

Look again at Exercise 1 in this unit.
You are the only Russian speaker out of a group of British people.
You have found out what they want.
Explain to the waiter what each of them wants to eat for each course:

Мистер Джо́унс хо́чет икру́ ...
Мисс Бенсон хо́чет ... (etc.)

Then you tell the waiter what you want:

Да́йте мне, пожа́луйста, ...

The drinks have already been ordered.

Are you hungry? Are you thirsty?

Ask a friend if he/she is hungry or thirsty.
Ask if he/she wants specific items of food or drink, choosing items from the menu in this unit.

● Playing with words

Word square

See how many items of food and drink you can find in the square.

А	С	К	А	Р	П	И	М
З	А	К	У	С	К	И	Ю
П	Л	О	В	И	П	К	С
Ж	А	Т	Л	И	У	Р	У
О	Т	Л	И	Р	Н	А	М
Ц	Ж	Е	М	Я	С	О	К
Й	Н	Т	О	С	С	У	П
Я	И	Ч	Н	И	Ц	А	К

Missing letters

Now here are some more items of food and drink. This time you have to insert the missing letters and then match the words on the left with the words or phrases on the right. The first one is done for you.

1 Шампа́нское   из помидо́ров
2 С_рд_ны   (кра́сная)
3 С_ла_   минера́льная
4 С_к   ру́сское (полусухо́е)
5 Би_шт_кс   с ма́слом
6 И_ра́   в ма́сле
7 Вод_   тома́тный
8 _ай   с лимо́ном
9 _ле_   н_т_ра́льный

Reading handwriting

Decipher the illustrated written forms and print the words beneath the photograph.

WHAT YOU KNOW

Saying what you want and what you want to do

Я хочу́	чай.
Хоти́те	сала́т?
	пи́во?

| Я хочу́ | есть |
| Хоти́те | пить? |

Asking for things

Да́йте (мне), пожа́луйста,	сок.
Мне, пожа́луйста,	ку́рицу.
	счёт.

What do you like with things?

Чай	с	лимо́ном
Суп	с	гриба́ми
Блины́	со	смета́ной

KEY VOCABULARY

вку́сно	tasty
вторы́е блю́да	main courses
есть	to eat
за́втрак	breakfast
заку́ски	hors d'oeuvre
за́нято	occupied
ко́фе	coffee
ма́сло	butter, oil
мя́со	meat
напи́тки	drinks
обе́д	dinner
пе́рвые блю́да	soup courses
пить	to drink
ры́ба	fish
Сади́тесь!	Sit down!
свобо́дно	free
сла́дкое	dessert
счёт	bill
у́жин	supper
чёрный хлеб	black bread
бе́лый хлеб	white bread

10

Going to church

Visiting art galleries and museums

Talking about things

Revision

The Church of Christ the Saviour

● Life in Russia

Russian churches

After the 1917 revolution the majority of the churches in Moscow and St Petersburg were used for a variety of non-religious purposes. Some were turned into museums, others used as warehouses, allowed to decay, or demolished. After the fall of communism many churches were returned to the church authorities and reinstated as working churches. **Храм Христа́ спаси́теля,** The Church of Christ the Saviour, built to celebrate Russia's victory over Napoleon in 1812, was destroyed by Stalin in 1931 and replaced by an open air swimming pool. Rebuilt and re-opened in 1996, it is now one of Moscow's largest churches.

A visit to a church during a service can be a very moving experience. The Orthodox church (**Правосла́вие**) has very different rituals from a Catholic or Protestant Christian service. The congregation is separated from the priest by a door and screen or iconostasis (**иконоста́с**) and there are no statues or three-dimensional images in the church. Instead the walls are covered with icons (**ико́ны**) which are venerated by the members of the congregation. The nave of the church is usually open, and the rich decorations add to the atmosphere.

The most famous icon painter was **Андре́й Рублёв** (early 15th century). His work is found on many church interiors in and around Moscow, and his masterpiece is the icon of the Trinity (**Тро́ица**). There were earlier icon painters, notably Theophanes the Greek (**Феофа́н Грек**), who came to Novgorod from Constantinople in the 1370s. Many icons are of unknown origin, with miraculous powers ascribed to them.

Don't expect to understand the words of the prayers. The language used is called *Church Slavonic*: it's related to Russian but the most you can expect to do is to pick out a few words. Listen out for **Бог** or **Бо́же** (*God*) and the verb **моли́ться** (*to pray*). Be aware that Russian church services can last a very long time and there are no seats!

If you are looking at religious buildings, you will need to know the following words:

собо́р	*cathedral*
це́рковь	*church*
храм	*church, cathedral*
монасты́рь	*monastery, convent*
ла́вра	*(large) monastery*

You'll find many **собо́ры** in the Kremlin in Moscow. The oldest and most famous is Assumption Cathedral (**Успе́нский собо́р**). Outside the walls of the Kremlin on Red Square lies St Basil's Cathedral (**Храм Васи́лия Блаже́нного**).

There are also many **монастыри́** in and around Moscow. One of the most important of these, **Новоде́вичий монасты́рь**, is close to the centre of Moscow. This is in fact a convent, as the Russian word, though related to the English *monastery*, can refer to a religious community either for men or for women. Many famous Russians are buried in the adjoining cemetery, including **Го́голь**, **Че́хов** and **Станисла́вский**. The tradition was continued in the communist period: there is a secular part of the cemetery where leading politicians such as **Хрущёв** and **Мо́лотов** were buried.

Novodevichi convent

If you're interested in church architecture, visit one of the towns in the **Золото́е кольцо́** (*Golden Ring*). North-east of Moscow you'll find the towns of **Влади́мир** and **Су́здаль**, home to many very old religious buildings. Possibly the most famous of all the monasteries near Moscow is Trinity-St Sergius (**Тро́ице-Се́ргиева Ла́вра**) in the town of **Се́ргиев Поса́д**, formerly **Заго́рск**. For many years in the communist period it housed the only seminary for training Orthodox priests.

Museums and art galleries

The best place to see icons is in the Tretyakov Gallery (**Третьяко́вская галере́я**) in Moscow. You can see the Virgin of Vladimir (**Влади́мирская богома́терь**) painted in the early 12th century and many of the works of Rublyov, Feofan Grek and others. There are also many paintings by Russian artists in the Tretyakov.

The Pushkin Museum (**Музе́й и́мени Пу́шкина**) in Moscow contains a large collection of world art, including Dutch paintings and French impressionists as well as Matisse and Picasso. Moscow's 'crown jewels' are on view in the Armoury Palace (**Оруже́йная пала́та**) in the Kremlin, along with many other precious artefacts from tsarist times.

The largest collection of art in Russia is in St Petersburg at the Hermitage (**Эрмита́ж**), which is housed in the Winter Palace. The collection of Dutch paintings is the largest in existence and these and other works are exhibited in 1000 rooms, so allow plenty of time!

● Language information

о *about*

The word **о** means *about* and is followed by the prepositional case ('**е**' form). It has an alternative form **об** used before most vowels.

Са́ша говори́т **о** Москве́.
Sasha is talking about Moscow.
Ната́ша говори́т **об** Эрмита́же.
Natasha is talking about the Hermitage.
Ни́на зна́ет **о** футбо́л**е**.
Nina knows about football.
Ми́ша зна́ет **об** А́нгли**и**.
Misha knows about England.

The word **в** sometimes has an alternative form **во**, e.g. **во Владивосто́ке**.

писа́ть *to write*

In Unit 8 you discovered the present tense forms of verbs. Inevitably some verbs have irregular forms. One such verb is:

писа́ть *to write*			
я	пишу́	мы	пи́шем
ты	пи́шешь	вы	пи́шете
он, она́	пи́шет	они́	пи́шут

ну́жно, на́до *must*

Мне на́до бежа́ть.   *I have to run.*
Вам (Тебе́) ну́жно прийти́ за́втра?
Do you have to come tomorrow?

The words mean literally *it is necessary*. Russians are saying: *It is necessary for me to run, Is it necessary for you to come tomorrow?*

They can also be used as the equivalent of the English *need*:

Э́то не то, что мне ну́жно (на́до).
It is not what I need. (Literally It is not what is necessary for me.)

You have already seen the forms **мне**, **тебе**
and **вам** in Unit 8. They are the dative case
of the words **я**, **ты** and **вы**, and mean *to* or
for me/you.

● Revision exercises

. . . .

EXERCISE 1

Read the following letter. It is written by a
young visitor to Moscow to a girl who is in
his class at school in Vladimir. Answer the
questions by ticking the correct box. The
first one is done for you.

Дорогая Оля!
Вот я и в Москве! У меня очень
хорошая комната в гостинице
«Националь», недалеко от Красной
площади. У меня в комнате есть
телевизор, радио и телефон. Всё,
что нужно. Сейчас по телевизору
идёт американский фильм. Очень
хороший фильм. Главную роль
играет очень красивая актриса,
англичанка. Как дела у тебя
дома? Как папа и мама? Моя мама
сейчас в Санкт-Петербурге, а папа
работает в Иркутске. Он очень
любит спорт и пишет, что играет в
теннис. Пиши! Мой адрес Москва
107642, гостиница «Националь»,
комната 524 Телефон (095) 298-
65-24.

Всего доброго,
Саша

New vocabulary

дорогой	*dear*
комната	*room*
гостиница	*hotel*
недалеко от	*not far from*
главный	*main*
роль	*part*
всего доброго	*all the best*

1 Где Саша?
А В Кремле
Б В гостинице «Москва»
В В гостинице «Националь» ✓
Г В театре

2 Где гостиница?
А В Санкт-Петербурге
Б Во Владимире
В В Америке
Г Недалеко от Красной
площади

3 Что Саша сейчас делает?
А Гуляет по Москве
Б Смотрит фильм по телевизору
В Читает американскую газету
Г Обедает в хорошем ресторане

4 Что идёт по телевизору?
А Американский фильм
Б Английский фильм
В Играет красивая англичанка
Г Он не говорит по-английски

5 Почему папа в Иркутске?
А Он смотрит телевизор
Б Он там работает
В Он играет в теннис
Г Он играет в футбол

6 Почему Саше нравится гостиница?
А Потому что он в Москве
Б Потому что в комнате
всё, что нужно
В Потому что папа играет в теннис
Г Потому что Оля красивая
англичанка

EXERCISE 2

Look at the picture above and complete the sentences by supplying the missing word from the box below. The first one is done for you.

1 На __столе́__ цветы́.
2 Оди́н мужчи́на _____ телеви́зор.
3 Оди́н мужчи́на _____ газе́ту.
4 По телеви́зору _____ футбо́льный матч.
5 Же́нщина говори́т _____ телефо́ну.

| идёт | по | смо́трит | столе́ | чита́ет |

EXERCISE 3

Here is a matching exercise, using some of the times you met in Unit 8, and the time zone chart in the same unit (page 62). For each item you are given the Moscow time and you have to say what time it is in another town by picking out the appropriate clock and putting its letter in the box. The first one is done for you.

1 Моско́вское вре́мя пятна́дцать часо́в. Ско́лько сейча́с вре́мени в Ирку́тске?
2 Моско́вское вре́мя двена́дцать часо́в. Ско́лько сейча́с вре́мени во Владивосто́ке?
3 Моско́вское вре́мя семна́дцать часо́в. Ско́лько сейча́с вре́мени в Волгогра́де?
4 Моско́вское вре́мя два́дцать оди́н час. Ско́лько сейча́с вре́мени в Санкт-Петербу́рге?
5 Моско́вское вре́мя семь часо́в. Ско́лько сейча́с вре́мени в О́мске?
6 Моско́вское вре́мя де́вять часо́в. Ско́лько сейча́с вре́мени в Новосиби́рске?
7 Моско́вское вре́мя шестна́дцать часо́в. Ско́лько сейча́с вре́мени в Магада́не?

EXERCISE 4

Here is a dialogue that takes place in a book shop between a shop assistant and a tourist. The shop assistant asks the tourist what he wants (**Что вы хоти́те?**)
Answer the questions on the next page.

Тури́ст:	Здра́вствуйте!
Де́вушка:	Здра́вствуйте! Что вы хоти́те?
Тури́ст:	У вас есть хоро́шие кни́ги о ру́сских собо́рах и монастыря́х?
Де́вушка:	Коне́чно, есть. Посмотри́те напра́во, там кни́ги о моско́вских собо́рах, а нале́во о собо́рах во Влади́мире и в Су́здале.
Тури́ст:	Хорошо́. Они́ на англи́йском языке́ и́ли то́лько на ру́сском?
Де́вушка:	То́лько на ру́сском.
Тури́ст:	А моя́ жена́ не чита́ет по-ру́сски.
Де́вушка:	У нас о́чень краси́вая кни́га о Рублёве. Она́ на англи́йском языке́. Там о́чень хоро́шие иллюстра́ции. Хоти́те посмотре́ть?
Тури́ст:	Хочу́. (*смо́трит на часы́*) Но мне сейча́с ну́жно бежа́ть. Я зайду́ за́втра.
Де́вушка:	За́втра магази́н открыва́ется в де́сять часо́в.
Тури́ст:	Большо́е вам спаси́бо. Зна́чит, до за́втра. До свида́ния!
Де́вушка:	Спаси́бо и до свида́ния!

c — a
— b
— c
— d
— e
— f
— g

New vocabulary

коне́чно	of course
(по)смотре́ть (на)	to look at
на англи́йском/ ру́сском языке́	in English/ Russian
то́лько	only
иллюстра́ция	illustration
часы́	watch
бежа́ть	run
зайти́ (зайду́, зайдёшь…)	call in
зна́чит	that means

1 What does the tourist want?
2 What does the shop assistant offer him?
3 What question does the tourist ask in response?
4 Which book does he choose?
5 Why doesn't he take it immediately?

EXERCISE 5

On your recording you will hear a number followed by a statement or question.
As soon as you hear the statement or question stop the recording and pick out the appropriate response below.
Put the number in the box.
The first one is done for you.
(It is a good idea to look first at the responses below and see if you can anticipate what sort of thing would fit before listening to each one.)

Хорошо́, а вы? ☐

Нет, сейча́с закры́т. ☐

Иди́те пря́мо, пото́м нале́во. [1]

Нет, то́лько лимона́д. ☐

Ничего́, а ты? ☐

Здра́вствуйте, о́чень рад. ☐

Нет, да́йте, пожа́луйста, ко́фе. ☐

Нет, не хочу́. Я сего́дня занята́. ☐

Нет, не моя́. ☐

Нет, да́йте, пожа́луйста, чай. ☐

О́ля, приве́т! Как дела́? ☐

EXERCISE 6

Look back at the metro map of St Petersburg in Unit 6. Your hotel is situated near the station **Технологи́ческий институ́т,** which is on the first (**пе́рвая ли́ния**) and second (**втора́я ли́ния**) lines. If you need a station on the third (**тре́тья ли́ния**) or fourth (**четвёртая ли́ния**) lines, you will need to change (**де́лать переса́дку**). You have to plan the number of stops to get to each of the stations (**ста́нция**) below from your station, **Технологи́ческий институ́т**. Go the shortest way each time.
Write the number of stops in the first column. If you have to change tick the second column. The first one is done for you.

1	Рыба́цкое	*9*	✓
2	Чёрная ре́чка		
3	Ла́дожская		
4	Академи́ческая		
5	пл. Алекса́ндра Не́вского		
6	Моско́вская		
7	Не́вский проспе́кт		
8	На́рвская		
9	Политехни́ческая		
10	Примо́рская		
11	Ломоно́совская		
12	Достое́вская		

Why do most of the station names end in **-ая**?
Try to work out the meaning of the station names.

A situation to remember

Staying in Moscow

You are staying in a nice hotel in Moscow. You have a television in your room and some beautiful flowers on the table. Tell this to your friend over the telephone. Tell him/her about the museums and churches in Moscow, and the nice food you have in the hotel restaurant. Say how much you like Moscow.

● Playing with words

Кроссво́рд

Note: This crossword consists mainly of words that you already know or can easily guess. New or difficult words are marked with an asterisk in the clues. If you have difficulty, solve them after you have solved the adjacent clues.

Across

1 Excuse me = **извини́те** or _____
7 And
10 _____ о́чень нра́вится смотре́ть телеви́зор
12 Aha! Russian style
14 Ско́лько _____ э́та ша́пка
16 Not the boxing kind of blow. More like a stunning drink.
17 Вам нра́вится _____ фильм
19 But
20 This is what happens before you get thrown into gaol*
22 Same as 19
23 Abbreviation for **Акаде́мия Нау́к** (Academy of Sciences)
24 In the Latvian capital = **в** _____
25 From*
27 – Как вы пожива́ете?
 – Спаси́бо _____ OK, Fine, Alright
29 So
33 Ива́н гуля́ет ____ Москве́
35 Как вам _____ Москва́?
37 Famous river in Rostov with Cossack connections
38 Not
39 Short for **О́льга**
41 State Universal Store
42 On, at or to
43 To go walking
45 Они́ love грибы́
51 You can drink пи́во here*
52 Russian choir. Starts with **x**
53 I'm for it = **я** (do this after 42 and 43 down)*
54 Volume or tome*
55 Моско́вское вре́мя двена́дцать _____

Down

1 _ _ _ **о** – it means beer
2 В _____ о́чень хоро́шее меню́
3 Let's drink **т** _ _ _
4 Я ____ телеви́зор
5 Genghis Khan was one – ends in **-ин**
6 Moscow University
7 And
8 Not
9 Ten
11 Russian girl
13 Same as 23 across
15 Metric ton (feminine)*
16 First syllable of the verbs to arrive and to come
18 ____ говоря́т о футбо́ле
21 ____ буфе́т откры́т в три часа́ (not за́втра)
22 Musical note (feminine)*
26 Nine
28 One o'clock or hour
30 Not breast-stroke. Ends in a **-ь***
31 Э́то вход. Мо́жно войти́? ____ , пожа́луйста.
32 The coldest place in Russia: **Верх** _ _ _ **ск**
33 Ива́н говори́т____-ру́сски
34 Ири́на студе́нтка. ____в университе́те.
36 Where samovars are made (near Tolstoy's home)
40 Musical note 'A'. (Do 39 and 43 across first)*
43 We get this from the North Sea – it's the first part of a newspaper
44 Russian Hooray! (guess!)
46 Short for **юрий**
47 What the Russians (and the French) shout for *Encore!* *
48 Э́то не ____ , что ну́жно
49 Short for **Ири́на**
50 Сего́дня____телеви́зору о́чень интере́сная програ́мма
51 _ _ ази́лия. Where the coffee comes from.

WHAT YOU KNOW

Talking about things
Он говори́т о Москве́.

Having to do things
Мне ну́жно (на́до) смотре́ть телеви́зор.

LANGUAGE REVIEW

Here are some words and phrases we have had in Units 6–10. Check that you understand what they mean. If you are not sure you know what they mean, look back to the unit where they first occurred: this is given on the right.

Как пройти́ на Кра́сную пло́щадь?	
Иди́те напра́во/нале́во/пря́мо.	6
У вас есть план метро́?	
Есть.	6
Покажи́те, пожа́луйста ... Да́йте, пожа́луйста ...	6
оди́н, два, три, четы́ре, пять, шесть, семь, во́семь, де́вять, де́сять, сто, ты́сяча	6
Как тебя́/вас зову́т?	
Меня́ зову́т Ната́ша.	7
Как ты пожива́ешь? Как вы пожива́ете?	7
Здра́вствуй! Здра́вствуйте!	7
кра́сный авто́бус, кра́сная ма́рка, кра́сное вино́, кра́сные авто́бусы	7
Мне хо́лодно, тепло́, жа́рко.	8
игра́ю, игра́ешь, игра́ет, игра́ем, игра́ете, игра́ют	8
говорю́, говори́шь, говори́т, говори́м, говори́те, говоря́т	8
Я иду́ по у́лице.	8
по телеви́зору, по ра́дио, по телефо́ну	8
Я люблю́ спорт. Мне нра́вится футбо́л.	8
хочу́, хо́чешь, хо́чет, хоти́м, хоти́те, хотя́т	9
чай с лимо́ном, огурцы́ со смета́ной	9
Са́ша говори́т о Москве́.	10
Мне на́до бежа́ть. Мне ну́жно прийти́ за́втра.	10

KEY VOCABULARY

гости́ница	hotel
дорого́й	dear
ко́мната	room
монасты́рь	monastery
но	but
ну́жно	must
о (об)	about
писа́ть	to write
собо́р	cathedral
то́лько	only
часы́	watch

Times and seasons

What Russians do in summer and winter

Saying when you do things

Making plans

● Life in Russia

The Russian winter (Ру́сская зима́)

Russians celebrate winter, rather than just cope with it. The temperature in Moscow can get down as low as minus 30 degrees Celsius, although it is not usually this cold for very long. Russians have adapted to these low temperatures and wear appropriate clothing. Traditional Russian headgear for the winter is **уша́нка**, a fur hat with ear flaps, although many young Russians now wear thick woolly hats instead. You will also need a warm coat (**пальто́**).

Houses and all public buildings are, of course, double-glazed and very well centrally heated. The inside of Russian buildings often seems too hot for the non-Russian. Make sure that, like Russians, you remove all your warm clothes when you go inside.

Theatres, museums and most public buildings in Russia are equipped with a cloakroom (**гардеро́б**), and you are always expected to check in your overcoat as you enter the building. When you enter someone's house you usually take off your coat, hat and your outdoor shoes. Slippers (**та́почки**) will usually be provided for visitors in a normal Russian household. When you go round palaces and stately homes, you will be required to put on **та́почки** over your outdoor shoes to protect the floors and carpets.

The national sport in winter is ice-hockey. Football is played in the summer, as grounds are not fit for play in the winter. The surface of rivers and lakes is frozen hard and skating is a popular pastime, as is skiing and tobogganing. Fishing is also a popular sport in winter. Anglers drill holes in the ice for their lines and may be seen sitting patiently waiting for a bite.

Useful words for winter activities:

игра́ть в хоккей	to play ice-hockey
ката́ться на лы́жах	to ski
ката́ться на конька́х	to skate
ката́ться на саня́х	to toboggan
лови́ть ры́бу	to fish

Ру́сское ле́то (Russian summer)

Russians who live in small flats in big cities like to get away as often as they can to the country. Moscow, for example, is surrounded by vast areas of woodland and it is here, in **Подмоско́вье**, that many Russians own or rent a dacha (**да́ча**). This can vary from a tiny single-storeyed wooden house with few facilities to a two-storeyed brick-built house with all the usual modern conveniences.

The dachas are often situated in beautiful countryside and are traditionally surrounded by a plot of land (**уча́сток**), on which the owners will grow potatoes (**карто́шка**) and other vegetables, as well as fruit such as apples, raspberries and gooseberries. Russians will not waste fresh vegetables and fruit. They are expert at pickling and salting vegetables and making **варе́нье**, a type of whole fruit jam. Some of the food that we talked about in Unit 9 may have come from the family's **да́ча**. However, young people today are often disinclined to work the land, and tend to buy fruit and vegetables from the shops. Many dachas have now become luxury second homes in the country for the more well-off Russians.

At the dacha, Russians might go for a swim (**купа́ться**) in the local river or lake, or simply sunbathe (**загора́ть**). Some of the very hardy will even swim in winter in sub-zero temperatures. They are known as **моржи́** (*walruses*), and have a theory that to swim in extreme conditions is good for the health. They also beat themselves with birch twigs for the same reason.

White nights (**Бе́лые но́чи**) are a feature of midsummer in northern Russia. During this period it never gets completely dark at night and in St Petersburg they celebrate with a music and theatre festival. Locals stay up all night and watch the bridges go up to let the big ships through. Otherwise, all the best plays and concerts are on in winter: most theatres and concert halls close in summer.

Summer or winter the public bath (**ба́ня**) is also a feature of Russian life, similar to a sauna or Turkish bath, and is often featured in films as a place where deals are fixed between businesspeople, sometimes of doubtful honesty. Don't confuse this word with **ва́нная**, which is a perfectly ordinary bathroom.

● Language information

Days of the week

понеде́льник	*Monday*	в понеде́льник	*on Monday*
вто́рник	*Tuesday*	во вто́рник	*on Tuesday*
среда́	*Wednesday*	в сре́ду	*on Wednesday*
четве́рг	*Thursday*	в четве́рг	*on Thursday*
пя́тница	*Friday*	в пя́тницу	*on Friday*
суббо́та	*Saturday*	в суббо́ту	*on Saturday*
воскресе́нье	*Sunday*	в воскресе́нье	*on Sunday*

To ask what the day is, say **Како́й сего́дня день?** The reply might be: **Сего́дня суббо́та** (*Today is Saturday*). If you ask **Когда́ вы бу́дете игра́ть в футбо́л?** (*When will you play football?*), the reply might be **В суббо́ту** (*On Saturday*). Simply put **в** in front of the word and change **-а** to **-у** when it occurs at the end of the word (the accusative case).

Months of the year and seasons

янва́рь	*January*	в январе́	*in January*	зима́	*winter*
февра́ль	*February*	в феврале́	*in February*		
март	*March*	в ма́рте	*in March*		
апре́ль	*April*	в апре́ле	*in April*	весна́	*spring*
май	*May*	в ма́е	*in May*		
ию́нь	*June*	в ию́не	*in June*		
ию́ль	*July*	в ию́ле	*in July*	ле́то	*summer*
а́вгуст	*August*	в а́вгусте	*in August*		
сентя́брь	*September*	в сентябре́	*in September*		
октя́брь	*October*	в октябре́	*in October*	о́сень	*autumn*
ноя́брь	*November*	в ноябре́	*in November*		
дека́брь	*December*	в декабре́	*in December*	зима́	*winter*

Russian uses capital letters much more sparingly than English. The months and days of the week are all written with a small letter in Russian.

Seasons don't need a separate word to indicate 'in'. They simply change the endings:

ЗИМО́Й – *in winter*   **ВЕСНО́Й** – *in spring*   **ЛЕ́ТОМ** – *in summer*   **О́СЕНЬЮ** – *in autumn*

Times of the day

у́тро	*morning*	у́тром	*in the morning*
день	*day*	днём	*during the day, in the afternoon*
ве́чер	*evening*	ве́чером	*in the evening*
ночь	*night*	но́чью	*at night*

Like the seasons, the times of the day don't need a word for 'in'. 'In the afternoon' is often translated by the phrase **по́сле обе́да**, which means literally *after dinner*.

First to tenth

Here are the numbers for first to tenth:

пе́рвый	*first*	шесто́й	*sixth*
второ́й	*second*	седьмо́й	*seventh*
тре́тий	*third*	восьмо́й	*eighth*
четвёртый	*fourth*	девя́тый	*ninth*
пя́тый	*fifth*	деся́тый	*tenth*

You should recognise higher numbers of this type without any difficulty.

Dates

Како́е сего́дня число́?
What date is it today?
Сего́дня шесто́е ма́рта (6-ое ма́рта).
Today is 6th March.
Сего́дня девя́тое января́ (9-ое января́).
Today is 9th January.

• •

EXERCISE 1
Look at the dates below. Fill in the boxes with the day, date and month, as in the first example.

пя́тница, шестна́дцатое ию́ня	*Fri*	*16*	*June*
вто́рник, деся́тое ноября́			
понеде́льник, два́дцать пя́тое апре́ля			
суббо́та, пе́рвое ию́ля			
среда́, тридца́тое декабря́			
воскресе́нье, трина́дцатое октября́			
четве́рг, два́дцать девя́тое января́			

Future with бу́ду, бу́дешь …

One way of talking about an event that is going to happen in the future is to use the forms **бу́ду**, **бу́дешь**, etc. combined with the infinitive (the form of the verb that you find in dictionaries). The infinitive usually ends in **-ть**.

Я бу́ду игра́ть в футбо́л.
I will play football. (or I will be playing football)
Ты бу́дешь смотре́ть фильм.
You will be watching the film.
Он (Она́) **бу́дет чита́ть** рома́н.
He (She) will be reading the novel.
Мы **бу́дем рабо́тать**.
We shall be working.
Вы **бу́дете гуля́ть**.
You will be taking a stroll.
Они́ **бу́дут обе́дать** в час.
They will have lunch at one.

You can tell the time that something will take place by simply using the word **бу́дет**. Here are some examples:

Матч бу́дет в пя́тницу.
The match will be (take place) on Friday.
Фильм бу́дет за́втра в 8 часо́в.
The film will be on tomorrow at 8 o'clock.
Бале́т бу́дет в суббо́ту в 7 часо́в.
The ballet will be on Saturday at 7 o'clock.

When you use these expressions, very often you are making plans for the future. To tell someone what you will be doing, you use **бу́ду** with the infinitive. Thus **я бу́ду рабо́тать** (*I shall be working*), **я бу́ду чита́ть** (*I shall be reading*), etc.

EXERCISE 2

The following exercise consists of sentences you might use when making plans. You have to put in the correct form of the day. The first one is done for you.

1 Saturday   В subbótu я бу́ду игра́ть в футбо́л.

2 Monday   В _____ я бу́ду смотре́ть телеви́зор.

3 Sunday   В _____ я бу́ду гуля́ть в па́рке.

4 Wednesday   В _____ я бу́ду рабо́тать в университе́те.

5 Friday   В _____ я буду́ обе́дать в рестора́не.

6 Thursday   В _____ я бу́ду чита́ть «Войну́ и мир».

7 Tuesday   Во _____ я бу́ду смотре́ть матч Дина́мо-Спарта́к.

Of, after, before and the genitive case

The word 'of' is not usually translated into Russian: simply use the genitive case: **1-ое ма́рта** (the first *of* March), **центр го́рода** (the centre *of* town). The forms of the genitive case are:

singular	
masculine and neuter nouns end in **-А**	часа́ ме́ста
masculine **ь** nouns end in **-Я**	января́
feminine nouns end in **-Ы**	ко́мнаты
or **-И** (ка nouns)	де́вушки
ь feminine nouns	о́сени

plural	
masculine nouns end in **-ОВ**	часо́в
feminine nouns remove **-а**	ко́мнат
neuter nouns remove **-о**	мест
some nouns add **-е** or **-о** to last syllable	де́вушек
ь nouns end in **ЕЙ**	царе́й

The genitive case is also used following **по́сле** *after* and **до** *before*: **по́сле обе́да** *after dinner*, **до у́жина** *before supper*.

Most Russian numbers are followed by a genitive case. **Два** (**две**), **три** and **четы́ре** (and all numbers ending in these words) use the genitive singular: **два часа́** (*two o'clock*); **пять** and above require the genitive plural: **пять часо́в** (*five o'clock*).

EXERCISE 3

In the following exercise, the endings have been left off some of the nouns. You will either need the genitive case, as explained above, or you may need the prepositional case, when following **в**, **на**, or **о**. Fill in the blanks with the correct form.

Мы за́втракаем в семь [1]час__. По́сле [2]за́втрак __ па́па рабо́тает. Он такси́ст. Он рабо́тает в [3]Москв__, в [4]це́нтр__ [5]го́род__ . До [6]обе́д __ мы гуля́ем в [7]па́рк__. Там о́чень краси́во. Мы обе́даем в два [8]час__.

По́сле [9]обе́д __ я смотрю́ телеви́зор. О́чень хорошо́!
Ве́чером в во́семь [10]час__ мы у́жинаем. По́сле [11]у́жин__ ма́ма рабо́тает на [12]ку́хн__, а па́па чита́ет журна́л о [13]футбо́л__.

◉ EXERCISE 4

Listen to the CD. A guide is describing to a group of tourists their itinerary for a stay in Moscow. They ask him questions about various events that are going to take place. You have the timetable in front of you, but there are some gaps in it. Fill in the gaps using the information on the recording.

суббо́та 8-ое ию́ля	
08.00–09.10	за́втрак
[1] _____	экску́рсия по Москве́
13.00	обе́д
14.30	[2] _____
[3] _____	Большо́й теа́тр
[4] _____	у́жин

воскресе́нье 9-ое ию́ля	
08.00–09.00	за́втрак
[5] _____	экску́рсия по Кремлю́
13.00	[6] _____

EXERCISE 5

Look at the following notices explaining when places are open. Some Russian shops still close for lunch. Some have a day when they do not open (**выходно́й день**). More and more shops are now opening every day: **без выходны́х**.

1 These are the hours of the Savings Bank (**Сберба́нк**).
   a When is it open on weekdays?
   b When is it open on Sundays?
   c When does it close for lunch?

2 When does the Smolensk shopping centre open
   a on weekdays?
   b on Sundays?

3 a On which days of the week can you buy contact lenses?
   b At what times is the shop open each day?

4 Look at the picture in the next column.
   a Which days does the post office open?
   b When does it close in the evening?
   c When does it close for lunch?

● Looking at words

Days of the week

Russians start the week with **понеде́льник**, which comes from **неде́ля** (*week*). **Вто́рник**, **четве́рг** and **пя́тница** come from the numbers **второ́й** (*second*), **четвёртый** (*fourth*), **пя́тый** (*fifth*). **Среда́** is the 'middle day': the Russian for *middle* is **сре́дний**. **Суббо́та** is related to English *sabbath*. **Воскресе́нье** originally meant *Resurrection*. It still does in modern Russian, although it is spelt slightly differently: **воскресе́ние**. It is the title of a novel by Tolstoy.

Сего́дня

Сего́дня is a two-part word: it literally means *of this day*. **Серо́** comes from an old word, **сей**, meaning *this*. You will only see it in a few words and idioms. The modern Russian for *this* is **э́тот**. **-дня** is the genitive case of the word **день**. Be careful, this word is pronounced *sevódnya*: this was mentioned in Unit 5. There are a number of places where **-ого** and **-его** are pronounced with a 'v' instead of a 'g': e.g. **ниче**г**о́**.

Russian version of 'h'

Russian does not have an 'h' sound. When it borrows words which have that sound, it often replaces it with a '**г**'. This may seem strange, until you listen to Russians from the south of the country, or Russian speakers in the Ukraine: they pronounce '**г**' quite close to an 'h'. The horizon in Russian is **горизо́нт**, and if you wish to exclaim 'Aha!', you write '**Ага́**!'.

EXERCISE 6

Here are some place names and the names of people (real and fictitious), where 'h' has been replaced by a Russian 'г'. Can you work out the English version?

1 Гонко́нг _____

2 Ги́тлер _____

3 Голла́ндия _____

4 Га́млет _____

5 Копенга́ген _____

● Reading

Summer and winter

EXERCISE 7

Read the following passage about how the Kalugin family spend their weekends in summer and winter. Then complete the table below in English. The first entry for **Ива́н Петро́вич** is done for you.

Ива́н Петро́вич Калу́гин о́чень лю́бит спорт. Но он не игра́ет в спорт, то́лько смо́трит спорт по телеви́зору. Зимо́й он хо́дит раз в неде́лю на стадио́н и смо́трит хокке́й. Он всегда́ но́сит (wears) тёплое (warm) пальто́ и ста́рую уша́нку. Ле́том ка́ждую (every) суббо́ту он рабо́тает на да́че, а ка́ждый ве́чер смо́трит футбо́л по телеви́зору.

Его́ жена́ Ири́на не лю́бит спорт. Ка́ждый год она́ покупа́ет (buys) абонеме́нт (season ticket) и слу́шает симфо́нии и конце́рты Чайко́вского и Шостако́вича в консервато́рии. Ле́том, когда́ нет конце́ртов, она́ рабо́тает с му́жем (husband) на уча́стке, а ка́ждый ве́чер чита́ет рома́ны.

Сын Бо́ря игра́ет в ша́хматы (chess) и зимо́й и ле́том: он рабо́тает на да́че то́лько, когда́ на́до. Его́ сестра́ Ма́ша лю́бит му́зыку. Она́ слу́шает рок-му́зыку с подру́гами (female friends). Ле́том, ка́ждую суббо́ту она́ то́же (also) на да́че, но она́ не рабо́тает на уча́стке: она́ лежи́т на со́лнце (lies in the sun) и загора́ет.

	зимо́й	ле́том
Ива́н	*goes to the stadium to watch ice-hockey*	
Ири́на		
Бо́ря		
Ма́ша		

Theatre posters

. . . .

EXERCISE 8

Look at the theatre advertisements from a Moscow paper for three theatres,
the Bolshoi, the Moscow Arts Theatre (**MXAT**) and the Rossiya concert hall.
Then answer the questions below.

пятница 15 сентября	суббота 16 сентября	воскресенье 17 сентября
Государственный академический большой театр		
Евгений Онегин, опера музыка П. И. Чайковского в 7.30 часов	Коппелия, балет музыка Л. Делиба в 7.30 часов	Борис Годунов, опера М. музыка П. Мусоргского в 7.00 часов
МХАТ (Московский художественный академический театр)		
Чайка, пьеса А.П. Чехова в 8.00 часов	Гамлет, пьеса Уильяма Шекспира в 7.30 часов	Воскресение, пьеса по роману Л. Н. Толстого в 7.30 часов
Государственный центральный концертный зал «Россия»		
Иисус Христос — суперзвезда А. Ллойд-Веббер в 7.30 часов	Хит Парад «Арлекино» в 8.00	Закрыто

1 a Where do opera fans go on Friday?
  b What will they see?
  c When does it start?
2 a Which play is on at the Moscow Arts Theatre on Sunday?
  b Who wrote the novel on which it was based?
  c When does it start?
3 Name two 'imports' from Britain in this theatre programme.
4 a Name the ballet on at the Bolshoi Theatre.
  b What day is it on?
  c Who wrote the music?
5 a The Moscow Arts Theatre is famous for its Chekhov productions. Which one can you see?
  b When is it on?
6 What will you see on Sunday at the Rossiya concert hall?

A situation to remember

Making plans

Imagine that you are making plans for tomorrow. Say what time you will have breakfast, lunch and dinner. What will you do before and after dinner?

Here are some things you are going to do:

– play football   – watch a film
– go for a walk in the town   – read a book
– sunbathe   – go for a swim or skate

Alternatively, if you want to go to the cinema, you cay say **Пойдём в кино!**
Let's go to the cinema!

A visit by Russians

Make a programme for a group of Russians who are visiting your town and read it out to them. Work with a fellow student if you have the chance.

Activities might be the theatre, a concert, dinner at a restaurant, shops (**магазины**), excursion to London. You should produce a timetable, as in Exercise 4.

93

Writing Russian (1)

Over the next six units we will show you how to write Russian letters. As soon as you can you should try writing everything with these forms, rather than printing.

There are some Russian letters which, when written, are easily recognised by an English speaker, but beware of using English variations as you write, as many of these would not be understood by a Russian. When you write, try to get as close as possible to the model. If you enjoy calligraphy you will enjoy the flourishes of written Russian, particularly of the large letters. We shall give you the letters which are difficult or new. Assume that the other letters are as you would expect them to be. Capital letters are given in brackets.

Examples

т is written *т Т*

и is written *и И*

п is written *п П*

н is written *н Н*

в is written *в В*

Now you try writing the words.

такси _____

такси

парк _____

парк

пианист _____

пианист

авиа _____

авиа

WHAT YOU KNOW

What you plan to do
я бу́ду   гуля́ть
вы бу́дете   рабо́тать

First, second, third ...
пе́рвый, второ́й, тре́тий, четвёртый, пя́тый

шесто́й sixth	девя́тый ninth	
седьмо́й seventh	деся́тый tenth	
восьмо́й eighth		

Days of the week, months of the year, seasons and times of the day
Како́й сего́дня день?
Сего́дня среда́.

Како́е сего́дня число́?
Сего́дня пя́тое января́.

When will you do it?
Когда́ вы бу́дете игра́ть   в футбо́л?
Я бу́ду игра́ть в футбо́л   в январе́.
                                весно́й.
                                у́тром.

Of, before, after
1-ое ма́я
по́сле обе́да
до у́жина

KEY VOCABULARY

ба́ня	bath house
весна́	spring
выходно́й день	day off
гардеро́б	cloakroom
да́ча	'dacha', cottage in the country
загора́ть	to sunbathe
зима́	winter
ката́ться на конька́х	to skate
ката́ться на лы́жах	to ski
ката́ться на саня́х	to toboggan
купа́ться	to swim
ле́то	summer
МХАТ	Moscow Arts Theatre
о́сень	autumn
по́сле обе́да	after dinner, in the afternoon
сын	son
та́почки	slippers

12

номер
двенадцать

Talking about the past

Famous names in literature

Чингисхан

Genghis Khan

The origins of Russia

● Life in Russia

Traders in old Novgorod

Early history

Slavic peoples were known in the days of the Roman Empire, but the origin of the Russian kingdom is believed by many historians to be in 862, when Rurik and his two brothers arrived. Rurik settled in Novgorod (**Но́вгород**). The founders of Russia were from Scandinavia, and it was not long before **Ки́ев** became the most important city-state, dominating all the tribes of eastern Slavs by the beginning of the 11th century.

In the 11th and 12th centuries Russia traded with the West and was not isolated until the invasion of the Mongol Tartars under Batu, the great-nephew of Genghis Khan, in 1244. The Tartars lived in encampments outside the towns, demanding homage and regular tribute from the Russian princes. This state of affairs lasted for two centuries, and was known as the 'Tartar Yoke' (**Тата́рское и́го**).

The establishment of Moscow as a city was in 1328 and its importance as the political and religious centre increased until it became acknowledged as the capital of the Russian state. Other important city-states of the period include **Но́вгород**, **Псков**, **Тверь** and **Влади́мир-Су́здаль**. Today they are important historical centres, much visited by tourists.

Useful words

Русь	*Rus', the name given to the country in this period*
князь	*prince*
тата́рин	*Tartar*

Ivan the Terrible, Boris Godunov and the first Romanovs

Ivan III (**Ива́н тре́тий**) was the first **царь** to call himself tsar of all Russia. He reigned from 1462–1505. In 1547 Ivan the Terrible (**Ива́н гро́зный**) was crowned in Moscow. He died in 1584. His name comes from his methods of dealing with the Boyars (**боя́ре**), as the nobility were called, and from his violent, suspicious unpredictability, which led to the murder of his son in a quarrel.

His reign was followed by the 'Time of Troubles' (**Сму́тное вре́мя**), which included the reign of **Бори́с Годуно́в** and finished in 1613 with the accession to the throne of **Михаи́л Фёдорович Рома́нов**, elected by a national assembly. He was the first in the line of Romanovs which came to a violent end after the 1917 Bolshevik revolution.

Ivan the Terrible

Boris Godunov

Peter the Great and St Petersburg

Peter the Great (**Пётр вели́кий**) came to the throne in 1682. He went on a fact-finding mission to the West, visiting and working in shipyards in Great Britain, Germany and Holland. Some of the time he tried to be incognito – a little difficult when you are well over two metres tall and followed around by a large retinue. Like **Ива́н гро́зный**, Peter had difficulties with his courtiers, the palace guard (**Стрельцы́**), and dealt with them severely on his return to Moscow.

Russia had fallen behind the West in the years of the Tartar Yoke and Peter set out vigorously to bring the country up-to-date. He reformed the army, and created a ruling class that was rewarded for service rather than birth. Besides his knowledge of ship-building and military matters, he developed an interest in surgery and dentistry, both of which he practised on a less than willing retinue.

Peter the Great

Peter's most spectacular achievement was the foundation in 1703 of St Petersburg (**Санкт-Петербу́рг**), his 'window on the West'. Designed mainly by Italian architects, the city is much more 'Western' than many other Russian cities, its many canals and bridges (**мосты́**) giving it the title of the Venice of the North. The statue of its founder stands proudly on the bank of the river Neva (**Нева́**). **Пу́шкин** wrote one of his most famous poems about it: «**Ме́дный вса́дник**» ('The Bronze Horseman'), in which the statue comes terrifyingly alive. St Petersburg became Peter's capital, and it remained the capital of Russia until the revolution in 1917.

The tsars from Peter onwards were buried in the St Peter and Paul Fortress (**Петропа́вловская кре́пость**) in St Petersburg. Previous tsars were buried in one of the cathedrals of the Moscow Kremlin. St Petersburg has had two other names: in 1914 its name was changed to **Петрогра́д**, and in 1924 it became **Ленингра́д** on the death of Lenin. After a referendum in 1991 the population of the city decided by a narrow majority to return to the old name of **Санкт-Петербу́рг**. During the second world war the siege of Leningrad was one of the most heroic episodes in the history of the Russian people.

Catherine the Great and the 19th century

Catherine II (**Екатери́на II**) took over the throne from her husband, Peter III. She reigned until 1796, and her attitudes were conditioned by the events in western Europe at the time – liberal philosophy followed by revolution.

The 19th century is the most important century in Russian music and literature. Europe at the start of the century was dominated by Napoleon, who made the mistake of invading Russia. The wars against Napoleon meant that many of the younger nobility, serving in the army, had been able to see parts of western Europe where serfdom had been abolished and autocracy overthrown. They began to want more freedom, and this led to a number of uprisings, one of which involved the Decembrists (**декабри́сты**) in 1825. The atmosphere became strongly anti-censorship and many of the 19th-century writers were in constant conflict with the authorities. The act which freed the serfs (**крепостны́е**) from bondage was passed in 1861, but the process went on until the end of the century, and its protracted nature deprived Russia of the gradual sort of industrial revolution that took place in the West.

Гла́вные да́ты ру́сской исто́рии

860–1240	Ки́евская Русь
1113–25	Влади́мир Монома́х, Князь (Ки́ев)
1147	Основа́ние Москвы́
1223	Чингисха́н и монго́льская а́рмия разби́ли славя́нскую а́рмию
1227	Смерть Чингисха́на
1240–1480	Тата́рское и́го
1533–84	Ива́н IV (Ива́н гро́зный)
1547	Ива́н IV стал царём
1598–1605	Бори́с Годуно́в, царь
1682–1725	Пётр I (Пётр вели́кий) царь
1697–8	Пётр на за́паде, в Голла́ндии и в А́нглии
1703	Основа́ние Санкт-Петербу́рга
1762-96	Екатери́на II
1812–14	Оте́чественная война́ с Наполео́ном
1861	Крестья́нская рефо́рма (освобожде́ние крестья́н)
1905	Револю́ция 1905-ого го́да
1914	Начала́сь Пе́рвая мирова́я война́
1917	Октя́брьская револю́ция
1918	Коне́ц мирово́й войны́ Нача́ло гражда́нской войны́
1922	Коне́ц гражда́нской войны́
1924	Смерть Ле́нина
1953	Смерть Ста́лина
1941–45	Вели́кая Оте́чественная война́
1958–64	Хрущёв
1985–91	Горбачёв
1991	Распа́лся Сове́тский Сою́з
1992–99	Е́льцин
2000	Пу́тин

EXERCISE 1

On the left is a list of some of the main dates in Russian history.
The questions below are designed to help you get information from the text.
Do not expect to understand every word. The questions are in order. Use them to work out some of the vocabulary.

1 When was Vladimir Monomakh prince of Kiev?
2 When was the founding of Moscow?
3 When did Genghis Khan defeat the Slav army?
4 When did he die?
5 What were the years of the Tartar Yoke?
6 What happened in 1547?
7 Who became tsar in 1598?
8 Who went where in 1697–8?
9 What happened in 1703?
10 What took place in 1812?
11 When was the peasant refor,m?
12 When did the October Revolution take place?
13 When was Lenin's death?
14 When was Stalin's death?
15 When did the Soviet Union end?
16 When did Putin become president?

Russians are very conscious of their historical identity. Everywhere you go you will see monuments, plaques and historical museums. Very often a museum devoted to a historical or literary personality will be in the house where they lived and worked. A plaque might have something like this on it:

> В этом доме жил и работал
> А. С. Пушкин.

If it were a woman who lived and worked there, it might read:

> В этом доме жила и работала
> Анна Ахматова.

● Language information

Past tense of verbs

читáть *to read*	
я, ты, он	читáл
я, ты, онá	читáла
мы, вы, они́	читáли

The past tense of **читáть** is formed by replacing **-ть** in the infinitive (dictionary form) by **-л** if a man was reading, by **-ла** if a woman was reading and by **-ли** if more than one person was reading. The forms from the verb **быть** (*to be*) are:

быть *to be*	
я, ты, он	был
я, ты, онá	былá
оно́	бы́ло
мы, вы, они́	бы́ли

The extra form is **бы́ло**, used with **оно́** (neuter) nouns.

EXERCISE 2

Look at the following passage and note the past tenses.

В прóшлом годý *last year* я **был** в Москвé. Погóда там **былá** óчень хорóшая. Мы **жи́ли** в гости́нице «Национáль» в цéнтре Москвы́. Я чáсто *often* **ходи́л** *walked* по гóроду. Нéсколько раз *several times* я **смотрéл** футбóльный матч. Однáжды *once* **игрáли** «Динáмо» Москвá и «Динáмо» Ки́ев. Пóсле э́того мáтча мы **поýжинали** в гости́нице, а потóм **потанцевáли**. Мне нýжно **бы́ло** рабóтать кáждый день. Я **рабóтал** в библиотéке *library*, где **читáл** интерéсные кни́ги.

1 How can you tell that the author is a man?
2 How would you have to change the text, if the author were a woman?

You may notice that some of the past tenses above have **по-** at the beginning. This usually indicates that the action is complete. Other prefixes occur, but **по-** is the most common. More details will appear in Unit 16.

EXERCISE 3

Here are some questions asking if someone is going to be somewhere tomorrow. You reply that they were there yesterday. The first one is done for you.

1 Онá зáвтра бýдет в Санкт-Петербýрге?
   Нет, онá __былá__ там вчерá.

2 Вы зáвтра бýдете в Ки́еве?
   Нет, я _____ там вчерá.

3 Они́ зáвтра бýдут в Москвé?
   Нет, они́ _____ там вчерá.

4 Вéра зáвтра бýдет здесь?
   Нет, онá _____ там вчерá.

5 Вáня бýдет на футбóле?
   Нет, он _____ там вчерá.

6 Ни́на и Кóля бýдут в ресторáне?
   Нет, они́ _____ там вчерá.

The verb to live

жить *to live*			
present tense			
я	живý	мы	живём
ты	живёшь	вы	живёте
он, онá	живёт	они́	живýт
past tense			
я, ты, он	жил		
я, ты, онá	жилá		
мы, вы, они́	жи́ли		

EXERCISE 4

Look at the diary below. It is also recorded on your CD. It is written by a young woman student, **Óльга**, at Moscow University (**студéнтка в Москóвском университéте**). Notice the endings of the verbs.

14ое мáя

Сегóдня я встáла в 7 часóв. Позáвтракала в буфéте. На зáвтрак бы́ли кóфе и яи́чница. Пóсле обéда читáла газéты в библиотéке. Вéчером смотрéла америкáнский фильм «Дóктор Живáго». Фильм стáрый, но óчень хорóший. Мне óчень понрáвился.

15ое мáя

Ýтром сидéла в кóмнате и читáла кни́гу по фи́зике. Потóм написáла письмó пáпе. Пообéдала в столóвой, éла шашлы́к. Пóсле обéда купи́ла грибы́ на ры́нке. Зáвтра бýдет экзáмен по фи́зике. Нýжно рабóтать!

16ое мáя

Сдалá экзáмен. Брат (Ви́тя) пи́шет, что бýдет рабóтать в бáнке. А я дýмала, что он бýдет учи́ться здесь, в Москвé.

New vocabulary

фи́зика	*physics*
встать	*to get up*
письмó	*letter*
столóвая	*canteen*
купи́ть	*to buy*
ры́нок	*market*
сдать	*to pass*
учи́ться	*to study*

Answer the questions in English.
1 What did Olga have for breakfast on 14th May?
2 What did she do after lunch?
3 What did she do in the evening? Did she enjoy it?
4 What subject is she studying?
5 What did she buy in the market?
6 Where is her brother going to work?

EXERCISE 5

Put in the correct form of an appropriate verb. If it happens **зáвтра** (*tomorrow*) you should use the future tense, if it happened **вчерá** (*yesterday*) you should use the past tense.
The first one is done for you.

1 Зáвтра мы ___бýдем обéдать___ в ресторáне.
2 Вчерá я _____ ромáн «Дóктор Живáго».
3 Зáвтра он _____ телеви́зор.
4 Сейчáс два часá. Сегóдня ýтром мы _____ в пáрке.
5 Вчерá вéчером Ни́на _____ на балалáйке.
6 Зáвтра вы _____ в футбóл.
7 Студéнтка вчерá _____ экзáмены.
8 Моя́ мáма всегдá _____ на кýхне.

● Looking at words

Verbs ending in -ся

A number of Russian verbs have the syllable **-ся** added on at the end. It originally meant *myself, yourself*, etc., although often this meaning has disappeared. Here are a few examples:

учи́ть	*to teach*
учи́ться	*to study* (literally *to teach yourself*)
роди́ть	*to give birth*
роди́ться	*to be born*
нра́виться	*to like* (literally *to please yourself*)

The ending **-ся** changes to **-сь** after vowels.

● Reading

Изве́стные ру́сские писа́тели 19-го ве́ка
Some famous 19th-century Russian writers

Никола́й Васи́льевич Го́голь роди́лся в 1809 году́. Он у́мер в 1852 году́. Он писа́л мно́го повесте́й и расска́зов, как наприме́р «Шине́ль» (*The Overcoat*). Он то́же писа́л пье́су «Ревизо́р»(*The Government Inspector*). Он мно́го лет писа́л рома́н «Мёртвые ду́ши»(*Dead Souls*) о крепостны́х, но не зако́нчил его́.

Алекса́ндр Серге́евич Пу́шкин роди́лся в 1799 году́. Он у́мер в 1837 году́. В Росси́и он са́мый изве́стный поэ́т, как Шекспи́р в А́нглии. Он писа́л стихи́, как наприме́р «Я вас люби́л», расска́зы «По́вести Бе́лкина» и рома́н в стиха́х «Евге́ний Оне́гин». Чайко́вский писа́л о́перу по э́тому рома́ну.

Ива́н Серге́евич Турге́нев роди́лся в 1818 году́. Он у́мер в 1883 году́. Он писа́л рома́ны, как наприме́р «Отцы́ и де́ти». В его́ рома́нах мы чита́ем о «ли́шнем челове́ке». Он то́же писа́л расска́зы и по́вести о любви́ и о приро́де.

Фёдор Миха́йлович Достое́вский
роди́лся в 1821 году́. Он у́мер в
1881 году́. Он писа́л мно́го рома́нов.
Его́ са́мые изве́стные рома́ны
«Преступле́ние и наказа́ние» (*Crime
and Punishment*), «Идио́т» и «Бра́тья
Карама́зовы». Он ча́сто писа́л о
го́роде Санкт-Петербу́рге, где он жил.

Лев Никола́евич Толсто́й роди́лся
в 1828 году́. Он у́мер в 1910 году́. Он
роди́лся в «Я́сной поля́не», недалеко́
от го́рода Ту́ла. Там сейча́с откры́т
музе́й. Все зна́ют его́ рома́ны «Анна
Каре́нина» и «Война́ и мир».

Анто́н Па́влович Че́хов роди́лся
в 1860 году́. Он у́мер в 1904 году́.
Он рабо́тал врачо́м. Пото́м писа́л
юмористи́ческие расска́зы и
расска́зы и пье́сы о жи́зни в Росси́и
до октя́брьской револю́ции: «Ча́йка»,
«Три сестры́», «Дя́дя Ва́ня» (*Uncle
Vanya*), «Вишнёвый сад» (*The Cherry
Orchard*). Он жил в Я́лте в Крыму́
и писа́л о ней в расска́зе «Да́ма с
соба́чкой» (*The Lady with the Little
Dog*). Он у́мер в Герма́нии.

New vocabulary

у́мер	(*from* умере́ть) *died*
са́мый	*most*
изве́стный	*famous*
поэ́т	*poet*
стихи́	*poetry*
наприме́р	*for example*
расска́з	*story*
мно́го	*many*
по́весть	(*long*) *story*
лет	*years*
ко́нчить	*to finish*
его́	*his, him*
приро́да	*nature*
любо́вь	*love*
брат	*brother*
все	*everyone*
врач	*doctor*
юмористи́ческий	*humorous*
жизнь	*life*
Крым	*Crimea*
ли́шний челове́к	*literally 'superfluous man', a recurring theme in 19th-century Russian literature: an idealist, a social misfit*

EXERCISE 6

1 Connect the two parts of the sentence to produce factually correct statements.
The first one is done for you.

a Лев Толстой   писа́л   рома́н «Преступле́ние и наказа́ние»

b Алекса́ндр Пу́шкин писа́л   рома́н «Отцы́ и де́ти»

c Ива́н Тургéнев   писа́л   пье́су «Три сестры́»

d Никола́й Го́голь   писа́л   рома́н «Война́ и мир»

e Фёдор Достое́вский писа́л   стихи́ «Я вас люби́л»

f Анто́н Че́хов   писа́л   пье́су «Ревизо́р»

2 What were the first names of the fathers of the above authors and composer?
Look them up in the first section.

3 Using the information in the above texts, answer the following questions in Russian.
The first one is done for you.

a Кто са́мый изве́стный поэ́т в Росси́и?   Пу́шкин

b Кто писа́л «Мёртвые ду́ши»?   _____

c Кто писа́л о Санкт-Петербу́рге?   _____

d Кто писа́л о ли́шнем челове́ке?   _____

e Кто роди́лся недалеко́ от Ту́лы?   _____

f Каку́ю (which) о́перу писа́л Чайко́вский? _____

g Каку́ю пье́су писа́л Го́голь?   _____

h Како́й рома́н писа́л Тургéнев?   _____

i Каки́е рома́ны писа́л Достое́вский?   _____ _____ _____

j Каки́е пье́сы писа́л Че́хов?   _____ _____ _____ _____

A situation to remember

What I did in Russia

Imagine that you are talking to your friend on the telephone discussing what you have been doing. You have been visiting Russia on a two-week excursion. You have been to the theatre several times, the cinema, and you liked the metro system but not the buses. You have been eating in the hotel, and the food has been very good.

Writing Russian (II)

Be careful of the height of the letters. There are fewer letters which go above and below the line in Russian. This gives printed and written Russian a different profile from English, and it takes a while to adjust to this.

Example

д is written *д Д*

з is written *з З*

х is written *х Х*

г is written *г Г*

Now you try writing the words.

водка _____
водка

зоопарк _____
зоопарк

Правда _____
правда

университет _____
университет

хоккей _____
хоккей

город _____
город

WHAT YOU KNOW

What you were doing

я/ты/он/Иван	чита́л
я /ты/она́/Ни́на	чита́ла
они́/Ива́н и Ни́на	чита́ли

I was, you were ...

быть	я был	
	она́ была́	
		там вчера́
	э́то бы́ло	
	мы/вы/они́ бы́ли	

to live

жить to live			
present tense			**past tense**
я	живу́	мы живём	я, ты, он жил
ты	живёшь	вы живёте	я, ты, она́ жила́
он, она́	живёт	они́ живу́т	мы, вы, они́ жи́ли

KEY VOCABULARY

век	century
вели́кий	great
война́	war
мирова́я война́	world war
оте́чественная война	'patriotic' war (on Russian territory)
все	everyone
вчера́	yesterday
год	year
в про́шлом году́	last year
жить	to live
изве́стный	famous
исто́рия	history
коне́ц	the end
купи́ть	to buy
нача́ло	the beginning
не́сколько раз	several times
получи́ть	to get, receive
расска́з	story
роди́ться	to be born
рома́н	a novel
са́мый	most
стихи́	poetry
умере́ть (*past* у́мер, умерла́ ...)	to die
ча́сто	often

Travelling by train

Russian towns

Going on foot or by vehicle

Travelling by train

● Life in Russia

Travelling by train

Russia has a highly developed train network, both local and long distance. Each large town has a number of mainline (terminal) stations, usually named after a major town or region.

• •

EXERCISE 1

Work out where you would travel to from the following stations.

a In Moscow
Ки́евский вокза́л
Ленингра́дский вокза́л★
Ку́рский вокза́л
Яросла́вский вокза́л

b In St Petersburg
Моско́вский вокза́л
Финля́ндский вокза́л
Балти́йский вокза́л
Варша́вский вокза́л

★Note that although the city is now called Санкт-Петербу́рг, the station name has not been changed.

• •

Russian has two words for a station. A mainline station is **вокза́л**. The word was borrowed from the English 'Vauxhall'. **Ста́нция** is used for an underground or a suburban railway station. The Russian for railway is **желе́зная доро́га**, literally 'iron road'.

When you arrive at a station, look for the following signs:

ПРИ́ГОРОДНЫЕ ПОЕЗДА́   *local trains*

ПОЕЗДА́ ДА́ЛЬНЕГО СЛЕ́ДОВАНИЯ *long distance trains*

You will also need to recognise the following words and phrases:

ОТПРАВЛЕ́НИЕ   *departure*
По́езд отправля́ется в 23.00. *The train departs at 11pm.*
ПРИБЫ́ТИЕ   *arrival*
По́езд прибыва́ет в 8.00.   *The train arrives at 8am.*

105

If travelling long distance, you should book in advance if possible. All seats on long distance trains are reserved and your carriage (**вагóн**) and seat (**мéсто**) will be indicated on the ticket. You will need your passport to book a long distance ticket and your name will appear on the ticket.

Russian trains are usually identified by numbers, but a few special trains also have names. If you are travelling between Moscow and St Petersburg, you may travel on the Red Arrow (**Крáсная стрелá**), the famous sleeper, which is painted red after its name, instead of the usual green.

Russian train carriages are divided into soft/ hard carriages (**мя́гкий/жёсткий вагóн**), the equivalent of the British first and second class. Distances in Russia are huge and Russian trains can travel very slowly, although the situation is improving as new trains are introduced. Some of them go at a reasonable speed. You can now do Moscow to St Petersburg in five hours.

Many train journeys are made overnight. If you wish to travel to what Russians call the 'Far East' (**Дáльний востóк**), for example to **Владивостóк**, you could be on the train for up to a week.

It is important to choose the appropriate type of sleeper. Sleeping cars can be either the basic open carriage in which you reserve a seat (**плацкáртный**), or you can travel on one with separate compartments – **купéйный**, from the word **купé**, *a compartment*. At the luxury end, there are two-berth compartments (the normal ones have four).

Each carriage on a long distance train has an attendant (**проводни́к**). It is their job to check your tickets when you get on. They may ask to see your passport to make sure the name on the ticket corresponds to that on your passport. They will also provide you with bed-linen (**бельё**). Be warned, the cost of the bed-linen is normally not included in your ticket and you will have to pay the **проводни́к** separately. He or she will often provide you with tea or coffee for a small fee. If nothing else, you should be able to get hot water.

Most Russians come prepared for a long journey. They bring food supplies with them, as a restaurant car (**вагóн-ресторáн**) is not always available. Russians also change out of their normal clothes into loose clothing, often into a track-suit, when travelling overnight by train.

EXERCISE 2

Listen to this dialogue, which takes place at a mainline railway station, and answer the questions that follow.

Тури́ст: Скажи́те, пожа́луйста, где здесь ка́сса?
Де́вушка: Куда́ вы е́дете?
Тури́ст: В Санкт-Петербу́рг.
Де́вушка: А когда́?
Тури́ст: Сего́дня.
Де́вушка: Ва́ша ка́сса бу́дет в большо́м за́ле, нале́во.
Тури́ст: Спаси́бо.

New vocabulary

Куда́ вы е́дете?   *Where are you going to?*
зал   *hall*

1   What is the tourist looking for?
2   Where is she going to?
3   Where can she buy a ticket?

EXERCISE 3

Now listen to her booking her ticket and answer the questions in English. You might find it useful to look at the timetable on page 108.

Тури́ст: Да́йте, пожа́луйста, оди́н биле́т в Санкт-Петербу́рг на сего́дня.
Де́вушка: Вам спа́льный ваго́н?
Тури́ст: Спа́льный.
Де́вушка: Вы хоти́те купе́йный?
Тури́ст: Да, купе́йный.
Де́вушка: У нас есть свобо́дные места́ на по́езде № 6 в 23 часа́ 10 мину́т. Есть ещё оди́н по́езд, № 2, отправле́ние в 23 часа́ 55 мину́т. Э́то ско́рый по́езд «Кра́сная стрела́».
Тури́ст: Так ... *(ду́мает)* Мне ну́жно быть в Санкт-Петербу́рге у́тром. Когда́ они́ прибыва́ют в Санкт-Петербу́рг?
Де́вушка: По́езд № 6 прибыва́ет в 7 часо́в 35 мину́т, № 2 – в 8 часо́в 25 мину́т.

Тури́ст: Да́йте биле́т на «Кра́сную стрелу́». С како́й платфо́рмы бу́дет по́езд?
Де́вушка: С пе́рвой.
Тури́ст: Спаси́бо.
Де́вушка: Пожа́луйста.

New vocabulary

на   *for*
ещё оди́н   *another*
ско́рый по́езд *fast train*
так   *so*
ду́мать   *think*
с   *from*

1   When does she want to travel?
2   What sort of carriage does she book?
3   What choice of trains does she have?
4   Which one does she select?
5   Which platform does it leave from?

The railway line from Moscow to St Petersburg is one of the oldest in Russia: it was built in 1851. It was originally called **Никола́евская желе́зная доро́га**, after **царь Никола́й I**. It is now called **Октя́брьская желе́зная доро́га**.

A departure board in St Petersburg

EXERCISE 4

Look at the timetable (**расписáние**) of trains from Moscow to St Petersburg.
Which train or trains would you choose to meet the conditions below?
Place the number of the train in the box. The first one is done for you.

Расписание:		Москва — Санкт-Петербург Октябрьская железная дорога											

км		20	10	30	158	48 В-Р	24 Ю	160 В-Р	14 А	28	26	6 И	2 КС	4
0	Москва Ленинградский	0105	0113	0156	1221	1226	1328	1718	2035	2200	2300	2310	2355	2359
167	Тверь					1421	1537	1850	2245	2355	0103			0202
331	Бологое	0505	1515	0611		1620	1745	2013	0051	0148	0302	0310	0344	0352
650	Санкт-Петербург Московский	0916	0920	1030	1720	2015	2236	2319	0515	0548	0710	0735	0825	0829

В-Р вагон-ресторан
Ю Юность   А Аврора   И Интурист   КС Красная стрела

1   Вы хотúте приéхать (*arrive*) в Санкт-Петербýрг вéчером.   `48`

2   Вы хотúте обéдать на пóезде.

3   Вы хотúте ýжинать на пóезде.

4   Вы хотúте приéхать в Тверь вéчером.

5   Вы хотúте приéхать óчень рáно (*early*) ýтром в Санкт-Петербýрг.

6   Пóезд отправлϯется в 10 часóв вéчера.

7   Пóезд прибывáет в Бологóе в три часá дéсять минýт нóчи.

8   Вы хотúте éхать на «Крáсной стрелé».

EXERCISE 5

Look at the following pictures taken in **Москóвский вокзáл** in St Petersburg and answer the questions that follow.

Photos 1 and 2:
a   Where are these trains going?
b   Are they express trains?
c   What are their numbers?

Photo 3   Where is this train going?

108

When you are in St Petersburg, you may want to visit some of the summer palaces situated in the small towns surrounding the city. To get there you will usually have to take a local train and then a bus. You may be able to go on foot (**пешко́м**) from the station.

This would be a good time to revise your numbers from Unit 6.

Photos 4 and 5:
Name the places you would be going if you followed these signs.

Local trains (**электри́чки**) connect the large towns with the surrounding villages. These trains are very basic, often with wooden seats. They go extremely slowly and stop frequently. Russians use them to go to their **да́ча**. Friday afternoon trains out of town and Sunday evening return ones are usually crowded with **да́чники**.

The price of a ticket on a local train depends on the zone (**зо́на**) you are travelling to. You do not need to book in advance. Give yourself time to queue at the **ка́сса** and name the station you want to go to.

⊚ EXERCISE 6

On the CD you will hear four conversations which take place between visitors who are staying with a family, and their host (**хозя́ин**) or hostess (**хозя́йка**).
Listen to each conversation and then:

a   underline where the visitor wants to go;
b   underline the station in St Petersburg he/she should depart from (**вокза́л**);
c   underline the local station (**ста́нция**) nearest to the palace;
d   write in how long it will take him/her;
e   write in either the number of the bus which will take him/her from the station to the palace, or write in 'on foot'.

	Куда́?	вокза́л	ста́нция	ско́лько мину́т	авто́бус №
1	Ломоно́сов Па́вловск Петродворе́ц Ца́рское Село́	Балти́йский Ви́тебский	Де́тское село́ Но́вый Петерго́ф Ораниенба́ум Па́вловск		
2	Ломоно́сов Па́вловск Петродворе́ц Ца́рское Село́	Балти́йский Ви́тебский	Де́тское село́ Но́вый Петерго́ф Ораниенба́ум Па́вловск		
3	Ломоно́сов Па́вловск Петродворе́ц Ца́рское Село́	Балти́йский Ви́тебский	Де́тское село́ Но́вый Петерго́ф Ораниенба́ум Па́вловск		
4	Ломоно́сов Па́вловск Петродворе́ц Ца́рское Село́	Балти́йский Ви́тебский	Де́тское село́ Но́вый Петерго́ф Ораниенба́ум Па́вловск		

You can also reach **Петродворе́ц** on a hydrofoil (**на метео́ре**). If you like boat trips, you can go on boat (**на теплохо́де**) along the rivers and canals of St Petersburg. There are also tourist boats that ply up and down the Moskva River (**Москва́-река́**) in Moscow – you get one of the best views of the Kremlin from one of these boats. You could also try a cruise down the Volga.

● Language information

Moving around

Russian distinguishes between going on foot and going in a vehicle.

идти́ *to go, come* (on foot)			
present tense			
я	иду́	мы	идём
ты	идёшь	вы	идёте
он, она́	идёт	они́	иду́т
past tense			
was going (on foot)			
он (я, ты)		шёл	
она́ (я, ты)		шла	
мы, вы, они́		шли	

е́хать *to go, come* (by vehicle)			
present tense			
я	е́ду	мы	е́дем
ты	е́дешь	вы	е́дете
он, она́	е́дет	они́	е́дут
past tense			
was going (in a vehicle)			
он (я, ты)		е́хал	
она́ (я, ты)		е́хала	
мы, вы, они́		е́хали	

Where are you living, where are you going?

– Где вы живёте?
Where do you live?
– Живу́ в це́нтре, на Тверско́й у́лице.

I live in the centre, on Tverskaya Street.
– Куда́ вы идёте?
Where are you going?
– Иду́ в центр, на рабо́ту.
I am going to the centre, to work.

Russian has two words for *where*. **Где** means *in* what place; **куда́** means *to* what place.

Going to a place

Russian has two words meaning *to*: **в** and **на** followed by the accusative case.

в is used with most place words.
на is used with words denoting an activity (e.g. **на рабо́ту**).
на is used with a few place words:

Я иду́   в це́нтр.
          на вокза́л.
          на по́чту.
          на Тверску́ю у́лицу.
          на Кра́сную пло́щадь.

на is sometimes also used to translate *for*: биле́т на по́езд *a ticket for the train*

Coming from a place

There are two words to translate *from*. The opposite of **в** is **из** and of **на** is **с**. Both prepositions meaning *from* are followed by the genitive case:

Я иду́   из це́нтра.
          с вокза́ла.
          с по́чты.

Be careful – **с** can also mean *with*. In this meaning it is followed by the instrumental case (see Unit 9).

Look at how Russian conveys the words *in, on, at, to, from*:

in, on, at в, на + prepositional case	to в, на + accusative case	from из, с + genitive case
Я живу́ **в** кварти́р**е** № 5.	Я иду́ **в** кварти́р**у** № 5.	Я иду́ **из** кварти́р**ы** № 5.
Я сейча́с **на** Кра́сной пло́щад**и**.	Я иду́ **на** Кра́сн**ую** пло́щад**ь**.	Я иду́ **с** Кра́сной пло́щад**и**.

If you are measuring distance from one place to another, use the two prepositions **от** and **до**. They are both also followed by the genitive case:

От Москвы́ до Санкт-Петербу́рга 650 киломе́тров.

Notice also the phrase **(не)далеко́ от** *(not) far from*.

● **Looking at words**

North, south, east, west

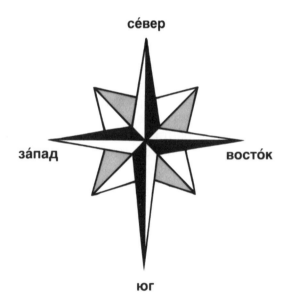

The four points of the compass – **се́вер** (*north*), **юг** (*south*), **за́пад** (*west*), **восто́к** (*east*) – are always used with **на** to mean *in* and *to*, and **с** to mean *from*.

Мой брат живёт **на** се́вер**е**.
My brother lives in the north.
Мы сейча́с е́дем **с** се́вер**а на** юг.
We are now going from north to south.

. . . .

EXERCISE 7
Complete the following sentences, adding direction words. The word **нахо́дится** means *is situated*. The first one is done for you.

1 Санкт-Петербу́рг нахо́дится на се́вере
   Росси́и.

2 Владивосто́к нахо́дится на _____
   Росси́и.

3 Му́рманск нахо́дится на _____
   Росси́и.

4 Ма́нчестер нахо́дится на _____
   А́нглии.

5 Сан-Франци́ско нахо́дится на _____
   Аме́рики.

6 Аберди́н нахо́дится на _____
   Шотла́ндии.

. . . .

Dividing words up

It is very important to look at the parts of a Russian word. It will help you to work out what words mean that you have never seen before. Here are some examples which start with **при-**:

прийти́	*to arrive (on foot)*
прие́хать	*to arrive (by vehicle)*
прибыва́ть	*to arrive (official)*
прихо́д	*arrival (on foot)*
прие́зд	*arrival (by vehicle)*
прибы́тие	*arrival (official)*

у- and **от-** have the opposite meaning: that of departure.

. . . .

EXERCISE 8

Can you work out what the following words mean?

1	уйти́	**4**	отъе́зд
2	уе́хать	**5**	ухо́д
3	отбыва́ть	**6**	отбы́тие

в- means into, **вы-** means out of.

. . . .

EXERCISE 9

Complete the table. The first one is done for you.

		Meaning	из	в
1	вы́йти	to go out (on foot)	✓	
2	вы́ехать			
3	вход			
4	вы́ход			
5	въезд			
6	вы́езд			

. . . .

ИДТИ́

Apart from meaning *to go on foot*, **идти́** has the following meanings:

1 *to be on* (of film, play, etc.)
Сего́дня идёт интере́сный фильм.
There is an interesting film on today.

2 *to rain, snow*
Идёт дождь.   *It is raining.*
Идёт снег.   *It is snowing.*

● Reading

Find out about Russia

Here are some notes in Russian about three cities of European Russia. Answer the questions which follow each passage in English.

Москва́

Москва́ – столи́ца Росси́и с 1918 го го́да. Здесь живёт о́коло девяти́ миллио́нов челове́к. В це́нтре го́рода нахо́дятся Кремль, Кра́сная пло́щадь и гла́вная у́лица – Тверска́я у́лица. Недалеко́ от це́нтра нахо́дится у́лица Но́вый Арба́т. На э́той у́лице мо́жно покупа́ть кни́ги в большо́м кни́жном магази́не «Дом кни́ги» и то́же мо́жно вку́сно обе́дать. Москва́ стои́т на Москва́-реке́.

New vocabulary

о́коло	*about*
стоя́ть	*to stand*
река́	*river*

1 How many people live in Moscow?
2 Give two reasons for going to New Arbat.

Санкт-Петербу́рг

В Санкт-Петербу́рге мно́го краси́вых зда́ний, музе́ев, собо́ров. У́лицы в Санкт-Петербу́рге прямы́е и широ́кие. Гла́вная у́лица го́рода – Не́вский проспе́кт. При коммуни́зме Санкт-Петербу́рг называ́лся Ленингра́дом. Здесь нахо́дится Эрмита́ж, о́чень большо́й музе́й и карти́нная галере́я, где вися́т карти́ны за́падных худо́жников. В Санкт-Петербу́рге мно́го рек и кана́лов. Гла́вная река́ – Нева́. Санкт-Петербу́рг – «Се́верная Вене́ция» Росси́и.

New vocabulary

зда́ние	*building*
прямо́й	*straight*
широ́кий	*wide*
при	*in the time of*
называ́ться	*to be called*
карти́нная галере́я	*art gallery*
карти́на	*picture*
висе́ть	*to hang*
худо́жник	*painter*

1 What sort of streets does St Petersburg have?
2 What is said about the Hermitage?
3 What is the name of the main street? Can you work out where it gets its name from?

Яросла́вль

К се́веро-восто́ку от Москвы́ на реке́ Во́лге стои́т ста́рый ру́сский го́род Яросла́вль. По́езд идёт пять часо́в от Москвы́ до Яросла́вля. Он оди́н из городо́в «Золото́го Кольца́» и здесь о́чень мно́го ста́рых зда́ний, наприме́р Спа́сский монасты́рь, постро́енный в шестна́дцатом ве́ке. Говоря́т, что Яросла́в Му́дрый основа́л го́род в 1010 г. Э́тот го́род ста́рше, чем Москва́. Сейча́с он не о́чень большо́й: там живу́т о́коло 600 ты́сяч челове́к.

New vocabulary

к	*to, towards*
постро́енный	*built*
говоря́т, что	*they say that*
му́дрый	*wise*
основа́ть	*to found*
ста́рше чем	*older than*

1 How do you get to Yaroslavl from Moscow? How long does it take?
2 When was
  a the Spasskiy monastery built?
  b the town of Yaroslavl founded?

A situation to remember

Your home town

You are being interviewed for a Russian newspaper. The reporter (**корреспондéнт**) wants to know about the town where you live. He or she asks you a number of questions. Answer them as fully as you can.

Скажи́те, пожáлуйста, в какóм гóроде вы живёте?

Где нахóдится гóрод?

Расскажи́те мне немнóжко (*a little*) о вáшем гóроде. Каки́е там здáния?

Как мóжно éхать отсю́да (*from here*) в ваш гóрод?

Скóлько часóв нáдо éхать?

Спаси́бо.

Find a partner. You are now a visitor from Britain to Moscow, St Petersburg or Yaroslavl. You meet a friendly person at a party. Ask him or her some questions about the town.

Writing Russian (III)

Three letters start with a hook:

л Л м М я Я

Make sure you do not miss out the hook when you join letters up. Look at the height of the letters in the examples.

Examples *дом красная лимонад*

ы is written *ы*

ю is written *ю Ю*

Now you try writing the words.

литр _____
литр

крокоди́л _____
крокодил

киломéтр _____
километр

А́нглия _____
Англия

вы́ход _____
выход

меню́ _____
меню

WHAT YOU KNOW

Going places
Кудá вы идёте?
Я иду́ на рабóту.

Кудá вы éдете?
Я éду в Москву́.

Coming from places
Я иду́ с рабóты.
Я éду из Москвы́.

Measuring distance
От Москвы́ до Санкт-Петербу́рга 650 киломéтров.

North, south, east, west
сéвер, юг, востóк, зáпад
Я живу́ на сéвере.
Я éду с сéвера на юг.

KEY VOCABULARY

вагóн	carriage
вокзáл	station (mainline)
востóк	east
дáча	dacha
éхать	to go (by vehicle)
зáпад	west
идти́	to go (on foot)
из + G	from
кудá	where to
от ... до + G	from ... to
отправлéние	departure
отправля́ться	to depart
пешкóм	on foot
пóезд	train
прибывáть	to arrive
прибы́тие	arrival
проводни́к/проводни́ца	attendant
рáно	early
с + G	from
сéвер	north
стáнция	station (suburban, underground)
электри́чка	train (local)
юг	south

Going to Russia

**Invitations and
visas**

**Arriving in and
leaving Russia**

Changing money

● Life in Russia

Getting a visa

To travel to Russia you will need a visa (**ви́за**). If you are going
on a package tour organised by a holiday company, your visa
will be arranged for you. All you will have to do is fill in a visa
application form (**ви́зовая анке́та**). If you are going in any other
way, you will need an invitation (**приглаше́ние**). The company
or educational institution arranging your visit will provide it.

Here is a sample invitation from a Russian university:

ПРИГЛАШЕНИЕ №	2Y9427990

на въезд в Российскую Федерацию

Вид визы	обыкновенная учебная	Кратность визы	однократная
Гражданство	ВЕЛИКОБРИТАНИЯ		
Государство постоянного проживания	ВЕЛИКОБРИТАНИЯ		
Въезд с	20.06.05 по 20.09.05	На срок (дней)	090
Фамилия	Smith/Смит		
Имя, отчество (имена)	Alan/Алан		
		Пол	муж
Дата, страна и регион рождения	20.04.1985/ВЕЛИКОБРИТАНИЯ Лондон		
Номер и дата выдачи паспорта	346954321 09.09.2003		
Цель поездки	Стажировка		
Приглашающая оганизация			
	МГ У		
Маршрут (пункты посещения)	МОСКВА С ПЕТЕРБУРГ		
Следует с детьми (до 16 лет)			
Дополнительные сведения			
Приглашение действительно до	20.09.2005		

М. П.   Орган, оформивший приглашение:

ГУВД 810

Подпись должностного лица

810   080-2 2065667   Дата   03.06.2005

EXERCISE 1

Read the invitation through and answer the questions which follow in English. Don't expect to understand every word.

1 Which Russian university has issued the invitation?
2 When does the course start?
3 How long does it last?
4 What is the name of the student?
5 Where was he born?
6 How old was he at the start of the course?

A private citizen can also obtain an invitation for you. Allow plenty of time, as Russian bureaucracy moves slowly. Your host in Russia has to fill in forms and hand them to an organisation called **ОВИР** (**Отде́л виз и регистра́ция иностра́нных гра́ждан,** *Visa Department and Registration of Foreign Citizens*). It will consider the application and eventually issue an official document (**извеще́ние**). You must send this to the consulate with your completed visa form.

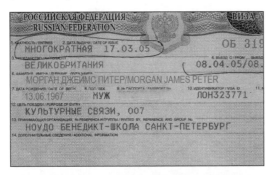

EXERCISE 2

Look at the two visas and answer the following questions:

1 Who has a single-entry visa and who a multi-entry one?
2 What is the purpose of Julia Thomas's visit to Russia?
3 What airport did she use to enter and leave Russia? (Hint: read the next paragraph before answering.)
4 What was James Morgan's reason for going to Russia?
5 Both were invited by the Benedict School. In which city is it situated?

New vocabulary

свя́зь   *link*

Russian airports

You will arrive through one of Moscow's international airports: **Шереме́тьево** or **Домоде́дово** or through St Peterburg's **Пу́лково** airport.

Your visa and passport will be checked by the border guard (**погра́ничник**). You should also have filled in a migration card (**миграцио́нная ка́рта**). The **погра́ничник** will keep part A, stamp and hand back part B to you. Do not lose it! You'll need it to register your passport and leave the country. After that, you'll need to collect your luggage (**бага́ж**). You'll probably need a trolley (**теле́жка**).

EXERCISE 3

Listen to the dialogue on your CD and answer the following questions.

Тури́ст:	Скажи́те, пожа́луйста, где теле́жки?
Пассажи́р:	Они́ вон там, нале́во, в углу́.
Тури́ст:	Там, где лю́ди стоя́т в о́череди?
Пассажи́р:	Да, да. Пойдёмте вме́сте. (*стоя́т в о́череди*)
Тури́ст:	Ой, ой, ой, как я не люблю́ стоя́ть в о́череди.
Пассажи́р:	Ничего́, ничего́. Бага́ж сейча́с бу́дет. Че́рез два́дцать мину́т.

	Вы зна́ете, что ну́жно плати́ть за теле́жку?
Тури́ст:	Нет! Как плати́ть? В А́нглии не пла́тят. У меня́ то́лько до́ллары и фу́нты.
Пассажи́р:	Ничего́. Да́йте им до́ллары.
Тури́ст:	А ско́лько сто́ит теле́жка?
Пассажи́р:	Не зна́ю. Год наза́д она́ сто́ила два до́ллара. А смотри́те, сейча́с беспла́тно! Вот э́то прогре́сс!

New vocabulary

вон там	over there
в углу́	in the corner
лю́ди	people
о́чередь	queue
вме́сте	together
плати́ть (за)	to pay (for)
че́рез	in (time)
Ско́лько сто́ит ...?	How much does it cost?
наза́д	ago
беспла́тно	free (of charge)

1 Where does the tourist find the trolleys?
2 Why is the man upset?
3 How long do they have to wait to get their luggage?
4 Has she got any roubles?
5 How does she decide to pay?
6 How much did the trolleys cost last year?

• •

After collecting your luggage, head for customs (**тамо́жня**), choosing from either the red channel (**кра́сный кана́л**) or, for most people, the green channel (**зелёный кана́л**). If you have anything especially valuable, such as a laptop, you'll need to fill in a customs declaration form (**тамо́женная деклара́ция**) in duplicate. Keep your stamped copy to hand in when you leave the country, as proof that you imported your laptop into Russia.

Changing money

There are various ways you can change foreign currency into roubles (**рубли́**). A cash machine (**банкома́т**) is one option – some will also give you US dollars. You can also get cash at many banks with a debit or credit card, showing your passport as ID.

If you want to change cash, US dollars or euros are the simplest. However, make sure that the notes are in good condition. Russians will often refuse any torn or very dirty notes. Look for one of these signs:

ОБМЕ́Н ВАЛЮ́ТЫ *change of currency*
ОБМЕ́ННЫЙ ПУНКТ *exchange point*

It's worth checking whether any commission (**коми́ссия**) is charged, and the different rates for the purchase (**поку́пка**) and the sale (**прода́жа**) of foreign currency. Questions to ask are:

Где мо́жно обменя́ть де́ньги?
Where can I change my money?
Ско́лько рубле́й за до́ллар?
How many roubles for a dollar?

You'll also be able to use your credit cards in large shops and restaurants in Moscow, St Petersburg and other large towns. However, their use is not as widespread as in the UK and you should not rely on them.

• •

EXERCISE 4

Look at the two pictures. If you can change currency there, tick the box.

1 What else can you buy?

2 When is the shop closed?

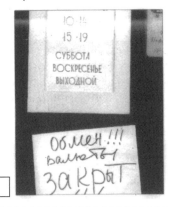

. . . .

⊙ EXERCISE 5

Mary is asking her host, Viktor, for advice about buying presents to take home. Listen to their conversation.

Мэри: Виктор, скажите, где можно купить подарки для детей и для мамы и для папы?

Виктор: У вас двое детей, да? Сын и дочка.

Мэри: Да. Сыну шесть лет, а дочке восемь.

Виктор: Что вы хотите? Игрушки, куклы.

Мэри: Да. Типичные русские игрушки и куклы.

Виктор: Знаете, в Москве старая, историческая улица: Арбат. Старый Арбат, не новый. Там стоят киоски. Продают игрушки, куклы, одежду. И матрёшки тоже продают. Всё есть.

Мэри: Хорошо. А как туда доехать?

Виктор: Можно на маршрутке, или на метро. Станция метро «Арбатская».

Мэри: Там можно купить диски и книги? Папа очень любит музыку, а мама – архитектуру. Я уже купила для неё книгу об архитектуре.

Виктор: Книги и диски лучше купить на Новом Арбате. Мама читает по-русски?

Мэри: Нет, купила книгу на английском языке.

New vocabulary

подарок	*gift*
для	*for*
двое детей	*two children*
дочка	*daughter*
сын	*son*
игрушка	*toy*
кукла	*doll*
матрёшка	*(nested) doll*
исторический	*historical*
продавать/продать	*to sell*
всё	*everything*
туда	*(to) there*
архитектура	*architecture*

Decide whether the following statements are true or false, adding a short explanation. The first one is done for you.

1 Mary only wants to buy presents for her children.

true ☐   false ☑

She also wants to buy her parents gifts.

2 Mary has two children.

true ☐   false ☐

3 Her daughter is older than her son.

true ☐   false ☐

4 She doesn't want toys or dolls.

true ☐   false ☐

5 The old Arbat is a street in Moscow.

true ☐   false ☐

6 There are lots of stalls on the old Arbat.

true ☐   false ☐

7 You can only get to the Arbat by metro.

true ☐   false ☐

8 Mary has already bought her mother a present.

true ☐   false ☐

9 Mary's mother reads Russian.

true ☐   false ☐

10 It's best to buy books on the old Arbat.

true ☐   false ☐

. . . .

● Language information

Describing things

Have a look again at the adjective endings explained in Unit 7, and then do Exercise 6.

EXERCISE 6

Here are three sets of adjectives and nouns. Link the adjectives up to the nouns. You will
need to look carefully at the ending. The first one is done for you.

1 ма́ленькая   теле́жки
   моско́вский   су́мка
   но́вые   аэропо́рт

2 де́тская   кана́л
   кра́сный   приглаше́ние
   университе́тское   игру́шка

3 хоро́шие   икра́
   чёрная   тамо́женник
   прия́тный   но́вости

My, your, our, his, her, its, their

The words for *my*, *your* and *our* change their endings, somewhat like adjectives, depending
on the gender of the noun:

	my	your (ты)	our	your (вы)	
Masculine	мой	твой	наш	ваш	дом
Feminine	моя́	твоя́	на́ша	ва́ша	кварти́ра
Neuter	моё	твоё	на́ше	ва́ше	письмо́ (*letter*)
Plural	мои́	твои́	на́ши	ва́ши	кни́ги

Его́ (*his*), **её** (*her*) and **их** (*their*) never change: **его́ дом**, **его́ кварти́ра**, **его́ письмо́**,
его́ кни́ги.

Закры́т, откры́т

Закры́т (*closed*) and **откры́т** (*open*) have the following forms:

Masculine	рестора́н	закры́т	откры́т
Feminine	апте́ка	закры́та	откры́та
Neuter	метро́	закры́то	откры́то
Plural	магази́ны	закры́ты	откры́ты

Would like to

Он хоте́л бы (Она́ хоте́ла бы) обменя́ть де́сять до́лларов.
He (She) would like to change ten dollars.
The plural form is **хоте́ли бы**. If **бы** appears in a sentence, you must always use the past
tense of the verb.
This is the *conditional* form of the verb, which you will see used in 'if' sentences.

119

EXERCISE 7

Devise answers to the following questions, as in the example.

Example

Question: Ни́на бу́дет в теа́тре сего́дня ве́чером?

Answer:

~~Он хоте́л бы~~		закры́т.
Она́ хоте́ла бы	пойти́, но теа́тр сего́дня	~~закры́та.~~
~~Они́ хоте́ли бы~~		~~закры́то.~~

1 Бори́с бу́дет в рестора́не сего́дня ве́чером?

Он хоте́л бы		закры́т.
Она́ хоте́ла бы	пойти́, но рестора́н сего́дня	закры́та.
Они́ хоте́ли бы		закры́то.

2 А́нна и Ка́тя бу́дут в библиоте́ке сего́дня ве́чером?

Он хоте́л бы		закры́т.
Она́ хоте́ла бы	пойти́, но библиоте́ка сего́дня	закры́та.
Они́ хоте́ли бы		закры́то.

3 Серге́й бу́дет в кино́ сего́дня ве́чером?

Он хоте́л бы		закры́т.
Она́ хоте́ла бы	пойти́, но кино́ сего́дня	закры́та.
Они́ хоте́ли бы		закры́то.

4 Моя́ сестра́ бу́дет на стадио́не сего́дня ве́чером?

Он хоте́л бы		закры́т.
Она́ хоте́ла бы	пойти́, но стадио́н сего́дня	закры́та.
Они́ хоте́ли бы		закры́то.

5 Воло́дя бу́дет в кафе́ сего́дня ве́чером?

Он хоте́л бы		закры́т.
Она́ хоте́ла бы	пойти́, но кафе́ сего́дня	закры́та.
Они́ хоте́ли бы		закры́то.

● Reading

Travelling around

Read the following excerpt from a Russian girl's essay for her school magazine.

В 2003 году́ мы жи́ли в Санкт-Петербу́рге. Па́па там рабо́тал в университе́те. Санкт-Петербу́рг – о́чень краси́вый го́род. Я о́чень люби́ла гуля́ть по Не́вскому проспе́кту, заходи́ть (call in) в ма́ленькое кафе́ и пить сок и́ли Пе́пси.

В 2004 году́ па́па чита́л ле́кции в Ло́ндонском университе́те и мы с ма́мой пое́хали в А́нглию. Там бы́ло о́чень интере́сно. Мы е́хали туда́ на самолёте. Гости́ница в Ло́ндоне была́ о́чень больша́я и комфорта́бельная. Мы бы́ли на Трафальга́рской пло́щади и на Да́унинг-Стрите, где нахо́дится резиде́нция премье́р-мини́стра.

Я хоте́ла бы пое́хать в Вашингто́н и в Нью-Йо́рк и посети́ть (visit) Бе́лый дом и Эмпа́йр стейт би́лдинг. Я хоте́ла бы подня́ться (go up) на 102-ой эта́ж!

EXERCISE 8
Answer the following questions in English.

1 Where did the girl's father work?
2 What did the girl like to do, when she lived in St Petersburg?
3 Why did they go to Britain?
4 Where did they stay?
5 What did they see in London?
6 Where else would she like to go?
7 What would she like to do there?

● Looking at words

Recognising adjectives

Russian commonly makes up new adjectives by adding either **-ный** (**-ной**) or **-ский** (**-ской**) to nouns:

интере́с	*interest*
интере́сный	*interesting*
го́род	*town*
городско́й	*municipal*

In English you can quite commonly put two nouns together to make up a phrase. In Russian you will make the first word into an adjective:

университе́тская ле́кция *university lecture*
мясно́й отде́л *meat section (in shop)*

The last letter of the noun may change when adding **-ный** or **-ский**:

поли́тика *politics*
полити́чный *politic*

EXERCISE 9
Translate the following phrases. Try not to look up any words in the dictionary.

1 а́томная эне́ргия
2 кни́жный магази́н
3 въездна́я ви́за
4 Не́вский проспе́кт
5 пивно́й бар
6 Собо́рная пло́щадь
7 телефо́нный разгово́р
8 библиоте́чный день

Flying

The syllable **-лёт-** or **-лет-** means *flying*. The word for a plane is made up of two roots: **сам** (*oneself*) and **лёт** (*flying*). Don't worry, Russian planes do have pilots! The word for *pilot* is **лётчик** – the ending **-чик** indicates a person, similar to *-er* at the end of English words. You will also see **сам-** at the beginning of some other words: e.g. **самова́р**, which literally means 'self boil'.

A situation to remember

Going through customs
Russian customs officers are normally not interested in what you are taking out of the country, but occasionally, they see something on their X-ray machines which arouses their suspicions and you may have to open your case. Here is a typical situation for you to recreate with a partner.

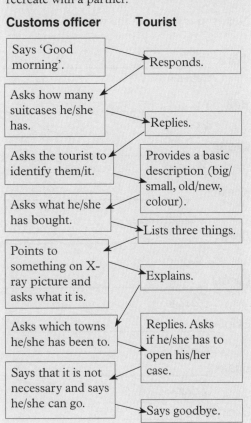

Writing Russian (IV)

Some of the capital letters are written with a flourish and give written Russian a more ornate appearance. Write all the words below with a capital letter. Note that **ь** is never the first letter in a word and is therefore not normally used as a capital. It is the same height as: *е   и   л*

Examples

Ф is written   *ф Ф*

Ч is written   *ч Ч*

ь is written   *ь*

Б is written   *б Б*

Э is written   *э Э*

Now you try writing the words.

Фо́то _____
фото

Чай _____
чай

Че́хов _____
Чехов

Кремль _____
Кремль

День _____
День

Грибы́ _____
Грибы

Бюро́ _____
Бюро

Бланк _____
Бланк

Экску́рсия _____
Экскурсия

My, your, his, her, our, their
мой дом
твоя́ кварти́ра
на́ше письмо́
ва́ши кни́ги
его́ дом
её кварти́ра
их письмо́

Open, closed
магази́н откры́т/закры́т
библиоте́ка откры́та/закры́та
кафе́ закры́то/откры́то
магази́ны закры́ты/откры́ты

Would like to
Он хоте́л бы (Она́ хоте́ла бы) обменя́ть де́сять до́лларов.

KEY VOCABULARY

бага́ж	luggage
до́ллар	dollar
за	for
ма́ленький	small
обме́н	exchange
обменя́ть	to change (money)
откры́ть	to open
о́чередь	queue
па́спорт	passport
письмо́	letter
плати́ть	to pay
пода́рок	gift
приглаше́ние	invitation
рубль	rouble
Ско́лько сто́ит ...?	How much does ... cost?
сувени́р	souvenir
су́мка	bag
тамо́женник	customs official
тамо́жня	customs
теле́жка	trolley
фунт	pound
чемода́н	suitcase

15

Russian schools

Universities

Revision

Revision

● Life in Russia

6 ме́сяцев → ЯСЛИ

3 го́да → ДЕТСКИЙ САД

СРЕДНЯЯ ШКОЛА

6 лет

17 лет → УНИВЕРСИТЕТ

МГУ

22 лет

The school system

Russians go to school (**шко́ла**) when they are six years old and most stay in full-time education till they are 17. They usually study at the same school for the whole of this period, at a **сре́дняя шко́ла**, literally *middle school*. These schools have numbers rather than names, a school in St Petersburg, for example, might be called **Сре́дняя шко́ла № 21, Моско́вского райо́на** (*district*).

Alongside the state system, big cities such as Moscow or St Petersburg have a wide range of private fee-paying schools. Many of them are now called **лице́й** or **гимна́зия**, words that were last used before the 1917 communist revolution to indicate a *grammar* or *high school*. Unlike the state schools, they usually have names, not numbers. Examples of private schools in Moscow are: **Гармо́ния** (*harmony*) **колле́дж XXI, Ренеса́нс**.

There is also a network of nursery schools (**я́сли**) and kindergartens (**де́тский сад**), both state and privately run.

Russia has a well established system of higher education institutions (**ву́зы**). At 17, on leaving school, students can go either to a university (**университе́т**) or to an institute (**институ́т**). Most courses last for five years and some lead to a job qualification. If, for example, you study at a **педагоги́ческий университе́т** or **институ́т**, you are trained as a teacher.

Entrance to a **вуз** is by examination and each **вуз** sets its own entrance examination. Examinations in Russia are usually oral. The student arrives and selects a **биле́т** (literally *ticket)* with a topic on it. He or she then has to answer questions on this topic from a panel of lecturers. Most prospective students will need the services of a **репети́тор** (*coach*) to give them private lessons. Without such help they are unlikely to get into university. The other way of getting into university is to join a **комме́рческий курс** (*commercial course*). These students will study alongside those that have passed the entrance examination. The only difference is that they have to pay for their course.

Teachers in both state schools and higher education are very poorly paid and many cities have serious recruitment problems. Many teachers and university lecturers only exist by having two or three jobs and giving private lessons as a **репети́тор**. If their subject is in demand (e.g. teaching

English), they will earn far more from their private work than they do from teaching in the state system.

The Russian education system uses a scale of five marks. The top mark is five (**пятёрка**). This is officially labelled **отли́чно** (*excellent*). Four (**четвёрка**) is **хорошо́** (*good*). Three (**тро́йка**) is **удовлетвори́тельно** (*satisfactory*). The lowest mark normally awarded is **дво́йка** (*two*). This is **неудовлетвори́тельно** (*unsatisfactory*).

Useful vocabulary

учи́тель, учи́тельница *teacher (m/f)*
преподава́тель, преподава́тельница
teacher (university, senior school)
учени́к, учени́ца *pupil (m/f)*
студе́нт, студе́нтка *student (m/f)*

If you are at school, university or an institute, use the verb **учи́ться**:

Я учу́сь в шко́ле № 23.
I go to school number 23.
Он у́читься в МГУ.
He is a student at Moscow University.
Вы рабо́таете и́ли у́читесь?
Are you working or are you a student?

● Language information

Years

В 2005 году́ (в две ты́сячи пя́том году́) – *in 2005*. '**году́**' is often abbreviated to '**г.**' To recognise years in Russian, listen out for **две ты́сячи** *two thousand* or **ты́сяча девятьсо́т**, *nineteen hundred*. The next number will give you the decade, and the final number, if there is one, the year: **пе́рвом, второ́м**, etc.

These numbers were given in Unit 11, and you can practise them in exercises 4–7.

● Looking at words

Number words

Russian has a set of special nouns related to numbers:

дво́йка from **два**
тро́йка from **три**
четвёрка from **четы́ре**
пятёрка from **пять**
шестёрка from **шесть**
семёрка from **семь**
восьмёрка from **во́семь**
девя́тка from **де́вять**
деся́тка from **де́сять**

As you can see from earlier in this unit, **дво́йка** to **пятёрка** are used to refer to marks at school and university. All of the above number words have other uses:

Cards: **деся́тка пик** is the ten of spades.
Bus, trolleybus and tram numbers: **Я е́ду домо́й на восьмёрке** (*I am going home on the number eight*). You will also hear **на восьмо́м авто́бусе (тролле́йбусе ...)**. Horse-driven vehicles: the most famous of them, **тро́йка**, has three.
Groups of people: The film *The Magnificent Seven* is **«Великоле́пная семёрка»** in Russian.

Abbreviations

Modern Russian makes a lot of use of abbreviations. You have already seen some of these. One word in this lesson is in origin an abbreviation: **вуз** stands for **вы́сшее уче́бное заведе́ние** *higher educational institution*.

EXERCISE 1

Here are some abbreviations we have had in the last few units. Can you remember what they mean in English?

1   МГУ (Моско́вский госуда́рственный университе́т)
2   ГУМ (Госуда́рственный универса́льный магази́н)

3   ОВИР (Отде́л виз и регистра́ция иностра́нных гра́ждан)
4   МХАТ (Моско́вский худо́жественный академи́ческий теа́тр)

Sometimes the abbreviations contain not just the first letters of the word but selected syllables.

EXERCISE 2

Each of the following is the name of an organisation. Can you work out what they are?

1   мосгортранс
2   минфин
3   госстрах
4   промстройбанк
5   ростелеком

New vocabulary

министе́рство	*ministry*
госуда́рство	*state*
страхо́вка	*insurance*
промы́шленность	*industry*
стро́ить	*to build*

You will regularly see theatres, concert halls, universities, etc. named after people. Look out for the abbreviation **им.**, short for **и́мени**, literally *of the name of*.

EXERCISE 3

Who are the following places named after?

В Москве́
1   Драмати́ческий теа́тр им. Н. В. Го́голя
2   Большо́й зал консервато́рии им. П. И. Чайко́вского
3   Моско́вский госуда́рственный университе́т им. М. В. Ломоно́сова

В Санкт-Петербу́рге
4   Академи́ческий Большо́й драмати́ческий теа́тр им. А. С. Пу́шкина
5   Филармо́ния им. Д. Д. Шостако́вича
6   О́перная сту́дия Консервато́рии им. Н. А. Ри́мского-Ко́рсакова
7   Музе́й антрополо́гии и этногра́фии им. Петра́ Вели́кого

125

● Revision exercises

EXERCISE 4

Here are some dates written out in words.
Write the figures in the space provided.

1 в тысяча двести двадцать третьем году

в __1223__ г.

2 в тысяча пятьсот сорок седьмом году

в _____ г.

3 в тысяча шестьсот пятом году

в _____ г.

4 в тысяча семьсот третьем году

в _____ г.

5 в тысяча восемьсот шестьдесят первом

году   в _____ г.

6 в тысяча девятьсот сорок первом году

в _____ г.

7 в тысяча девятьсот девяносто девятом

году   в _____ г.

EXERCISE 5

All the dates in Exercise 4 refer to events
listed in the table of events in Unit 12 (page
98). Answer the question **Что случилось?**
(What happened?) in Russian or English:

1 Что случилось в тысяча двести двадцать
третьем году?

2 Что случилось в тысяча пятьсот сорок
седьмом году?

3 Что случилось в тысяча шестьсот пятом
году?

4 Что случилось в тысяча семьсот третьем
году?

5 Что случилось в тысяча восемьсот
шестьдесят первом году?

6 Что случилось в тысяча девятьсот сорок
первом году?

7 Что случилось в тысяча девятьсот
девяносто девятом году?

EXERCISE 6

Here are three jumbled lists.
Once again you need to refer to the list of
dates in Unit 12 on page 98.
Connect one item from the left-hand
column with one from the centre and one
from the right-hand column to make a
sensible statement.
The first one is done for you.

1 В 1227 г.	Пётр Великий	первая мировая война.
2 В 1914 г.	кончилась	Екатерина II.
3 В 1697 г.	умер	татарское иго.
4 В 1945 г.	началась	Чингисхан.
5 В 1480 г.	умерла	поехал в Голландию.
6 В 1796 г.	кончилось	великая отечественная война.

⊙ EXERCISE 7

Listen to the recording on your CD, giving
information about events that took place in
particular years of the 20th century.
Listen out for **в тысяча девятьсот**, the
equivalent of nineteen hundred.
Fill in the table below in English.

	Year	Event
1		
2		
3		
4		
5		

EXERCISE 8

Read through the letter on the next page
from **Ваня**, a student in **МГУ**, to his friend
Боря, who is training to be a teacher at
the **педагогический университет** in St
Petersburg (**РГПУ им. Герцена**). Then do
the exercises.

Москва́
среда́ 12-ое октября́ 2005 г.

Дорого́й Бо́ря,

Вот я и в Моско́вском Университе́те. Мы [1] _i_ ле́кции и семина́ры две неде́ли
наза́д. На́шего профе́ссора по фи́зике [2] __ Бори́сов, Ива́н Никола́евич.
Вчера́ он [3] __ о́чень интере́сную ле́кцию о ко́смосе. По́сле ле́кции мы [4] __
в студе́нческой столо́вой, а пото́м [5] __ телеви́зор. Америка́нский пиани́ст
[6] __ конце́рт Чайко́вского. За́втра мы бу́дем [7] __ в лаборато́рии, а ве́чером
бу́дем [8] __ в библиоте́ке. Мне ну́жно [9] __ о́чень мно́го рабо́тать, но я то́же [10] __
занима́ться _play_ спо́ртом. Здесь мы [11] __ в волейбо́л, хокке́й, те́ннис.
Как ты [12] __ в РГПУ им. Ге́рцена?

Приве́т ма́ме и па́пе
Ва́ня

1 Here is a list of the words that have been missed out.
Put the letter of the correct word in the space provided in the text.
The first one is done for you.

a смотре́ли **b** зову́т **c** игра́ем **d** у́жинали **e** у́чишься **f** чита́ть
g рабо́тать **h** чита́л **i** бу́дет **j** на́чали **k** игра́л **l** бу́ду

2 Answer the following questions in Russian.
  a В како́м ме́сяце (_month_) начали́сь ле́кции?   **d** Где Ва́ня бу́дет за́втра?
  b Как зову́т профе́ссора?   **e** По телеви́зору игра́ет англи́йский
  c В како́й день профе́ссор чита́л ле́кцию?   пиани́ст?
                                                          f В како́м го́роде у́чится Бо́ря?

EXERCISE 9

Look at the table, showing
how long it takes by plane
(**на самолёте**) and by train
(**на по́езде**) and giving you
information about the zone
time (**поясно́е вре́мя**) for
the destination (**пункт-
назначе́ния**). Then do the
task on page 128.

Пункт назначения (от Москвы)	Время в пути		Поясное время
	на самолёте	на поезде	
ВЛАДИВОСТОК	9.55	170	+ 7 часов
ВОЛГОГРАД	1.35	18.15	+ 1 час
ВОЛОГДА	1.15	7.32	Московское время
ИРКУТСК	6.50	80.04	+ 5 часов
КАЗАНЬ	1.20	14.45	+ 2 часа
КРАСНОДАР	2.25	26.06	+ 1 час
ЛИПЕЦК	1.05	14.00	Московское время
НИЖНИЙ НОВГОРОД	1.10	6.55	+ 1 час
САНКТ-ПЕТЕРБУРГ	1.20	5.59	Московское время

A travel agent has a list of people returning from a conference in Moscow. Their means of transport (**вид тра́нспорта**) and departure time (**отправле́ние**) are listed. She uses the table on page 127 to work out when each participant will arrive home. She has done the first one, you do the rest.

Пассажи́р	вид тра́нспорта	отправле́ние	го́род	прибы́тие
Ле́вин	самолёт	семь часо́в	Волгогра́д	9.35
Алексе́ева	по́езд	во́семь часо́в	Во́логда	
Сега́ль	самолёт	де́вять часо́в	Ирку́тск	
Моро́зова	по́езд	де́сять часо́в	Ли́пецк	
Есе́нин	самолёт	оди́ннадцать часо́в	Владивосто́к	
Петро́ва	по́езд	двена́дцать часо́в	Санкт-Петербу́рг	

LANGUAGE REVIEW

Look at the words and phrases below. If you don't remember what they mean, look back at the unit given on the right.

понеде́льник, вто́рник, среда́; в понеде́льник, во вто́рник, в сре́ду	11
янва́рь, февра́ль, март; в январе́, в феврале́, в ма́рте	11
зимо́й, весно́й, ле́том, о́сенью; у́тром, днём, ве́чером, но́чью	11
пе́рвый, второ́й, тре́тий	11
1-е ма́рта, университе́т О́ксфорда	11
по́сле обе́да, до у́жина	11
два часа́, пять часо́в	11
За́втра я бу́ду рабо́тать.	11
он чита́л, она́ чита́ла, они́ чита́ли	12
был, была́, бы́ло, бы́ли	12
живу́, живёшь, живёт, живём, живёте, живу́т	12
учи́ться, роди́ться	12
иду́, идёшь, идёт; е́ду, е́дешь, е́дет	13
где, куда́	13
Я иду́ в центр/из це́нтра. Я иду́ на вокза́л/с вокза́ла.	13
се́вер, юг, восто́к, за́пад; на се́вере, на ю́ге, на восто́ке, на за́паде	13
прихо́д, ухо́д, вы́ход, вход; прие́зд, отъе́зд	13
мой, твой, наш, ваш, его́, её, их	14
закры́т, закры́та, закры́то, закры́ты; откры́т, откры́та, откры́то, откры́ты	14
хоте́л бы, хоте́ла бы, хоте́ли бы	14

KEY VOCABULARY

вуз	higher educational institution	преподава́тельница	teacher, lecturer (*f*)
		учи́тель	teacher (*m*)
институ́т	institute	учи́тельница	teacher (*f*)
ме́сяц	month	учени́к	pupil (*m*)
преподава́тель	teacher, lecturer (*m*)	учени́ца	pupil (*f*)
		шко́ла	school

16

Advertising

Opinions

Comparisons

More about shopping

Shopping in the Arbat

● Life in Russia

Advertising

Russia has changed from a country where there was once no advertising (**рекла́ма**) for consumer goods, to one which has adverts everywhere: on the street, in the metro, on radio, in newspapers and magazines. The state TV channels all show adverts and corporate programme sponsorship is commonplace.

It is interesting to compare prices (**це́ны**) with those in the UK. Some things, such as bread, will be cheaper (**деше́вле**). Other goods, such as imported alcohol or cars (**автомоби́ли**), will be more expensive (**доро́же**), due to high import duty. The price for expensive goods is often quoted in **y.e.** (see Unit 6), but you will pay in roubles.

Here are some typical advertisements. Don't expect to understand every word in them.

EXERCISE 1

Adverts **a** and **b** are offering a repair service.

1 What does **a** offer to repair?
2 When is the shop open?
3 What does **b** repair?
4 They offer concessions (**льго́ты**). What two other things do they offer to encourage you to use their services?

a

b

EXERCISE 2

Look at advertisement **c** and answer the following questions:

1 What does the company sell?
2 What is the company's name?

c

FANтастические каникулы

Международный языковой центр
English for All
приглашает тебя принять
участие в конкурсе

Расскажи нам о своих самых ярких,
самых зажигательных, веселых каникулах
и получи приз –

**Поездку в Великобританию
в языковую школу
«English by the Sea», г. Скарборо
на 3 НЕДЕЛИ!**

Ждем твоих писем по адресу:
129233 г. Москва, ул. Тверская, 22
e-mail: study@engall.ru
Подробности читай на сайте
www.engall.ru

EXERCISE 3

Look at the poster opposite. It contains a typical mixture of Russian and English words. This an advert for a competition in which you have to describe your most exciting holiday.

1   Who is sponsoring the competition?
2   Where exactly will you go if you win?
3   How long will you go for?

. . . .

EXERCISE 4

This is an advertisement for business electronic products. You will see that the advertisement has mixed English and Russian. It gives (**даёт**) a guarantee on all goods (**товáры**). It promises the lowest prices (**сáмые нúзкие цéны**) and big discounts (**скúдки**). Name as many items as you can which the company sells. You should be able to work out at least ten. If you wanted to fax them, which number would you use?

Writing Russian (v)

We have saved the most ornate letters till last:

Examples

Ж ж	is written	_Ж_
Ш ш	is written	_ш_
Щ щ	is written	_щ_
Ц ц	is written	_ц_

Now you try writing the words.

Этаж   _____

Этаж

Хорошо   _____

Хорошо

Цирк   _____

Цирк

Щи   _____

_Щи_

Женщина   _____

Женщина

Шашлык   _____

Шашлык

● Language information

Imperfective and perfective verbs

Russian verbs have two forms or *aspects: imperfective* and *perfective*.
Here are some examples of the way they are used:

Imperfective	**Action in progress** Я **сиде́л** до́ма и **чита́л** газе́ту. *I was sitting at home and reading the newspaper.*
Imperfective	**Action repeated** Ка́ждый день я **чита́л** газе́ту. *Every day I used to read a newspaper.*
Perfective	**Action complete on one occasion** Я **прочита́л** газе́ту и **пошёл** в го́род. *I read the newspaper and went to town.*

Russians make up these forms in a variety of ways. Sometimes they add a prefix at the beginning of the word:

чита́ть/**про**чита́ть *to read*   писа́ть/**на**писа́ть *to write*

Sometimes they change the ending:

расска́**зывать**/рассказа́**ть** *to tell* (*a story*)
отправ**ля́ть**ся/отпра́**виться** *to depart*

You will find both forms given in the vocabulary list at the end of the book.

Comparing things

You have seen a number of words which compare things.
Such comparative forms end in **-e** or **-ee**:

хоро́ший	*good*	лу́чше	*better*
плохо́й	*bad*	ху́же	*worse*
большо́й	*big*	бо́льше	*bigger, more*
ма́ленький	*small*	ме́ньше	*smaller, less*
дорого́й	*dear*	доро́же	*dearer*
дешёвый	*cheap*	деше́вле	*cheaper*
интере́сный	*interesting*	интере́снее	*more interesting*

Than is usually translated by the word **чем**:

Москва́ бо́льше, чем Санкт-Петербу́рг.   *Moscow is bigger than St Petersburg.*

EXERCISE 5

Это де́ло вку́са

It's a matter of taste

Here are some statements about various nationalities and places.

Match the first part on the left to the ending that best completes the sentence. The first one is done for you.

1	В Шотла́ндии	бо́льше лю́бят вино́, чем пи́во.
2	Во Фра́нции	бо́льше икры́, чем в Ита́лии.
3	Англича́не	ме́ньше лю́бят хлеб, чем рис.
4	В Кита́е	ме́ньше лю́бят чай с лимоном, чем с молоком. (milk)
5	Америка́нцы	бо́льше лю́бят ви́ски, чем во́дку.
6	В Росси́и	бо́льше лю́бят бейсбо́л, чем кри́кет.

EXERCISE 6

Each time, the second person in the dialogue below disagrees with the first. Supply the missing word and the nationality of the person making the statement. The first one is done for you.

1 – У вас в А́нглии библиоте́ки лу́чше, чем в Москве́?

   – Нет, <u>ху́же.</u> <u>(англича́нин)</u>

2 – Скажи́те, у вас в Нью-Йо́рке бо́льше автобусов, чем в Москве́?

   – Нет, _____ (_____)

3 – Скажи́те, у вас в Росси́и ме́ньше пьют, чем в Япо́нии?

   – Нет, _____ (_____)

4 – Как вы ду́маете, у вас в Шотла́ндии ме́ньше пьют ви́ски, чем в Аме́рике?

   – Нет, _____ (_____)

Prefer

You have come across the expressions **мне нра́вится** (*I like*) and **мне о́чень нра́вится** (*I very much like*). The phrase **мне бо́льше нра́вится** means *I like more*, or *I prefer*. The opposite of this would be **мне ме́ньше нра́вится** (*I like less*). **Мне бо́льше всего́ нра́вится** means *More than anything (else) I like.*

EXERCISE 7

In this exercise the second speaker always chooses something different from what is suggested by the first one. You have to fill in the blanks. The first one is done for you.

1 Муж: Вот в меню́ есть мя́со и ры́ба. Мне, пожа́луйста, мя́со.

   Жена́: А мне <u>бо́льше</u> <u>нра́вится</u> ры́ба.

2 Муж: Мо́жно пое́хать и́ли на авто́бусе и́ли на тролле́йбусе. Пое́дем на авто́бусе!

   Жена́: Нет, лу́чше _____ _____ _____.

3 Жена́: Фильм идёт в воскресе́нье и четве́рг. Пойдём в воскресе́нье.

   Муж: Нет, лу́чше _____ _____ _____.

4 Муж: Сего́дня интере́сная програ́мма по телеви́зору. Я не хочу́ идти́ в теа́тр.

   Жена́: А я _____ _____ в теа́тр.

5 Жена́: Что вам бо́льше нра́вится: о́пера или бале́т? Я хоте́л бы послу́шать о́перу.

   Муж: А мне _____ _____ бале́т.

Agreeing

If you want to agree with someone, you say **я согла́сен**, if you are a man, and **я согла́сна**, if you are a woman.
To ask them if they agree, you say **Вы согла́сны?**
When you have agreed, you might say **Мы согла́сны**.

Opinions

When you want to say what you think, you might use the expression **я ду́маю** (*I think*), or **мне ка́жется** (*it seems to me*), or **по-мо́ему** (*in my opinion*).

To ask someone what they think, you say:

Как вы ду́маете?   *What do you think?*
Как по-ва́шему?   *What is your opinion?*

● Looking at words

Giving yourself time to think

Russian, like English, is full of little words and phrases which do not have a great deal of meaning. They are used to fill in time, while you decide on the next thing to say.
Зна́ете (*you know*) is used like this in the dialogue between the Muscovite and the two women from Edinburgh in the listening section later in this unit. Other expressions Russians use are:

ну	*well*
вот	*here*
ла́дно	*OK*
мне ка́жется	*it seems to me*
что́ ли	*well*
так	*so*
по-мо́ему	*in my opinion*
зна́чит	*it means*

These translations are provided as a guide only. If you translate such phrases into English too literally, they will sound artificial. They are extremely useful for the foreign learner, as they may give you time to think of the correct ending!

Russian proverbs

Russians are very fond of using proverbs and sayings. Many of them make use of the comparative forms we discussed in the 'language information' section. Here are some common ones:

Лу́чше по́здно, чем никогда́
Better late than never

Ти́ше е́дешь – да́льше бу́дешь
More haste, less speed (literally *the quieter you go, the further you'll be*)

В гостя́х хорошо́, а до́ма лу́чше
There's no place like home (literally *it is good visiting, but it is better at home*)

Лу́чше сини́ца в руке́, чем жура́вль в не́бе
A bird in the hand is worth two in the bush (literally *it's better to have a blue tit in your hand than a crane in the sky*)

● Listening

Meeting Russians

Russians are very curious about the West, and will be very curious about you and how you live. They may ask very searching questions about the details of your life, some of which can sometimes appear rude, but are usually not intended to be so. Russians, like Ivan in the recording, can hold views which it is difficult to change.

In the following dialogue, recorded on your CD, two British women are visiting Moscow and staying in a flat with Russian friends. They are introduced to a very inquisitive Russian friend of the family. He tries to engage them in conversation, but gets put in his place!

Ива́н: Извини́те, отку́да вы?

А́нна: Из Великобрита́нии!

Ива́н: Вы отли́чно говори́те по-ру́сски.

А́нна: Спаси́бо.

Ива́н: Вы студе́нтки?

А́нна: Да.

Ива́н: Я тоже студе́нт. Прости́те, меня́ зову́т Ива́н Бори́сович. Фами́лия Бело́в.

А́нна: Я А́нна, а э́то Мэ́ри.

Ива́н: О́чень прия́тно. Вы из Ло́ндона?

Мэ́ри: Нет, из Эдинбу́рга.

Ива́н: Интере́сно. Ну, как дела́ у вас в А́нглии.

Мэ́ри: Мы не из А́нглии, а из Шотла́ндии.

Ива́н: Для нас э́то то же са́мое.

Мэ́ри: А я не согла́сна.

Ива́н: Скажи́те, у вас в А́нглии – то есть, в Шотла́ндии, же́нщины лю́бят ви́ски?

Мэ́ри: Нет, я ви́ски не люблю́.

Ива́н: Я ви́жу, у вас во́дка. Зна́ете, у нас же́нщины лю́бят вино́, шампа́нское, пи́во, кокте́йли, да́же, мо́жет быть, и конья́к, а во́дку – нет, никогда́.

А́нна: Э́то де́ло вку́са. Во́дка мне бо́льше нра́вится, чем ви́ски.

Ива́н: Нет, по-мо́ему, э́то не де́ло вку́са. Де́ло в том, что у нас же́нщины ме́ньше пьют, чем у вас.

А́нна: Мо́жет быть.

Ива́н: Коне́чно. А скажи́те, е́сли вы из Шотла́ндии, почему́ вы не в шотла́ндской ю́бке? Говоря́т, что там да́же мужчи́ны но́сят ю́бки. Э́то пра́вда?

Мэ́ри: Ну, что вы говори́те! Э́то не так!

В Шотла́ндии солда́ты но́сят ю́бки. И пото́м э́то национа́льный костю́м. Иногда́ по пра́здникам мужчи́ны но́сят ю́бки. Вот и всё!

Ива́н: А милиционе́ры?

Мэ́ри: Извини́те, но уже́ шесть часо́в. У нас биле́ты в теа́тр.

А́нна: Пье́са начина́ется в семь часо́в.

Ива́н: У вас нет ли́шнего биле́та?

А́нна: К сожале́нию, нет. До свида́ния.

Ива́н: До свида́ния. Всего́ до́брого. Вы бу́дете здесь за́втра ве́чером?

Мэ́ри: Я ду́маю, нет.

New vocabulary

Великобрита́ния	*Great Britain*
отку́да	*where from*
то же са́мое	*same*
то есть	*that is*
кокте́йль	*cocktail*
да́же	*even*
мо́жет быть	*perhaps*
никогда́	*never*
де́ло в том, что	*the fact is that*
коне́чно	*of course*
е́сли	*if*
ю́бка	*skirt*
солда́т	*soldier*
иногда́	*sometimes*
пра́здник	*holiday*
милиционе́р	*policeman*
уже́	*already*
начина́ться	*to begin*
к сожале́нию	*unfortunately*
всего́ до́брого	*all the best*

⊙ EXERCISE 8

Answer the following questions.

1 Where are the British women from?
2 What do Russian women like to drink?
3 Why does the Russian student think it's not just a matter of taste?
4 Why is the Russian student surprised at the way they are dressed?
5 What do they tell him about this?
6 Where are they going?

A situation to remember

It's cheaper in Moscow

Your friend wants to buy a television
(**купи́ть телеви́зор**).

Devise a conversation to convince him/her
that it is cheaper to buy it in Moscow than in
St Petersburg.

You tell him/her how much a television costs
in Moscow.

He/she admits it is dearer in St Petersburg.
However, he/she prefers the shops in St
Petersburg.

Don't forget that if you need time to think,
you can add one or more of the words or
phrases from the *Looking at words* section of
this unit.

You can invent similar conversations by
selecting a different item of technical
equipment from the 'Savar Electronics'
advertisement. You could think of other
reasons for shopping in St Petersburg: you
live there, they give a guarantee, you don't
like Moscow, it costs a lot of money to go
to Moscow (**до́рого сто́ит пое́хать в
Москву́**), etc.

WHAT YOU KNOW

Comparing things
Москва́ бо́льше, чем Санкт-Петербу́рг

Expressing preferences
мне бо́льше нра́вится теа́тр

Agreeing and disagreeing

я	(не)	согла́сен
		согла́сна
мы		согла́сны

Expressing your opinion
Я ду́маю, что в Москве́ деше́вле.
Мне ка́жется, что у нас доро́же.
По-мо́ему, в Петербу́рге лу́чше.

KEY VOCABULARY

бо́льше	bigger, more
деше́вле (дешёвый)	cheaper (cheap)
доро́же (дорого́й)	dearer (dear)
ду́мать	to think
ка́жется	it seems
к сожале́нию	unfortunately
лу́чше	better
ме́ньше	smaller, less
никогда́	never
по-мо́ему	in my opinion
по-ва́шему	in your opinion
согла́сен, согла́сна, согла́сны	agree
това́р	goods
то есть	that is
то же са́мое	the same (the same thing)
ху́же	worse
цена́	price
чем	than
ю́бка	skirt

17

Holidays and celebrations

Public and other holidays

Congratulations and greetings

More on travel

● Life in Russia

Public holidays

Russians enjoy a number of public holidays (**прáздники**), which can last more than one day. The current official holidays are:

1-ое и 2-ое января́	Нóвый год
7-ое января́	Рождествó (*Christmas*)
23-е января́	День защи́тника отéчества (*Armed Forces Day*, lit. *Day of the Defender of the Fatherland*)
8-ое мáрта	Междунарóдный (*international*) день жéнщин
1-ое/2-ое мáя	День весны́ и трудá (literally *Day of Spring and Labour*).
9-ое мáя	День побéды (*Victory Day*) celebrating the end of the Second World War in Europe.
12-ое ию́ня	День незави́симости Росси́и (*Russian Independence Day*). This commemorates the creation of the Russian Federation in 1991 after the collapse of the Soviet Union.
4-ое ноября́	Деньóнар дного еди́нства (*Day of National Unity*) Originally a holiday to celebrate the anniversary of the 1917 revolution on November 7th, recently moved to November 4th.

Russian holidays follow a similar pattern to ours in the West. They tend not to work on Sundays, have one break in the winter and another at Easter, with a longer spell in the summer, in August. If you want to check what the official holidays are in any particular year, they are always shown in red on a Russian calendar.

Be careful if you are going to Russia around these public holidays, as it can sometimes be difficult to get things done when places are closed. Two periods to avoid, if you are going on business, are the first weeks of January and May. Many Russians take advantage of two public holidays close together and do not return to work for the intervening period.

By far the most important religious feast is Easter (**Пасха**), which sometimes coincides with our Easter, but not always. Russian Christians at Easter greet one another with **Христо́с воскре́с** (*Christ is risen*). This is related to the word **воскресе́ние** (*Resurrection*). (See Unit 11.)

The Russian Orthodox church (**Правосла́вие**) still follows the Julian calendar. The Gregorian calendar was adopted in Britain in 1752 but was not introduced into Russia until 1918, after the communist revolution. Since 1900 the Julian calendar has been 13 days behind the Gregorian one. This is why the October revolution had its anniversary in November and why Orthodox Russians celebrate Christmas on January 7th.

Holidays

Russians will usually go away in August. They either go to their dacha, to Sochi, a seaside resort (**куро́рт**) on the Black Sea (**Чёрное мо́ре**), or to the Crimea (**Крым**), which is now part of Ukraine. Many Russians travel abroad (**за грани́цу**). Many travel agencies (**тураге́нтство**) arrange package tours (**путёвка**) to places such as Turkey (**Ту́рция**) or Cyprus (**Кипр**) as they are reasonably priced (**досту́пный**).

The Russian for *holiday*, if you are working, is **о́тпуск**; if you are a student, you have **кани́кулы**. On holiday your aim is to have **о́тдых** (*relaxation*) and **развлече́ние** (*entertainment*).

EXERCISE 1

Look at the advertisement to the right and answer the following questions:

1 What two countries can you go to for 20,689 roubles?
2 Where can you go for 10,709 roubles?
3 How much does it cost to go to Cyprus?
4 How much is a holiday in Tenerife?
5 What two towns in Austria are on offer?
6 What are the most expensive destinations on offer?
7 Which four countries have tours offered, but no price advertised?

EXERCISE 2

Look at the poster for the Atlas travel company and answer the following questions.

1 What kind of holiday does Atlas specialise in?
2 How many features of Atlas holidays can you name?
3 Name as many as you can of the ten destinations they have on offer.
4 What are the costs of an Atlas holiday like?
5 Complete the slogan:
'Travel (**Путешéствуйте**) with Atlas
_____,'

Greeting people

Here are some useful phrases for greeting Russians, many of which you have met earlier in the course:

Здрáвствуй! (ты)/Здрáвствуйте! (вы)	*Hello.*
Привéт!	*Hi.*
Как ты поживáешь?/Как вы поживáете?	*How are you?*
Как делá?	*How are things?*
Дóброе ýтро!	*Good morning.*
Дóбрый день!	*Good afternoon.*
Дóбрый вéчер!	*Good evening.*

Apart from these phrases, you will need to know the following construction:

Поздравля́ю Поздравля́ем	вас	с Но́вым го́дом! с Рождество́м! с Днём побе́ды.

These phrases mean literally *I (We) congratulate you with New Year/Christmas/Victory Day.* If you wish, you can simply say **Поздравля́ю вас с пра́здником!** (*Happy holiday!*)
You can often miss out the word **поздравля́ю** or **поздравля́ем** and say simply **С Но́вым го́дом!** etc.

You can also use this same formula for congratulating people on birthdays (**день рожде́ния**), weddings (**сва́дьба**) or name day (**имени́ны**), the religious feast day of the person's patron saint.

Here are some greetings cards. Russians use the word **откры́тки**, which also means *postcards*.

EXERCISE 3
Work out which holiday or event each card is celebrating.

The last card uses spelling that disappeared with the reform of the Russian alphabet in 1918, shortly after the foundation of the Soviet Union. If you see books printed pre-1918, you may notice hard signs (**ъ**) at the end of words and several unfamiliar letters. Nowadays, you'll sometimes see the hard sign used for effect, e.g. in the title of the financial newspaper **Коммерса́нтъ**, or restaurants trying to recreate the atmosphere of Tsarist Russia, e.g. **Пу́шкинъ**.

Wishing people well

Russians are often very eloquent when wishing people success, happiness, etc. Here are some sample phrases:

Желáю вам счáстья и успéхов.
I wish you happiness and success.
Желáю вам вы́здороветь.
I hope you recover. (literally I wish you to recover)
(Sometimes the phrase **желáю вам** can be omitted.)

Счастли́вого пути́!   *Have a good journey.*
Всегó хорóшего! or Всегó дóброго!   *All the best.*

. . . .

EXERCISE 4

Here are some phrases wishing people a variety of things.
When do you think they would be used?

1 Желáю вам сдать экзáмен.
2 Прия́тного аппети́та!
3 Поздравля́ем тебя́ с днём рождéния!
4 Успéхов вам!
5 Дóлгих (*long*) лет жи́зни!
6 Спокóйной нóчи!
7 Прия́тного сна! (sleep)

. . . .

EXERCISE 5

On the right is a handwritten card from a Russian friend. Read it and answer the questions.

1 What was the reason for writing the card?
2 What three things is she wishing her friend?

. . . .

Letter writing

Here are some more greetings, this time at the start and finish of a letter in Russian.

Intimate
Ми́лая Тáня!
Целýю и обнимáю!

Informal
Дорогóй Бóря!
С привéтом!

Formal
С уважéнием!
Уважáемый Ивáн Петрóвич!

С привéтом!   *Regards*
С уважéнием!   *With respect*
          (*Yours sincerely*)
Целýю и обнимáю!   *I kiss and embrace you.*

(Russians are much more demonstrative in the way they express affection! This is a standard expression, perhaps translatable by something like 'All my love'.)

Other phrases you will see in letters are:

Передáйте емý (горя́чий) привéт
Give him my (warmest) greetings
Бýдьте здорóвы
Keep well! (literally be well)
Всегó дóброго *All the best*

Поздравля́ем Вас с наступаю́щим
Нóвым 2006 гóдом!
Желáем Вам успéхов, здорóвья и
нóвых поéздок в Петербýрг.

Ирина

EXERCISE 6

Here is a letter with the expressions of greeting omitted. You have to fill them in. Pay attention to the dates when you fill in the first two items.

Notice also that the **ты** form is used, causing the woman to write **передай** instead of **передайте**.

New vocabulary

муж	*husband*
сказáть	*to say*
получить	*to receive*
встречáться	*to meet*
рáньше	*earlier, previously*

Дорогáя Сáша!

Я всегдá дýмаю о тебé в э́то врéмя гóда! Ты, как и я, родилáсь 2-го января́. С ¹_____ _____и с
²_____ _____! Как твой муж?
Передáй ему ³_____ _____.
Мúла мне сказáла, что твой сын сдал экзáмены в прóшлом годý. ⁴_____!
Он дéлает большúе успéхи! У меня есть хорóшие нóвости. Муж получúл рабóту в Москвé. Мы с тобóй чáсто бýдем встречáться, как и рáньше.
⁵_____ ýю и _____ áю
⁶_____ _____

Тáня

● Language information

Case forms used in greetings

The phrase **поздравляю вас** is followed by **с** and the instrumental case. We have seen the noun endings for the instrumental case in Unit 9. Adjectives end in **-ым** if the noun is masculine or neuter; they end in **-ой** if the noun is feminine:

Поздравля́ю вас (acc) с Нóвым годом! (instr) *Happy New Year!*
Сын поздрáвил родúтелей (acc) с серéбряной свáдьбой. (instr)
The son congratulated his parents on their silver wedding.

The greeting phrase after **желáю вам** is in the genitive case.
The genitive noun endings were given in Unit 11.

Adjectives ending in the genitive are:

Masculine and neuter	**-ОГО (-ЕГО)**	Всегó дóброго!	*All the best!*
Feminine	**-ОЙ (-ЕЙ)**	Спокóйной нóчи!	*Good night.*
Plural	**-ЫХ (-ИХ)**	большúх успéхов	*great success*

The endings **-ого** and **-его** are pronounced as if they were spelt -ово and -ево.

Verbs of going

In Unit 13 we saw the two verbs **идти** (*to go on foot*) and **éхать** (*to go by vehicle*). There are two further verbs: **ходúть** (*to go on foot*) and **éздить** (*to go by vehicle*). They are used either when you are walking or driving *round* (**по**) a place:

Я ходúл по магазúнам.   Я éздил по гóроду.
I walked around the shops   *I drove round town.*

or when you have made a round trip *there and back*:

Вчерá я ходúл в кинó.   В прóшлом годý я éздил в Россúю.
I went to the cinema yesterday.   *Last year I went to Russia.*

● Looking at words

Verbs ending in -овать

There are numerous verbs ending in **-овать**, borrowed from other European languages. The meaning should be obvious from English: for example, **организова́ть** (*to organise*), **фотографи́ровать** (*to photograph*).

. . . .

EXERCISE 7

Look at the following verbs and work out what they mean.

1 драматизи́ровать   4 плани́ровать
2 эмигри́ровать   5 регули́ровать
3 регистри́ровать   6 пакова́ть

Note that the present tense of a verb like **целова́ть** (*to kiss*) is **я целу́ю, ты целу́ешь, он/она́ целу́ет, мы целу́ем, вы целу́ете, они́ целу́ют**. Verbs ending in **-овать** normally form their present tense in this way.

. . . .

весь

Весь (**вся, всё**) means *all* and is an adjective. The feminine is **вся**, accusative **всю** and neuter **всё**:

весь день   *all day*
всю ночь   *all night*
всё утро   *all morning*

Всё also means *everything* and *all the time* (short for **всё вре́мя**):

Он зна́ет всё. *He knows everything.*
Он всё ду́мает о Та́не. *He thinks about Tanya all the time.*

The genitive form **всего́** is found in greetings: **всего́ до́брого/хоро́шего** *(all the best)*. **Все** is the plural, so you would say **все ру́сские** *(all Russians)*. It also means *everybody*, as in **все зна́ют э́то** *(everyone knows that)*. Two useful related words are **всегда́** *(always)* and **совсе́м** *(completely)*.

● Listening

Travelling round Europe

. . . .

⊛ EXERCISE 8

Listen to the passage recorded on your CD. Two Russians have returned to work after the summer holiday. Answer the questions which follow.

Ири́на: Здра́вствуйте, Ива́н Никола́евич! Ну, как дела́?

Ива́н: Ири́на Матве́евна, здра́вствуйте! Как вы пожива́ете?

Ири́на: Спаси́бо, хорошо́, а вы?

Ива́н: То́же хорошо́. А скажи́те, куда́ вы е́здили ле́том?

Ири́на: Ива́н Никола́евич, как вам сказа́ть. По всей Евро́пе е́здили!

Ива́н: Интере́сно. А вы бы́ли в Пари́же?

Ири́на: Коне́чно. Там о́чень краси́во. Дома́ элега́нтные.

Ива́н: Как мы там вку́сно обе́дали! Скажи́те, вы на маши́не бы́ли?

Ири́на: Коне́чно, на маши́не. Пото́м из Фра́нции мы пое́хали в Ита́лию.

Ива́н: Ваш муж говори́т по-италья́нски, не пра́вда ли?

Ири́на: Нет. Фами́лия на́ша италья́нская, но не говори́м.

Ива́н: В Ита́лии, мне ка́жется, доро́же жить?

Ири́на: Нет, до́рого, но в Пари́же то́же до́рого. В Ита́лии бензи́н о́чень до́рого сто́ит.

1 Where did Irina go in the summer?
2 How did she travel?
3 What did she think of Paris?
4 Why does Ivan Nikolayevich think Irina's husband can speak Italian?
5 What did she say about Italy?

. . . .

● Reading

. . . .

EXERCISE 9

Here is an article adapted from a Russian newspaper. Try to answer the questions that follow it. It contains a number of words and constructions that you may not have met. Do not expect to understand all of the article.

Some key words are given at the end. Look at these and make your best guess at the information in the passage.

Старты и финиши

Москвич Сергей Долматов, набрав 10,5 очка, вышел победителем юношеского первенства мира по шахматам, завершившегося в австрийском городе Граце. На втором месте — теперь уже экс-чемпион мира его земляк Артур Юсупов, отставший от Долматова на 0,5 очка. Третье место занял датчанин Енс Фриз-Нильсен.

Победой русских спортсменов закончилась 16-я велогонка «Тур де Л'авенир» по дорогам Франции. Победителем состязаний (1590 км) стал Сергей Сухорученков из Самары — 42 часа 26 мин. 28 сек. Следующие три места заняли также наши спортсмены — Рамазан Галялетдинов из Самары, москвич Сергей Морозов и победитель велогонки Мира-95 Александр Аверин из Самары.

New vocabulary

очкó	*point*
ю́ный	*young*
велосипéд	*bicycle*
гóнки	*race*

1 What did Dolmatov win?
2 Where did it take place?
3 What can you learn about Yusupov?
4 What was the surname of the man who came third?
5 Where did the bicycle race take place?
6 Who won the bicycle race and what was his time?
7 Who were the runners-up and which towns did they come from?

A situation to remember

Passing on greetings and presents
You have arrived in Russia on 9th May, a public holiday. Your Russian friends **Бóря**, **Натáлья** and **Ви́ктор**, who are living in England, have asked you to pass on their best wishes to their friend **Вáня** and his family. They have also given you a large present to pass on (**передáть**). You phone **Вáня**. His wife **Óля** answers. Relay the phone conversation.

144

● Playing with words

Кроссво́рд

Across

1 C____ _____ ! First greeting of the year
10 What Russians sometimes say for in
11 She
12 Constrictor or neck-wear
13 **Евге́ний Оне́гин**, for example
15 Along the street _____ у́лице
17 **Апре́ль_____ию́нь**
18 **Не пра́вда_____?**
19 Nets or networks: after 8, 9, 10 and 19 down you will untangle this one!
20 Sometimes about
21 Sometimes with **зоо-**, but usually not.
22 **Он купи́л пода́рок_____10 до́лларов.**
23 Russian Helen
25 **C_____ _____!**
30 **Покажи́те мне го́род на ка _____!**
32 **Я о́чень люблю́ на́ши русск _____ блю́да!**
33 **Е́сли у вас нет де́нег, вы́пишите, пожа́луйста _____**
34 Fashion
35 Sometimes used for and
36 Moscow sports club
38 I told them = **Я _____ сказа́л**
39 Outside
40 An alternative to **электри́чество**
41 King Arthur had a round one
42 **Он мне пи́шет о _____** (short for 23)
43 A new place in the New World, and historic city
45 German name. Nothing to do with Turkey
48 Aspect or view
50 Three-horse sled
51 He
52 A Russian in Unit 16 thought Scots wore this
53 **В аэропорту́ мо́жно ви́деть _____**

Down

1 More emphatic than a
2 Clear soup – **буль _____**
3 _____ **нра́вится смотре́ть футбо́л?**
4 **Воло́дя _____** (my) **брат**
5 Gala
6 The place where you register
7 **От семи́ ___ восьми́ бюро́ закры́то**
8 **Пуччи́ни** might have written this
9 Not an obvious way of travelling
10 **В столи́це Ита́лии**
12 Cinderella went to one of these
14 An avenue or path in a park. Looks like an alley but isn't
15 Congratulations!
16 About Mr Chekhov
19 Shops may give this to encourage you to buy
21 **Целу́ю и обнима́ю! _____ приве́т ма́ме и па́пе**
24 **Споко́йной _____ !**
26 They are very kind = **Они́ о́чень _____**
27 **Они́ не брат и сестра́, а муж и _____**
28 Sheet music = __ты
29 Novel by Dostoevsky
31 Pupil but not of the eye
37 Somewhere Russians go to rest – **кур __ р __ .**
40 Hill or mountain
41 Juice
44 Strong spirit
46 **тот, ___ , то** = that
47 They are here!
49 What a Russian bride and groom will say
51 ___ **Москвы́ до Ло́ндона бо́льше чем 2000 киломе́тров**

WHAT YOU KNOW

Greetings

до́брое у́тро	до́брый день	до́брый ве́чер
Поздравля́ю вас	с Рождество́м с Но́вым го́дом	с днём рожде́ния
Жела́ю вам	споко́йной но́чи	всего́ хоро́шего/до́брого
С приве́том	С уваже́нием	

Verbs of going

Я ходи́л по магази́нам.
Вчера́ я ходи́л в кино́.
В про́шлом году́ я е́здил в Росси́ю.

KEY VOCABULARY

весь, вся, всё, все	all
встреча́ться	to meet
день рожде́ния	birthday
е́здить	to go (by vehicle)
жела́ть	to wish
ми́лый -ая -ое	dear
муж	husband
переда́ть	to pass on
пра́здник	holiday
про́шлый: в про́шлом году́	last, last year
ра́ньше	earlier, previously
Рождество́	Christmas
сказа́ть	to say
уважа́емый	respected, dear (letters)
уваже́ние	respect
ходи́ть	to go (on foot)
ча́сто	often

Expressing feelings

The Russian soul
«Ру́сская душа́»

Getting medical help

Parts of the body

● Life in Russia

The Russian Soul – «Ру́сская душа́»

It often seems to Western observers that the behaviour and emotions of Russians can be extreme. Extremes of sadness and depression, extremes of excitement and joy, extremes of tenderness and violence are all reflected in the works of Russian authors. Some put this down to the climate, others to the geography of the country and others to the Russian 'soul' – **ру́сская душа́**. No doubt all of these play a part. The atmosphere and air of futility in plays by Chekhov (**Че́хов**), the introspection and suffering in Dostoyevsky (**Достое́вский**), the physical involvement of Tolstoy (**Толсто́й**), the 'laughter through tears' in Gogol (**Го́голь**), all give the work of these writers a peculiarly 'Russian' flavour. The use of folk songs by composers, particularly Glinka (**Гли́нка**) and Tchaikovsky (**Чайко́вский**), also reflects Russian life, and it is this reflection of reality which has been the constant feature of Russian creative art since the beginning of the 19th century.

It is perhaps the Russians' love of realism that made Dickens and Graham Greene two of their most popular English authors, and Steinbeck and Hemingway are also widely read. On a lighter note, Russians have long been devotees of Agatha Christie.

147

Russian medical services

Doctors are very poorly paid and medicines are often in short supply. It can sometimes help to gain access to a doctor if you are willing to provide an appropriate 'gift'. Doctors will prescribe medication, which you can get from a chemist's (**аптека**). Russians have to pay for their medicines and the cost can be high, especially for imported medicines. Pensioners and people classed as invalids can get free or subsidised prescriptions, when they are available.

In the big cities, there is also a range of private clinics, catering for the foreign business community as well as wealthy Russians. They are often staffed by foreign doctors and they will all speak English. It is essential to have good medical insurance (**страховка**) if you travel to Russia. You will then be able to use the facilities of the private clinics and have your bill sent straight to your insurance company.

If you are in a place where there are no private clinics, you will have to go to the nearest local health centre (**поликлиника**). They may refer you to a hospital (**больница**).

If you are ill, you will need to be able to answer some important questions:

Как вы себя чувствуете?
How are you? (literally *How do you feel yourself?*)
Я чувствую себя плохо.
I feel ill. (literally *bad*)
You only use this phrase when inquiring about a person's health. The normal greetings are: **Как дела?** or **Как вы поживаете?**

Что у вас болит?   *What is hurting you?*
У меня болит голова. *I have a headache.*
У меня болит живот. *I have a pain in my stomach.*

If more than one part of the body hurts, use the form **болят**:

У меня болят голова и живот.
I have a headache and a pain in my stomach.

Note that the Russian construction means literally *belonging to me hurts the head/stomach*. English has a variety of ways of indicating the pain.

EXERCISE 1
Here are some complaints from a patient. Can you work out how an English speaker would express the complaint? Note that Russian has only one way of expressing this idea, English has several.

1   У меня болит горло. *throat*
2   У меня болит рука. *arm*
3   У меня болит нос. *nose*
4   У меня болит нога. *leg*
5   У меня болит зуб. *tooth*

If your teeth are causing problems, you should go to a **зубной врач** (*dentist*).

You may also be concerned as to whether your temperature (**температура**) is high (**высокая**). You may want to tell the doctor how warm you feel:

Мне холодно. *I feel cold.*
Мне тепло.   *I feel warm.*
Мне жарко.   *I feel hot.*

You may fall ill (**заболеть**) with the flu (**грипп**) or simply a cold (**простуда**). You may get a prescription (**рецепт**) for some medicine (**лекарство**) or tablets (**таблетки**).

The word for doctor is **врач**; **доктор** is only used when addressing a doctor. In the following dialogue the **медпункт** (medical unit) tells the tourist that a **врач** will come. When he comes, the patient calls him **доктор**.

. . . .

💿 **EXERCISE 2**

Listen to the dialogue on your tape. It is about someone who falls ill in a hotel in Moscow. The hotel has its own **медпункт**, and the lady at the service desk (**бюро обслуживания**) is very helpful, as are the floor supervisor (**дежурная**) and the doctor (**врач**).

Answer the questions which follow.

Турист набирает номер

Пауза

– Бюро обслуживания.
– Скажите, пожалуйста, что мне делать? Мне кажется, я заболел.
– Даю вам медпункт.

Пауза

– Медпункт.
– Я говорю из номера 345. Мне кажется, у меня высокая температура. И очень болит горло.
– Так. Понятно. Что ещё?
– Голова тоже болит, но не очень.
– Так. Врач будет у вас через полчаса. Я думаю, что это простуда. Закажите через дежурную чай с лимоном. Это иногда очень помогает.
– Спасибо.

Через пять минут. Дежурная приходит.

– Здравствуйте. Вот вам чай с лимоном.
– Спасибо.
– Заболели, да? Врач сейчас будет. Пейте чай. Если хотите что-нибудь ещё, позвоните.
– Спасибо большое.

Врач приходит.

– Можно?
– Пожалуйста, входите.

Врач входит в комнату

– Здравствуйте. Я уже знаю, что у вас болит горло.
– И голова.
– А как аппетит?
– Аппетита совсем нет.

– Покажите, пожалуйста горло. Скажите «А-а-а»
– А-а-а.
– Гм. Посмотрим, какая у вас температура. Вот термометр.

Пауза

– Да, у вас есть температура, но не очень высокая.
– Это грипп, доктор?
– Нет, простуда. Я вам выпишу рецепт. Принимайте эти таблетки три раза в день. Вы должны лежать, отдыхать. Завтра я буду у вас. Если вам будет хуже, позвоните опять в медпункт.

New vocabulary

понятно	*understood*
через полчаса	*in half an hour*
закажите	*order*
через	*through*
помогать	*to help*
пейте	*drink*
что-нибудь	*anything*
позвонить	*to ring*
отдыхать	*to relax*
опять	*again*
высокий	*high*

1 Who does the tourist ring first?
2 To whom is he referred?
3 What are his symptoms?
4 What does he do before the doctor comes?
5 What does the doctor do?
6 Does the tourist have a high temperature?
7 What is the treatment?

. . . .

⊙ EXERCISE 3

Ива́н Петро́вич wants to see a doctor and has been recommended to **Ната́лья Петро́вна Воло́дина**. He rings up health centre Nº 23 to make an appointment, only to find she no longer works there. He is given the number of where they think she works. It takes quite a few phone calls to find her. Russian health centres are usually referred to by number and not name.

Listen to the CD and then fill in the table. The first one is done for you.

	поликли́ника №	телефо́н
1	22	298 66 38
2		
3		
4		
5		

Which health centre does Dr Volodina work in?

They also use the same form to express a variety of feelings:

Нам ску́чно.	*We are bored.*
Ему́ хорошо́.	*He feels fine.*
Мне пло́хо.	*I feel ill.*
Ей сты́дно.	*She is ashamed.*

EXERCISE 4

Put the numbers in the appropriate boxes. The first one is done for you.

1	I'm hot	Мне хо́лодно	2
2	I'm cold	Мне жа́рко	
3	I'm ashamed	Мне хорошо́	
4	I feel worse	Мне лу́чше	
5	I'm ill	Мне пло́хо	
6	I'm bored	Мне тепло́	
7	I feel good	Мне ску́чно	
8	I feel warm	Мне сты́дно	
9	I feel better	Мне ху́же	

● Language information

Expressing temperature and feelings

As we have seen earlier, when Russians say how hot or cold they are, they use the forms **Мне хо́лодно** (*I'm cold*), **Мне тепло́** (*I'm warm*), **Мне жа́рко** (*I'm hot*). They are saying literally *it is cold to me*. The phrase *to me* is translated by a dative case. These phrases are most commonly used with pronouns:

я	I	dative	мне	мы	we	dative	нам
ты	you	dative	тебе́	вы	you	dative	вам
он	he	dative	ему́	они́	they	dative	им
она́	she	dative	ей				

150

EXERCISE 5

On the left you have some English sentences. Show how you would translate them into Russian by linking the words and phrases.

The first one is done for you.

1	He feels good.	Мне	плóхо
2	You (fam.) feel hot.	Им	теплó
3	You feel warm.	Емý	жáрко
4	We feel ill.	Тебé	хýже
5	I feel cold.	Вам	скýчно
6	You are bored.	Нам	стыдно
7	She feels better.	Емý	хорошó
8	He feels worse.	Вам	хóлодно
9	They are ashamed.	Ей	лýчше

Notice that you can change these expressions into questions simply by adding a question mark. In speech you make your voice go up on the word you are questioning. Look at the line above the phrase: it indicates where to raise your voice.

Вам плóхо?

Russians often ask negative questions. The meaning is the same, it just sounds less aggressive.

Вам не плóхо?

To refresh your memory on how to ask questions, listen to Track 26 on your CD.

EXERCISE 6

Here are three pictures and three captions. Which caption goes with which picture?

1 Вам не жáрко?
2 Мне скýчно.
3 Ей хóлодно.

Instructing, requesting, advising

Russian has a special form of the verb called the imperative which is used when giving people instructions, making requests and giving advice. The informal (**ты**) form ends in **-и** (or **-й** after a vowel); the formal (**вы**) form, which is also used when addressing more than one person, ends in **-ите** (or **-йте** after a vowel). It is formed from the present tense root. You have already seen some of these forms:

покажи	покажите	*show*
извини	извините	*excuse me*
прости	простите	*excuse me*
скажи	скажите	*tell me*
дай	дайте	*give*

The words **здрáвствуй** and **здрáвствуйте** (*hello*) originally were advice to 'be healthy'.

You may have noticed some of these forms in the dialogue in Exercise 2: the tourist is told to order (**закажите**) and a little later to drink (**пéйте**) the tea. The tourist tells the doctor to come in (**входите**), who in turn tells the tourist to take (**принимáйте**) the tablets twice in the conversation. He is twice encouraged to ring (**позвоните**) if there is a problem. You will also see examples of **скажите** and **покажите**.

a   b   c

If you wish to encourage a group of people to do something, you may use a form ending in **-ем**, **-ём** or **-им**. This is the same as the **мы** form of the future tense. In the dialogue the doctor says **посмо́трим** (*let's have a look*). In Unit 4 we saw the form **пойдём** (*let's go*).

You will also hear the forms **Пошли́!** and **Пое́хали!** when you are giving instructions to a group of people or to a bus driver to start moving. This is a colloquial idiom, which means literally *We have gone!* or *We have set off!*

EXERCISE 7

Pick out a suitable imperative from those listed on the right and put its letter in the correct space. The first one is done for you.

1	Рестора́н о́чень популя́рный. _*d*_ стол.	**a** позвони́те
2	Е́сли за́втра тебе́ бу́дет ху́же, _____ в медпу́нкт.	**b** покажи́те
		c пойдём
3	_____ чай с лимо́ном. О́чень помога́ет.	**d** закажи́те
4	Я не люблю́ теа́тры. Лу́чше _____ в кино́.	**e** пе́йте
		f посмо́трим
5	Сего́дня о́чень интере́сный фильм. _____ телеви́зор.	**g** позвони́
6	_____ 23543 67. Там живу́т Ива́н и Та́ня.	**h** извини́те
7	_____ , пожа́луйста, вы не зна́ете где здесь рестора́н?	**i** откро́й
		j закро́йте
8	Мне хо́лодно. _____ , пожа́луйста, дверь. (door)	
9	Е́сли тебе́ жа́рко, _____ дверь.	
10	Не хочу́ э́ту кни́гу. _____ , пожа́луйста, вот э́ту.	

Should

Another way of giving advice is not to use the imperative form, but simply to tell someone what they ought to do. The doctor in the dialogue says **вы должны́ лежа́ть**, **отдыха́ть** (*you should lie down, relax*). **До́лжен** is an adjective, i.e. it changes according to the person it describes. Thus **должна́** is what you would use for a woman, and **должны́** for a plural.

EXERCISE 8

See if you can direct the people via the right boxes. The first one is done for you.

1	Та́ня
2	Ива́н
3	То́ля и И́ра
4	Ни́на Никола́евна
5	Студе́нт
6	Учени́ца
7	Ва́ня
8	Англича́нин
9	Мы
10	Она́
11	Он
12	Вы

до́лжен

должна́

должны́

чита́ть э́ту кни́гу.

● Looking at words

The root 'бол-'

We have already seen three words with this root:

боли́т *to hurt* (part of the verb **боле́ть**)
заболе́ть *to fall ill*: literally *to begin* (**за-**) *to be ill*
больни́ца *hospital*

Боле́знь means *an illness* and **он бо́лен, она́ больна́, вы больны́** are ways of saying that *he is ill, she is ill, you are ill.* **Больно́й** is a male patient and **больна́я** a female patient.

Parts of the body

голова́ *head*

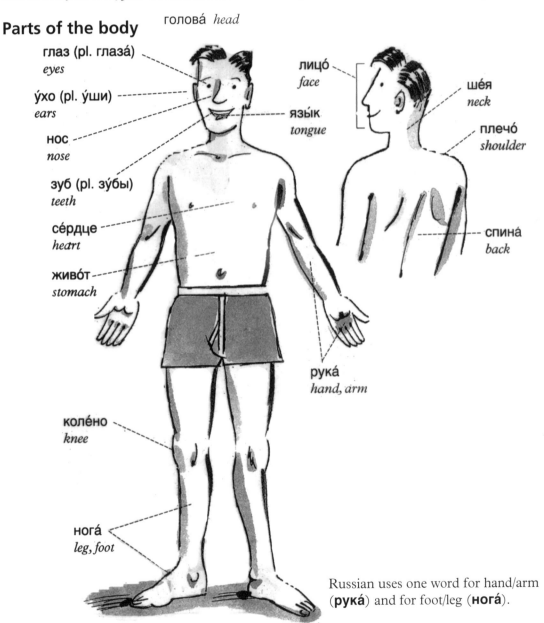

глаз (pl. глаза́) *eyes*

у́хо (pl. у́ши) *ears*

нос *nose*

зуб (pl. зу́бы) *teeth*

се́рдце *heart*

живо́т *stomach*

лицо́ *face*

язы́к *tongue*

ше́я *neck*

плечо́ *shoulder*

спина́ *back*

рука́ *hand, arm*

коле́но *knee*

нога́ *leg, foot*

Russian uses one word for hand/arm (**рука́**) and for foot/leg (**нога́**).

153

A situation to remember

Ringing a doctor

Devise a telephone conversation as follows:

Your friend is ill and you have to ring the health centre to try and get a doctor.

You are not sure what is wrong with her, but you think it might be something to do with her stomach. She has a pain in her stomach and one in her arm, as well as a headache.

At the moment she is lying down in her room in the hotel.

The person you speak to asks if she has had dinner.

You answer that she hasn't. She has had tea with lemon, but nothing else (**больше ничего**).

Complaining

You have an ache or pain. If you are working with another student, take it in turns to say what is wrong with you. Indicate the part of the body that hurts and say **У меня́ боли́т _____** .

Your friend may be able to suggest a solution: ringing the doctor, lying down, resting, taking tablets, etc.

WHAT YOU KNOW

Expressing how you feel

Мне	хо́лодно.
Вам, тебе́	тепло́.
Нам	жа́рко.
Ему́	ску́чно.

Как вы себя́ чу́вствуете?	Хорошо́.
	Пло́хо.

Something hurts

Что у вас боли́т?	У меня́ боли́т	зуб.
		го́рло.
		нога́.

Instructing, requesting, advising

Позвони́те за́втра.
Откро́йте рот.
Посмо́трим.

Should

он	я	ты	до́лжен	
она́	я	ты	должна́	лежа́ть, отдыха́ть
они́	мы	вы	должны́	

KEY VOCABULARY

боле́ть (боли́т)	to hurt
заболе́ть (perfective)	to fall ill
больни́ца	hospital
врач	doctor
высо́кий(-ая,-ое,-ие)	high; tall
дава́ть (даю́)	give (I give)
дежу́рная	woman on duty (floor supervisor)
душа́	soul
набира́ть но́мер	to dial the number
пе́йте (from пить)	drink!
позвони́ть	to ring
поликли́ника	health centre
помога́ть	to help
посмо́трим	Let's have a look!
пошли́, пое́хали	Let's go!
принима́ть	to take
ску́чно	bored
сты́дно	ashamed
че́рез полчаса́	in half an hour
чу́вствовать себя́	to feel

Russian flats

Finding your way
to a Russian home

Addressing a letter
to Russia

Visiting a Russian home

● Life in Russia

Russian flats

Most Russians live in small flats (**кварти́ры**) in large apartment blocks. Typical blocks of flats have five or nine storeys (**пятиэта́жный** or **девятиэта́жный дом**) and are often in new districts (**райо́ны**) that have been developed since the second world war. These **райо́ны** are full of tall blocks of flats that stretch as far as the eye can see.

They were built in response to a chronic housing shortage, for vast numbers of Russians who were living in overcrowded flats in city centres. This development was funded by the state and, under the old regime, most Russians lived in **госуда́рственные кварти́ры** (*state flats*). Some were built by co-operatives (**кооперати́вы**). Central heating (**центра́льное отопле́ние**) was provided by a boiler, which supplied heating not just for a single apartment block but for a whole district. Rents were extremely low, as were charges for electricity, gas and telephones (**электри́чество, газ, телефо́н**). Prices are now rising for all services, and local telephone calls, which used to be free, are now being charged for in many big cities.

Russian flats typically have a **гости́ная** (*living room*), **спа́льня** (*bedroom* – they may have one or two), **ку́хня** (*kitchen*), **ва́нная** (*bathroom*) and **туале́т** (*toilet*). The **гости́ная** will often double

155

as a bedroom: the **дива́н** (*sofa*) that you sit on may open out into someone's bed. They usually have double entrance doors and many Russians are installing steel doors for extra security. Flats are categorised by the number of rooms (excluding kitchen and bathroom) that they have. Russians will talk of **одноко́мнатная**, **двухко́мнатная**, **трёхко́мнатная кварти́ра** (*one, two, three room flat*).

Russians who can afford it now have the opportunity to buy their own flats from the state, which they can then sell on the open market. Flats in big cities, such as Moscow and St Petersburg, can fetch high prices.

In Moscow many rich Russians are now buying their own homes, which they call **котте́джи**. There are new estates being built on the edge of Moscow for the well-off, and older buildings near to the centre are being gutted and rebuilt to luxury European standards. Moscow has become a very expensive place to live if you don't qualify for a state flat.

On the right are some adverts from a local Moscow paper. People are looking to buy and sell property, as well as let, rent and exchange flats etc. Essential words to know are:

покупа́ть/купи́ть	*to buy*	Куплю́	*I will buy*
продава́ть/прода́ть	*to sell*	Продаю́	*I am selling*
снима́ть/снять	*to rent, hire*	Снима́ем	*We are renting*
		Сни́мем	*We will rent*
сдава́ть/сдать	*to rent out*		
меня́ть на	*to exchange for*	Меня́ю	*I exchange*
с допла́той	*with extra payment*		

EXERCISE 1

Read the advertisements and give the phone number or numbers to ring if you want to do the following:

1 buy a flat near a metro station.
2 rent out your flat in the centre of Moscow.
3 rent an office.
4 exchange a room for a flat, with extra payment.
5 exchange a one room flat for a larger one, with extra payment.
6 buy a room.
7 buy a plot of land in the country to grow your own vegetables.

Russian addresses

Here are some typical Russian addresses:

Садо́вая у́лица, д. 25, корп. 2, кв.137
Не́вский проспе́кт, д. 236, кв. 343
Можа́йское шоссе́, д. 367, корп. 1, кв. 423
Боя́рский переу́лок, д. 53, кв. 98

Abbreviations: **д. (дом)**, **корп. (ко́рпус)**, **кв. (кварти́ра)**.

Дом gives you the number of the building, or complex of buildings. Each building can be quite large and you may have to walk further than you think to find your **дом**. If **дом** refers to more than one apartment block, you will be given the block (**ко́рпус**) number. Finally, you will need the flat number. Sometimes addresses are written in an abbreviated form. The first address on our list could be written **Садо́вая у́лица, 25 - 2 - 137**.

Проспе́кт is a main street in a town. **У́лица** is an ordinary street. **Переу́лок** is a side street. **Шоссе́** is a main road leading out of town. The name of the **шоссе́** shows you the direction: in our example it leads to the small town of **Можа́йск**, on the Moscow River, near to the site of the Battle of Borodino, where Napoleon defeated the Russian armies in 1812.

You will need to know on which floor (**эта́ж**) someone lives. The question to ask is:

На како́м этаже́ вы живёте?
What floor do you live on?

Be careful: Russians start counting floors from the ground, which they call the 'first'. The Russian **второ́й эта́ж** is our first floor, etc. The answers you can expect are:

на пе́рвом этаже́	*on the ground floor*
на второ́м этаже́	*on the first floor*
на тре́тьем этаже́	*on the second floor*
на четвёртом этаже́	*on the third floor*

The entrance to Russian flats is not normally directly from the street. You usually have to find the entrance into a **двор** and from there find the appropriate **подъе́зд** (*entrance*). To go into many of these **подъе́зды** you have to tap in a code (**код**) to release the door lock.

Addressing an envelope

Russians write the address (**а́дрес**) in the reverse order, compared with English. You start with the country (**страна́**), if outside Russia, then the town (**го́род**). This is followed by the street. Finally you write the person.

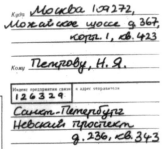

Most Russian envelopes are pre-printed with sections labelled **Куда́** (*where to*), **Кому́** (*who to*), and a section on the right to insert the **и́ндекс** (*post code*). There is a space under the address for the **и́ндекс и а́дрес отправи́теля** (*sender*). There is often a drawing as decoration. In the sample on page 157, it shows Russians' love of mushrooms. There are even dotted lines drawn to help you write the six figures of a Russian **и́ндекс** in the correct way with detailed instructions on the reverse of the envelope.

Внимание!
Образец написания цифр индекса:

0123456789

· ·

EXERCISE 2
No doubt, when you return home, you will want to write a letter to your host family. Here is another Russian envelope, this time with a picture of a church. Address it to the family you were staying with. Use one of the addresses given on page 157.

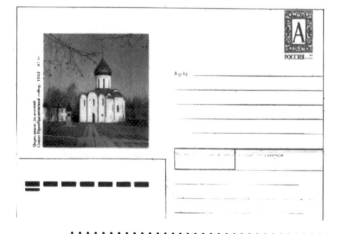

· ·

● Language information

Future tense
You have already seen one way of talking about the future:

Я бу́ду жить в Москве́.
I will live in Moscow.

This is the *imperfective* future: you are saying that you *will be living* in Moscow. Very often you need to talk about doing something that will be complete in the future. You do this by taking the perfective verb and using forms that look like the present tense. Compare the following two sentences:

Imperfective, present
Сейча́с мы **е́дем** в Москву́.
We are now going to Moscow.

Perfective future
За́втра мы **пое́дем** в Москву́.
Tomorrow we will go to Moscow.

You saw some examples of the future tense in the advertisements in Exercise 1:

Куплю́ *I will buy*
Сни́мем *We will rent*

Approximate time
Приду́ часо́в в пять.
I will come at about five o'clock.
На́до идти́ мину́т де́сять.
You have to walk for about ten minutes.

If Russians want to say that you are coming at *about* five o'clock or that something will take *about* ten minutes, they simply put the number after the noun.

⚙EXERCISE 3

Sarah is visiting St Petersburg for the first time. She has been invited to go and see a Russian friend, **Воло́дя**, whom she has known for a number of years. This is how she makes the arrangements to go and visit him. Listen to the phone conversation and answer the questions that follow.

Са́ра: (набира́ет но́мер) Девятьсо́т два́дцать семь во́семьдесят четы́ре ноль три. До́брое у́тро!

Воло́дя: Алло́!

Са́ра: Алло́! Воло́дя? Это Са́ра.

Воло́дя: А Са́ра! Ты прие́дешь к нам сего́дня ве́чером, да? Ната́ша пригото́вит нам вку́сный украи́нский борщ. Мы вы́пьем рю́мку во́дки и поговори́м. Ты здесь надо́лго? Мо́жет быть пое́дем вме́сте в Но́вгород? Я куплю́ биле́ты в теа́тр. Ты лю́бишь бале́т?

Са́ра: Так, сего́дня ве́чером я к тебе́ пое́ду. Мы всё реши́м тогда́. В кото́ром часу́ мне прие́хать?

Воло́дя: Часо́в в семь. Ты зна́ешь наш а́дрес?

Са́ра: Зна́ю. Балка́нская у́лица, дом пятьдеся́т два, кварти́ра но́мер де́вять. А как туда́ дое́хать? Это далеко́ от це́нтра?

New vocabulary

к + dative	to (see)
гото́вить/пригото́вить	to cook
рю́мка	glass (small)
говори́ть/поговори́ть	to have a talk
надо́лго	for a long time
реша́ть/реши́ть	to decide
тогда́	then, at that time
В кото́ром часу́	At what time

1 What is Volodya's phone number?
2 What are they going to eat?
3 Who will do the cooking?
4 What are they going to drink?
5 What suggestions has Volodya got to entertain Sarah?
6 At about what time is she expected?

⚙EXERCISE 4

Listen to a bit more of the conversation between Sarah and **Воло́дя** and answer the questions which follow.

Воло́дя: К сожале́нию, мы живём далеко́ от це́нтра, в но́вом райо́не. А где ты живёшь?

Са́ра: В гости́нице «На Садо́вой». Мой телефо́н три́ста девятна́дцать девяно́сто шесть девяно́сто оди́н.

Воло́дя: Это где? На Садо́вой у́лице?

Са́ра: Да, да. Очень удо́бно. Ме́тров пятьсо́т от метро́.

Воло́дя: Зна́ю. Лу́чше е́хать на метро́. Там две ста́нции: Садо́вая и Сенна́я пло́щадь. Тебе́ нужна́ ста́нция Сенна́я пло́щадь. На́до е́хать до коне́чной ста́нции Ку́пчино.

Са́ра: Без переса́дки?

Воло́дя: Без переса́дки. Это мину́т два́дцать, два́дцать пять.

Са́ра: От метро́ мо́жно пешко́м?

Воло́дя: Мо́жно. Ты идёшь пря́мо, ми́мо остано́вки тролле́йбуса и трамва́я. Пото́м ты свернёшь напра́во: э́то уже́ Балка́нская у́лица. Около метро́ там дом двадца́тый и́ли два́дцать второ́й. А наш дом пятьдеся́т второ́й. Та́кже мо́жно сесть на тролле́йбус. От метро́ идёт тролле́йбус но́мер семь.

Са́ра: Ско́лько остано́вок до твоего́ до́ма?

Воло́дя: Три. Договори́лись?

Са́ра: Договори́лись.

Воло́дя: До ве́чера.

Са́ра: До ве́чера.

New vocabulary

удо́бный	convenient
коне́чный	last
ми́мо	past
свора́чивать/сверну́ть	to turn off
сади́ться/сесть	to get on the bus (lit. to sit down)
договори́лись	agreed

1 Where is Sarah staying?
2 What is her telephone number?
3 What's the easiest way to get to Volodya's?
4 Does she have to change trains?
5 How long does it take on the metro?

159

EXERCISE 5

We now rejoin Sarah. She has found her friend's flat, rings the doorbell (**звони́т в дверь**), the door opens ...

Воло́дя: Входи́, входи́. Снима́й пальто́ и проходи́ в гости́ную.

Са́ра: Я та́кже сниму́ ту́фли.

Воло́дя: Не на́до. Ты наш гость.

Са́ра: На́до. На у́лице идёт дождь.

Воло́дя: Вот тебе́ та́почки. Проходи́ в гости́ную.

Са́ра: Я купи́ла тебе́ пода́рок из А́нглии, нет, не из А́нглии, из Шотла́ндии. Вот, пожа́луйста.

Воло́дя: А что э́то? Зна́ю. Спаси́бо, Са́ра, э́то моё люби́мое ви́ски. Ну проходи́, проходи́.

Са́ра: А где Ната́ша?

Воло́дя: Она́ ещё гото́вит: она́ ско́ро придёт. Сади́сь.

Са́ра: Ско́лько у тебя́ книг! Э́то не гости́ная, а библиоте́ка!

Воло́дя: Я предлага́ю тост за твой прие́зд, за твоего́ му́жа, за твои́х бра́тьев, за твои́х сестёр, за всех мои́х шотла́ндских и америка́нских друзе́й ...

Са́ра: Хва́тит! Дава́й вы́пьем за тебя́, за Воло́дю и за на́шу хозя́йку Ната́шу! Но где она́?

New vocabulary

снима́ть/снять (сниму́)	*to take off (clothes)*
проходи́ть	*to go through*
ту́фли	*shoes*
люби́мый	*favourite*
предлага́ть тост	*to propose a toast*
хва́тит	*enough*

1 We looked at imperatives in Unit 18. How many you can find in this dialogue, including repeats?
2 Why does Sarah insist on taking off her shoes?
3 Where is Natasha?
4 What is Sarah's first impression of Volodya's living room?
5 Who does Volodya propose a toast to?
6 Who does Sarah want to drink to?

Toasts

The Russian construction is:

Предлага́ю тост за ... *I propose a toast to ...*
Дава́й(те) вы́пьем за ... *Let us drink to ...*

The word **за** (*to, for*) is followed by the accusative case, which for nouns denoting human beings is often identical to the genitive case. Only feminine nouns in the singular have their own form. Here are some examples:

за моего́ бра́та
за мою́ сестру́
за госте́й
за ва́ше (твоё) здоро́вье

Look at Volodya's toasts at the end of the previous conversation for some more examples.

EXERCISE 6

You are being entertained by some Russian friends, who have already raised their glasses several times to toast you and all their friends in Britain. Now it is your turn to propose a toast. Here are some suggested toasts: you may need them all during the course of the evening! Translate them into Russian.

1 to my Russian friends
2 to Vanya
3 to Sasha
4 to your health
5 to the hostess
6 to happiness
7 to your birthday

● Looking at words

Saying goodbye

Instead of saying «**До свида́ния**» Russians will often use a more specific phrase consisting of **до** and a time word in the genitive case. The conversation for Exercise 4 ends with **до ве́чера** (*till the evening*). A common phrase is **до встре́чи** (*until we meet*; literally *until a meeting*).

. . . .

EXERCISE 7

Here are some more examples of phrases which finish conversations. Work out for each one when the speakers hope to meet again.

1	до за́втра	5	до утра́
2	до суббо́ты	6	до Но́вого го́да
3	до Рождества́	7	до среды́
4	до Па́схи		

. . . .

Agreeing

If you make an arrangement, Russians usually conclude the discussion with the word **Договори́лись!** (literally *we have agreed*). The other person repeats this to confirm the arrangement. **Воло́дя** and Sarah do this when making the arrangements for her to visit.

Friends

The standard word for a friend is **друг**. It has a special plural form **друзья́**. If you are referring to a female friend, Russians use **подру́га** instead.

A situation to remember

Lost in St Petersburg
Actually Sarah got lost! She turned the wrong way out of the underground. Look at the map of the area and you will see where she is. Devise a conversation between Sarah and a passer-by and get some directions to Volodya and Natasha's flat.

Giving directions
Volodya has decided to visit Britain once again.
He has arranged to come and see you.
Find out where he is living.
Tell him where you live.
Explain that he has to go by bus.
Tell him how many stops.
Describe your house – is it big, small?
Is it a bungalow? (**одноэта́жный дом**)
How many storeys does it have?
(**двухэта́жный/трёхэта́жный дом ...**)
How long will it take him?

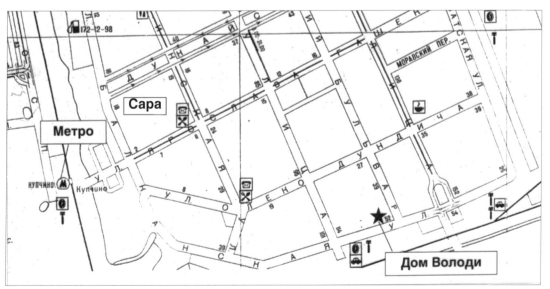

WHAT YOU KNOW

Talking about the future
Я пое́ду в Москву́.
Я куплю́ кварти́ру.
Я бу́ду жить в Москве́.

Approximate time
Приду́ часа́ в два.
Вы идёте мину́т пять.

Drinking people's health
Предлага́ю тост за на́шего дру́га!
Дава́йте вы́пьем за ва́ше здоро́вье!

Agreeing and saying goodbye
Договори́лись!
До за́втра!
До встре́чи!

KEY VOCABULARY

в кото́ром часу́	at what time
ва́нная	bathroom
гости́ная	living room
гото́вить/пригото́вить	to cook
дива́н	settee
дом: пятиэта́жный дом	five-storeyed building
друг (pl. друзья́)	friend
ко́рпус	block
кварти́ра:	
двухко́мнатная кварти́ра	two-roomed flat
меня́ть (на)	to exchange for
покупа́ть/купи́ть	to buy
продава́ть/прода́ть	to sell
сдава́ть/сдать	to rent out
ско́ро	soon
снима́ть/снять	to let (flat); take off (clothes)
спа́льня	bedroom
ту́фли	shoes
Хва́тит!	Enough!
эта́ж: на пе́рвом этаже́	on the ground floor

Revision

Moscow v
St Petersburg

Revision exercises

Peter and Paul Fortress,
St Petersburg

Leningrad station, Moscow

● Life in Russia

Moscow or St Petersburg?

Rivalry between St Petersburg and Moscow has existed since
the former was founded as the Russian capital (**столи́ца**), and
intensified when it lost that status at the start of the Soviet state.
Inhabitants of St Petersburg will tell you that it is the Northern
Capital (**се́верная столи́ца**) of Russia. Certainly it rivals, many
would say surpasses, Moscow in the excellence and beauty of its
historic buildings, and the atmosphere is quite different. Moscow
is, of course, much older than St Petersburg, and because it was
formed by the gradual amalgamation of villages (**дере́вни**), it has
evolved in a less organised way. St Petersburg was built more on a
grid system typical of Western architecture of the early 18th century.

Hermitage, St Petersburg

Moscow Kremlin

Although the patchwork effect of the succeeding styles can still be seen in Moscow, particularly in collections of buildings such as the Kremlin, one has to go to the area around Moscow (**Подмоско́вье**) to see the beautiful wooden houses (**и́збы**) which used to be the typical Russian homes. During the Soviet period there was a conscious attempt, partly for propaganda reasons, to replace all wooden houses with blocks of flats (**жилы́е дома́**). Many other tall buildings (**высо́тные зда́ния**) were built during the Stalin era, including the university and several ministries (**министе́рства**).

● Language information

You have met all the cases of nouns in the singular, and most of them in the plural. Here are some of the plurals you have met up to now.

Nominative case
грибы́, тури́сты, но́вости, заку́ски, но́чи, поезда́

Genitive (of) **case**
теа́тров, музе́ев, мину́т, зда́ний

Dative (to or for) **case**
к друзья́м, по у́лицам

Instrumental (by or with) **case**
с гриба́ми, с де́вушками

Prepositional case
на лы́жах, на конька́х

The endings of the accusative case are identical to the nominative case (if the nouns refer to inanimate objects) or to the genitive case (if they refer to people or animals).

As you will see, there is a variety of endings in the nominative and genitive. The dative, instrumental and prepositional are always **-ам -ами -ах** or **-ям -ями -ях**.

Adjectives are even simpler! They are the same for all three genders in the plural. In the dative, instrumental and prepositional they have **-ым -ыми -ых** (or **-им -ими -их**): **интере́сным кни́гам** (*interesting books*), **интере́сными кни́гами, (в) интере́сных кни́гах; ру́сским маши́нам** (*Russian cars*), **ру́сскими маши́нами, (о) ру́сских маши́нах.** In the nominative they have **-ые (-ие): интере́сные кни́ги, ру́сские маши́ны** and the genitive **-ых (-их): интере́сных кни́г, ру́сских маши́н.** Once again, the accusative is like the nominative or genitive case.

EXERCISE 1

Read the following passage: a letter from two Russian visitors to London written to their children back home in Moscow. Answer the questions which follow.

1 Underline the plural nouns, adjectives and pronouns in the passage.
2 Which city was having the better weather: Moscow or London?
3 Why were they surprised to see a play in English?
4 After the theatre where did they go?
5 Why didn't they eat in a typical British restaurant?
6 What other special features did dad mention?

Дороги́е мои́!

Вот мы с ма́мой в Ло́ндоне! Здесь о́чень интере́сно, но пого́да не така́я хоро́шая, как у вас в Москве́. Мы бы́ли во мно́гих интере́сных места́х. Здесь о́чень мно́го хоро́ших теа́тров. Вчера́ мы смотре́ли пье́су «Дя́дя Ва́ня» — по-англи́йски! Актёры о́чень хорошо́ игра́ли. Пото́м мы пошли́ в кита́йский рестора́н. Я съел суп из кра́бов, а пото́м креве́тки с гриба́ми и с ри́сом. Все там пи́ли кита́йский чай. Ма́ме там бы́ло хорошо́, а мне не́ бы́ло. Я люблю́ на́ши ру́сские блю́да! Хоте́ли пообе́дать в типи́чном англи́йском рестора́не, но ка́жется, здесь все рестора́ны и́ли кита́йские, и́ли францу́зские, и́ли италья́нские!

Авто́бусы здесь кра́сные, двухэта́жные, и их о́чень мно́го. Здесь о́чень мно́го такси́. Они́ больши́е, чёрные.

Ну, нам пора́! Бу́дьте здоро́вы! Целу́ем!
Па́па и ма́ма.

● Revision exercises

EXERCISE 2

The inhabitants of St Petersburg and those of Moscow usually disagree about which is the better city. Here is a conversation in which this is apparent.
Eleven words have been missed out.
At the end of the passage you will find these eleven words – but not in the correct order.
Fill each space with the correct word from the box below.

A: Мне ка́жется, что в Санкт-Петербу́рге жить о́чень прия́тно. У́лицы у нас широ́кие, зда́ния краси́вые.
B: Пра́вда, но в Москве́ то́же хорошо́.
A: Да, здесь хорошо́, но в Санкт-Петербу́рге ¹лу́чше. Там краси́вые дворцы́ ...
B: В Москве́ дворцы́ (palaces) то́же ² _____ . Мне о́чень ³ _____ жить в Москве́. Москва́ ⁴ _____ Росси́и.
A: Коне́чно, Москва́ хоро́ший го́род, а я о́чень ⁵ _____ Санкт-Петербу́рг.
B: Я то́же. Но в Москве́ ⁶ _____ теа́тров, ⁷ _____ кинотеа́тров, ⁸ _____ рестора́нов.
A: Пра́вда, у нас ⁹ _____ рестора́нов, но они́ не ¹⁰ _____ чем моско́вские рестора́ны. Как тебе́ ка́жется?
B: Я ¹¹ _____ , что ты бо́льше лю́бишь Санкт-Петербу́рг, а я Москву́. Вот и всё!

столи́ца	ме́ньше	бо́льше
ху́же	краси́вые	нра́вится
лу́чше	бо́льше	люблю́
ду́маю	бо́льше	

EXERCISE 3

When you have completed Exercise 2 and corrected your responses, answer the following questions in English.

1 Where does the conversation take place?
2 Which person speaks first?
3 Why does the person from St Petersburg think her city is better?
4 What does she say about the restaurants in St Petersburg?

EXERCISE 4

If you go to Russia, you are bound to have to fill in forms. At the airport, you will have to fill in a migration card, at the hotel you will be asked to fill in another form. Here is a typical form (**анкéта**):

```
                  А Н К Е Т А

Фамилия  4 . . . . . . . . . .  Имя . . . . . . . . . .  Отчество . . . . . . . . . . .

Дата рождения . . . . . . . . . . . . .  Место рождения . . . . . . . . . . . .

Адрес . . . . . . . . . . . . . . . . . . . . . . . . . . . . . . . . . . . . . . . . . . .

. . . . . . . . . . . . . . . . . . . . . . . . . . . . . . . . . . . . . . . . . . . . . . .

Имя отца . . . . . . . . . . . Отчество отца . . . . . . . . . . . . . . . . . . . . . .

Национальность . . . . . . . . . . . . . . . . . . . . . . . . . . . . . . . . . . . . . .

Профессия . . . . . . . . . . . . . . . . . . . . . . . . . . . . . . . . . . . . . . . . .
```

Here are some answers, all jumbled up. Insert the number against each one in the appropriate place. The first one is done for you.

1 ул. Чайкóвского 5 кв. 18
2 Никúта
3 Москвá
4 Сýслова
5 Никúтична
6 Áнна
7 Петрóвич
8 студéнтка
9 16-ое апрéля, 1986 гóда
10 рýсская

Now you try to fill in the form, giving your own details.

EXERCISE 5 Greeting people

Look at the list of greetings and place the number of the appropriate picture in the box.

С Нóвым гóдом! ☐

С днём рождéния! ☐

С прáздником! ☐

Приятного аппетúта! ☐

Поздравляю! ☐

EXERCISE 6

Fill in the greetings in the sentences below. You should be able to
work them out from the context.

1 В де́вять часо́в я пошёл в бюро́.

«_____ _____» сказа́л дире́ктор.

«_____ , Ива́н Серге́евич, как вы

_____?»

2 В рестора́не.

– Вот ваш бифште́кс.

– Спаси́бо.

– _____ _____ !

– _____

3 –До свида́ния, и _____ до́брого!

– _____

4 – Уже́ по́здно. Тебе́ пора́ (*time
to*) спать.

– _____ _____

....

EXERCISE 7 Feeling well and feeling ill
Choose the appropriate alternative.

1 Ива́н бо́лен. Он чу́вствует себя́

хорошо́.
сты́дно.
пло́хо.

2 Ни́на больна́. У

него́
вас
неё

боли́т го́рло.

3 Закро́йте окно́. Мне здесь о́чень

хо́лодно.
жа́рко.
тепло́.

4 Врач вы́писал мне реце́пт, и я пошёл в

медпу́нкт.
магази́н.
апте́ку.

5 В апте́ке мне да́ли

во́ду.
лека́рство.
температу́ру.

☉ EXERCISE 8

A man is arranging a birthday party for his sister and wants to order some drinks. He rings up a big supermarket, hoping to get a discount (**скидка**) or something free (**бесплатно**) if he orders in bulk.

Listen carefully to your CD and then answer the questions. Try to answer in Russian.

Ива́н:	Алло́, э́то магази́н «Седьмо́й контине́нт?
Де́вушка:	Да, «Седьмо́й контине́нт».
Ива́н:	В суббо́ту организу́ю вечери́нку для сестры́ – э́то её день рожде́ния. Хочу́ заказа́ть вино́ и во́дку.
Де́вушка:	Хорошо́. Како́е вино́ вы хоти́те? У нас сто ви́дов. Вы хоти́те францу́зское и́ли неме́цкое?
Ива́н:	Мне, пожа́луйста, хоро́шее францу́зское кра́сное вино́.
Де́вушка:	Рекоменду́ю Кот ду Рон. Отли́чное вино́.
Ива́н:	А ско́лько сто́ит буты́лка?
Де́вушка:	Четы́реста пятьдеся́т рубле́й. Ско́лько буты́лок вы хоти́те?
Ива́н:	Шесть. Вы дади́те мне ски́дку на шесть буты́лок?
Де́вушка:	Нет. Мы даём ски́дку то́лько на двена́дцать. Даём одну́ буты́лку беспла́тно.
Ива́н:	Ла́дно, возьму́ двена́дцать буты́лок. А скажи́те, пожа́луйста, кака́я у вас есть во́дка?
Де́вушка:	У нас есть «Столи́чная», «Ру́сский станда́рт» и та́кже и́мпортная во́дка.
Ива́н:	Мне, пожа́луйста, и́мпортную. «Абсолю́т» есть?
Де́вушка:	Есть. Четы́реста девяно́сто рубле́й за буты́лку. Ско́лько вам буты́лок?
Ива́н:	Я возьму́ пять. Я прие́ду в пя́тницу в оди́ннадцать утра́. Ла́дно?
Де́вушка:	Ла́дно. До пя́тницы. До свида́ния.

1 Почему́ Ива́н организу́ет ве́чер?
2 Что он хо́чет заказа́ть?
3 Ско́лько ви́дов вин в магази́не?
4 Како́е вино́ де́вушка рекоменду́ет?
5 Ско́лько сто́ит вино́?
6 Ско́лько буты́лок зака́зывает? Почему́?
7 Кака́я во́дка у них есть?
8 Кака́я во́дка бо́льше нра́вится Ива́ну?
9 Ско́лько сто́ит буты́лка э́той во́дки?
10 Когда́ Ива́н прие́дет в магази́н?

LANGUAGE REVIEW

Here is a list of words and constructions that you have met in the previous five units. If you do not know what they mean, you need to look back at the unit given on the right.

Я сиде́л до́ма и чита́л газе́ту.	**16**
Я прочита́л газе́ту и пошёл в го́род.	**16**
Ка́ждый день я чита́л газе́ту.	**16**
Москва́ бо́льше, чем Санкт-Петербу́рг.	**16**
Мне бо́льше нра́вится Санкт-Петербу́рг.	**16**
Он согла́сен. Она́ согла́сна.	**16**
Поздравля́ю вас с Но́вым го́дом!	**17**
Жела́ю вам больши́х успе́хов!	**17**
Я ходи́л по магази́нам.	**17**
В про́шлом году́ я е́здил в Росси́ю.	**17**
всё у́тро, весь день, всю ночь	**17**
Нам ску́чно. Ему́ хорошо́. Мне жа́рко.	**18**
Покажи́те кни́гу! Принима́йте табле́тки!	
Позвони́ за́втра!	**18**
Та́ня должна́ чита́ть э́ту кни́гу.	**18**
Сейча́с мы е́дем в Москву́. За́втра мы пое́дем в Москву́.	**19**
Приду́ часо́в в пять.	**19**
Предлага́ю тост за моего́ бра́та.	**19**

Alphabet: transliteration and pronunciation guide

Russian

Capital	Small	Transliteration	Approximate pronunciation (when different or unexpected)
А	а	A	
Б	б	B	
В	в	V	
Г	г	G	'v' when between two vowels as in -его, -ого
Д	д	D	
Е	е	YE*	'ye' as in *yet*
Ё	ё	YO**	
Ж	ж	ZH	like 's' in *pleasure*
З	з	Z	
И	и	I	like 'ee' in *sweet*
Й	й	I or Y	like 'y' in *boy*
К	к	K	
Л	л	L	
М	м	M	
Н	н	N	
О	о	O	
П	п	P	
Р	р	R	rolled (Scottish)
С	с	S	
Т	т	T	
У	у	U	'oo' in *boot*
Ф	ф	F	
Х	х	KH	'h' but hard, like Scottish *loch*
Ц	ц	TS	
Ч	ч	CH	but occasionally 'sh' as in что
Ш	ш	SH	
Щ	щ	SHCH	
Ъ	ъ	hard sign***	
Ы	ы	Y	like 'y' in *physio*
Ь	ь	soft sign***	
Э	э	E	'e' in *Edward*
Ю	ю	YU	
Я	я	YA	

* Initially and after vowels except, y otherwise E

** In all positions except after ч and щ, when o is used.

*** May be written ' or omitted.

This is not, strictly speaking, a guide to pronouncing Russian, although it may be used as an approximate guide. If you do use it this way, you should take care not to change the sounds in an English way. For example, an English speaker might be tempted to pronounce the Russian word KOSMOS as if it had a 'z' where the first 's' is. A nearer approximation to the Russian might be given by representing the word as 'KOSSMOSS'. There are many other examples of this sort of thing.

You should always try to get your pronunciation as near to the Russian as you can by imitating the sound you hear on the recording. Train yourself to listen without looking at the text, and pay particular attention to the stress, indicated with an accent in the transcriptions. The sound under the stress always carries its full value, but vowels in other positions often sound very different from what you would expect, e.g. the 'o' sounds in **хорошо́**. If the transcription system produces a misleading pronunciation, an alternative is given in brackets. Note that KH is the transcription for the Russian **х** and ZH for the Russian **ж**.

Approximate pronunciation guide for alphabet Units 1–5

Unit 1

1 KOMÉTA (KOMYÉTA)
2 APPARÁT
3 SAMOVÁR
4 KÁSSA
5 TEÁTR
6 ÁTOM
7 METRÓ
8 ÓPERA
9 SPORT
10 PARK
11 TAKSÍ
12 PIANÍST
13 VINÓ
14 MOSKVÁ
15 RESTORÁN
16 ORKÉSTR
17 ÁVIA
18 MÁRKA
19 NET (NYET)
20 STOP
21 PÁSPORT

Unit 2

1 VODÁ
2 VÓDKA
3 LIMONÁD
4 LITR
5 KILÓ
6 KILOMÉTR
7 UNIVERSITÉT
8 KÓKA-KÓLA
9 PÉPSI
10 PRÁVDA
11 KROKODÍL
12 KAVKÁZ
13 ZOOPÁRK
(ZO-OPÁRK)
14 DOM
15 DÁTA
16 KVAS
17 APTÉKA
18 MARS
19 KIÓSK
20 TOLSTÓY
21 VOYNÁ I MIR
22 ROSSÍYSKY
23 UKRAÍNA
(UKRAÉENA)
24 ZDRÁVSTVUYTE
(ZDRÁSTVUYTE)

Unit 3

1 FUTBÓL
2 KLUB
3 VKHOD
4 KOSTYÚM
5 MENYÚ
6 PEREKHÓD
7 TELEFÓN
8 BULÓN (BULYÓN)
9 KAFÉ
10 BYURÓ
11 FÓTO
12 KREML'
13 FIL'M
14 YÚMOR
15 AVTÓBUS
16 BUFÉT
17 UZBÉK
18 KLÍMAT
19 DINÁMO
20 STADIÓN
21 SPARTÁK
22 TORPÉDO
23 LOKOMOTÍV
24 REMÓNT
25 ADMINISTRÁTOR
26 KHOKKÉY
27 KINÓ

Unit 4

1 GÓROD
2 TELEGRÁMMA
3 GOD
4 TURÍSTY
5 AEROFLÓT
6 SAMOLYÓT
7 EKSKÚRSIYA
8 IZVÉSTIYA
9 GAZÉTA (GAZYÉTA)
10 ROSSÍYA
11 GUM
12 EKSPRÉSS
13 ENÉRGIYA
14 PROGRÁMMA
15 VÝKHOD
16 VYKHODÍT'
17 GRIBÝ
18 ÓL'GA
19 MAY
(like English 'my')
20 NEDÉLYA
21 RYAD
22 BLANK
23 EM-GE-Ú (EM GE ÓO)
24 MÉSTO (MYÉSTO)

Unit 5

1 CHÉKHOV
2 CHÁIKA
3 MASHÍNA
4 ELEKTRÍCHESTVO
5 INFORMÁTSIYA
6 BIFSHTÉKS
7 SHASHLÝK
8 DEMONSTRÁTSIYA
9 MATCH
10 BOLSHÓY TEÁTR
11 MOSKVÍCH
12 ETÁZH
13 MÓZHNO
14 KHOROSHÓ
15 SHOSSÉ
16 TSVETÝ
17 VÉCHER
18 NOCH'
19 KRÁSNAYA
PLÓSHCHAD'
20 SHCHI
21 SHÁPKA
22 ZHÉNSHCHINA
23 TSIRK (TSYRK)
24 PÓCHTA
25 TSENTR
26 KONTSÉRT
27 POD'YÉZD

Grammar notes

1 Genders

Russian has three genders – masculine, feminine and neuter. Usually the gender can be recognised from the ending (see page 171).

2 Cases

Russian nouns, adjectives and pronouns have six cases. This means that words change their endings according to their function in a sentence. The cases are as follows:

● NOMINATIVE. The 'naming' case. This is the one you will find in a dictionary. It is used for the subject of the sentence.

● ACCUSATIVE. This is used for the direct object of a sentence and after some prepositions, mostly indicating movement: notably **в** (*into*), **на** (*onto*) and **че́рез** (*across)*. It is also used in many time expressions, either on its own or with a preposition.

● GENITIVE. The 'possession' case, or the 'of' case. It is used with a large number of prepositions (**из, от, до, с, у,** etc.) and after numerals.

● DATIVE. The 'to'/'for' case (e.g. **Он дал мне кни́гу** – *He gave (to) me a book*, **Он купи́л мне кни́гу** – *He bought (for) me a book*). It is used after some prepositions including **к** (*towards)* and **по** (*along)*.

● INSTRUMENTAL. The 'with' or 'by' case. It is used on its own to indicate the instrument used (e.g. **Он писа́л карандашо́м** – *He was writing with a pencil)* and after some prepositions, including **с** – *with* (**чай с лимо́ном**, *tea with lemon*, **сала́т с гриба́ми**, *salad with mushrooms)*. It is also used on its own with certain time expressions – **ве́чером, весно́й**, etc.

● PREPOSITIONAL (sometimes called LOCATIVE). The 'place' case. Only used after the prepositions **в** (*in)*, **на** (*on)*, **о** (*about)*, **при** (*in the time of)*.

3 Prepositions

All cases except the nominative may have prepositions in front of them, i.e. they may be 'governed' by a preposition. Here is a list of some of the main prepositions with their cases:

ACCUSATIVE	**в** (*into)*, **на** (*onto)*, **за** (*in exchange for)*, **че́рез** (*across)*
GENITIVE	**у** (*by/at)*, **из** (*out of)*, **от** (*from)*, **до** (*as far as/up to)*, **с** (*from)*, **для** (*for)*, **БЕЗ** (*without)*
DATIVE	**к** (*towards)*, **по** (*along, about)*, etc.
INSTRUMENTAL	**с** (*with)*, **под** (*under)*, **над** (*above)*, **ЗА** (*for)*
PREPOSITIONAL (LOCATIVE)	**в** (*in)*, **на** (*on)*, **о** (*about)*

4 Endings: nouns

You can normally tell which gender a noun is by looking at the ending of the nominative singular case. Here is a table of all the nominative singular endings grouped by gender.

	Masculine	Feminine	Neuter
hard endings	consonant	-а	-о
soft endings	-й	-я	-е
soft endings		-ия	-ие
soft endings	-ь	-ь	

The endings in the table appear in nouns which are of Russian origin or in nouns which have become 'Russified' (**футбо́л**, **чай**, **маши́на**, etc.). Words which have not (yet) changed in form often do not change their endings at all (**такси́**, **кино́**, **кенгуру́**, etc.).

5 Spelling rules

Russian also has a number of spelling rules, which do not allow certain vowels to occur after certain groups of consonants. Two rules that will help in working out the correct endings on nouns and adjectives are:

Spelling rule 1: after г, к, х, ж, ч, ш, щ write **И** in place of **Ы**

Spelling rule 2: after ж, ч, ш, щ, ц write **Е** in place of unstressed **О**

Note that if the **о** is the stressed syllable, it does not change.

6 Tables

Notice that 'hard' and 'soft' types are parallel, in that they involve a difference of one letter only and this is a corresponding vowel. Here is a list of vowels to help you:

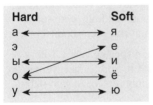

The arrows indicate the corresponding vowels. Thus **Ни́на** in the accusative is **Ни́ну**, whereas the accusative of **Та́ня** is **Та́ню**, etc. Note that **э** occurs mainly in words of foreign origin and never in endings.

7 Nouns: masculine

	Singular	Plural
Nom.	теа́тр	теа́тры
Acc.	теа́тр*	теа́тры*
Gen.	теа́тра	теа́тров
Dat.	теа́тру	теа́трам
Instr.	теа́тром	теа́трами
Prep.	(в) теа́тре	(в) теа́трах
Nom.	музе́й	музе́и
Acc.	музе́я*	музе́и*
Gen.	музе́я	музе́ев
Dat.	музе́ю	музе́ям
Instr.	музе́ем	музе́ями
Prep.	(о) музе́е	(о) музе́ях

* In inanimate nouns in both singular and plural the accusative is identical to the nominative; in animate nouns it is identical to the genitive.

Note that masculine nouns in **-ь** behave like **музе́й** except that they end in -**ей** in the genitive plural.

8 Nouns: feminine

	Singular	Plural
Nom.	ко́мната	ко́мнаты
Acc.	ко́мнату	ко́мнаты*
Gen.	ко́мнаты	ко́мнат
Dat.	ко́мнате	ко́мнатам
Instr.	ко́мнатой	ко́мнатами
Prep.	(в) ко́мнате	(в) ко́мнатах

Feminine nouns ending in **-я** behave very much like those in **-а**, but they have 'soft' endings, e.g. **Та́ня → Та́ню** (accusative) **→ с Та́ней** (instrumental). The ones in **ия** have **-ий** in the genitive plural and **-ии** in the dative and prepositional singular.

	Singular	Plural
Nom.	пло́щадь	пло́щади
Acc.	пло́щадь	пло́щади*
Gen.	пло́щади	площаде́й
Dat.	пло́щади	площадя́м
Instr.	пло́щадью	площадя́ми
Prep.	(на) пло́щади	(на) площадя́х

* In inanimate nouns in the plural the accusative is identical to the nominative; in animate nouns it is identical to the genitive.

9 Nouns: neuter

Notice that many of the neuter nouns we have used in the course do not change their endings (**кино́, метро́, Дина́мо, кило́, фо́то, кафе́, бюро́, Торпе́до**). Such nouns will be marked *indec* in the vocabulary. One that does change is **ме́сто** (*place*).

	Singular	Plural
Nom.	ме́сто	места́
Acc.	ме́сто	места́
Gen.	ме́ста	мест
Dat.	ме́сту	места́м
Instr.	ме́стом	места́ми
Prep.	(в) ме́сте	(в) места́х

The singular of neuter nouns is very much like the masculine singular. Neuter nouns are always inanimate. The genitive plural is very much like feminine in **-a** (it has a 'zero' ending). Notice also the stress shift in the plural. This avoids confusion between the genitive singular and the nominative plural.

	Singular	Plural
Nom.	зда́ние	зда́ния
Acc.	зда́ние	зда́ния
Gen.	зда́ния	зда́ний
Dat.	зда́нию	зда́ниям
Instr.	зда́нием	зда́ниями
Prep.	(в) зда́нии	(в) зда́ниях

If you want to learn these by heart it would help if you take note that in all instances the dative, instrumental and prepositional plural are similar in form. The same is true with adjectives. Most, but not all, noun types are listed above. If you want a comprehensive list, you should consult any standard grammar of Russian.

10 Pronouns

Singular

Nom.	я	ты	он (оно́) она́	
Acc.	меня́	тебя́	его́	её
Gen.	меня́	тебя́	его́	её
Dat.	мне	тебе́	ему́	ей
Instr.	мной	тобо́й	им	ей (ею)
Prep.	(обо) мне	(о) тебе́	(о) нём	(о) нём

Plural

Nom.	мы	вы	они́
Acc.	нас	вас	их
Gen.	нас	вас	их
Dat.	нам	вам	им
Instr.	на́ми	ва́ми	и́ми
Prep.	(о) нас	(о) вас	(о) них

Notice that when the pronoun begins with a vowel and is governed by a preposition, **н** is added, e.g. **о нём**, **у них** (genitive), etc.

11 Possessive pronouns

	Masculine		Neuter	Feminine	Plural
Nom.	мой		моё	моя́	мои́
Acc.	*as nom. or gen.*		моё	мою́	*as nom. or gen.*
Gen.	моего́			мое́й	мои́х
Dat.	моему́			мое́й	мои́м
Instr.	мои́м			мое́й	мои́ми
Prep.	моём			мое́й	мои́х

	Masculine		Neuter	Feminine	Plural
Nom.	ваш	ва́ше	ва́ше	ва́ши	
Acc.	*as nom. or gen.*		ва́ше	ва́шу	*as nom. or gen.*
Gen.	ва́шего			ва́шей	ва́ших
Dat.	ва́шему			ва́шей	ва́шим
Instr.	ва́шим			ва́шей	ва́шими
Prep.	ва́шем			ва́шей	ва́ших

твой has the same forms as **мой** and **наш** has the same forms as **ваш**.

12 Adjectives

These are much simpler than nouns, in that there are not as many classes, and the plural is the same for all three genders. Masculine and neuter are very much alike, so we have put them together.

	Masculine	Neuter	Feminine	Plural
Nom.	интере́сный	интере́сное	интере́сная	интере́сные
Acc.	*as nom. or gen.*	интере́сное	интере́сную	*as nom. or gen.*
Gen.	интере́сного		интере́сной	интере́сных
Dat.	интере́сному		интере́сной	интере́сным
Instr.	интере́сным		интере́сной	интере́сными
Prep.	интере́сном		интере́сной	интере́сных

Notice in the feminine the last four endings are the same, and notice the similarity between the adjectival and noun endings, with **-ы** taking the place of **-a** in dative, instrumental and prepositional plural.

Many adjectives end in **-кий** and, following spelling rule 1, will replace all occurrences of the vowel **ы** with **и**. Some adjectives end in **-жий**, **-чий**, **-ший** or **-щий** and will not only replace **ы** with **и**, but also **o** with **e**:

	Masculine	Neuter	Feminine	Plural
Nom.	хоро́ший	хоро́шее	хоро́шая	хоро́шие
Acc.	*as nom. or gen.*	хоро́шее	хоро́шую	*as nom. or gen.*
Gen.	хоро́шего		хоро́шей	хоро́ших
Dat.	хоро́шему		хоро́шей	хоро́шим
Instr.	хоро́шим		хоро́шей	хоро́шими
Prep.	хоро́шем		хоро́шей	хоро́ших

There are a few 'soft' adjectives, e.g. **вече́рний**, which means that you have a straight substitution of **я** for **а**, **е** for **о**, **и** for **ы** and **ю** for **у**. Thus **вече́рняя газе́та** and **я чита́л вече́рнюю газе́ту**, etc.

Some adjectives have a short form, which is much simpler than the long form, but it is only used in one case, the nominative. For example:

Рестора́н откры́т.	*The restaurant is open.*
Кафе́ закры́то.	*The cafe is closed.*
Апте́ка закры́та.	*The chemist is closed.*
Они́ откры́ты.	*They are open.*

13 Adverbs

They are usually derived from adjectives, by taking off the ending and adding **-о**.

хоро́ший	хорошо́	*well*
плохо́й	пло́хо	*badly*
интере́сный	интере́сно	*interestingly*

14 Comparison

We have used a few short forms of the comparative, as follows:

хорошо́	лу́чше	*better*
пло́хо	ху́же	*worse*
большо́й	бо́льше	*bigger, more*
ма́ленький	ме́ньше	*smaller, less*

followed by a simple genitive or **чем** (*than*).

15 Verbs: present and past tense

The infinitive ends in **-ть** – **рабо́тать**, **гуля́ть**, **говори́ть**, **смотре́ть**, etc. Verbs that end in **-ать** or **-ять** usually have a present tense like **чита́ть** (first conjugation). Those that end in **-ить** have present tense forms like **говори́ть** (second conjugation). Those that end in **-еть** are more difficult to predict, although many common verbs, such as **смотре́ть**, are second conjugation. Look at the examples below.

Present tense			
чита́ть		**говори́ть**	
я	чита́ю	я	говорю́
ты	чита́ешь	ты	говори́шь
он	чита́ет	он	говори́т
мы	чита́ем	мы	говори́м
вы	чита́ете	вы	говори́те
они́	чита́ют	они́	говоря́т
stem	чита-	stem	говор-

In some verbs the stem is slightly different from the infinitive form. If you know the first and second persons singular, you can usually guess the rest. The stress stays fixed from the 'ты' form onwards, and, in such verbs, a stressed ending results in **-ё**. Look at the examples below.

е́хать		**идти́**	
я	е́ду	я	иду́
ты	е́дешь	ты	идёшь
он	е́дет	он	идёт
мы	е́дем	мы	идём
вы	е́дете	вы	идёте
они́	е́дут	они́	иду́т

There are one or two exceptions to the above, notably the following:

хоте́ть	
я	хочу́
ты	хо́чешь
он	хо́чет
мы	хоти́м
вы	хоти́те
они́	хотя́т

Past tenses are usually formed from the infinitive, by taking away **-ть** and adding **-л**, **-ла**, **-ло**, **-ли** depending on the gender and number of the persons involved.

я, ты (m.), он, Ива́н	чита́л,	говори́л
я, ты (f.), она́, Ве́ра	чита́ла,	говори́ла
мы, вы, они́, Ива́н и Ве́ра	чита́ли,	говори́ли

оно́ After **оно́**, or neuter nouns, the past tense ends in **-ло**, e.g. **оно́ бы́ло**, **ра́дио Москва́ говори́ло**. (Exception **идти́ → шёл шла шло шли**.)

16 Verbs: imperatives

Imperatives are formed by taking the stem of the present tense: if it ends in a vowel, add **-й** for the **ты** form or **-йте** for the **вы** form. If it ends in a consonant, add **-и** or **-ите** for the **ты** and **вы** forms respectively. Thus:

ты	**вы**	
чита́й	чита́йте	*read!*
говори́	говори́те	*speak!*
иди́	иди́те	*go!*

If you want to say *Let us do it*, use the **мы** form of the perfective future: **Пойдём** (*Let's go!*).

17 Verbs: aspects

Most Russian verbs have two aspects, the imperfective and the perfective. The imperfective is used for the present tense, the compound future (**я бу́ду/ он бу́дет чита́ть**, etc.) and the past tense. The perfective is used for the simple future and the past.

Aspects are a very complex area of Russian grammar. Only a general indication of when to use each aspect can be given here. You should consult a more detailed Russian grammar if you want further details. The imperfective is used to indicate an action in progress or an action performed on more than one occasion, the perfective is used when stressing that an action is complete on one occasion.

Here are a couple of examples of aspect pairs:

Imperfective: покупа́ть смотре́ть е́хать
Perfective: купи́ть посмотре́ть пое́хать

We have included both aspects of common verbs in the vocabulary.

18 Numerals

1	оди́н	30	три́дцать
2	два, две (f.)	40	со́рок
3	три	50	пятьдеся́т
4	четы́ре	60	шестьдеся́т
5	пять	70	се́мьдесят
6	шесть	80	во́семьдесят
7	семь	90	девяно́сто
8	во́семь	100	сто
9	де́вять	200	две́сти
10	де́сять	300	три́ста
11	оди́ннадцать	400	четы́реста
12	двена́дцать	500	пятьсо́т
13	трина́дцать	600	шестьсо́т
14	четы́рнадцать	700	семьсо́т
15	пятна́дцать	800	восемьсо́т
16	шестна́дцать	900	девятьсо́т
17	семна́дцать	1,000	ты́сяча
18	восемна́дцать	2,000	две ты́сячи
19	девятна́дцать	3,000	три ты́сячи
20	два́дцать	4,000	четы́ре ты́сячи
21	два́дцать оди́н	5,000	пять ты́сяч
22	два́дцать два	1,000,000	миллио́н
23	два́дцать три		

After **оди́н/одна́/одно́** the nominative sing. is used; after **два/две**, **три**, **четы́ре** (and numerals ending in these words) the genitive singular is used. After numerals other than these, the genitive plural is used.

19 Word building

As you will have seen from our regular *Looking at words* section in the course, it is often possible to make a guess at the meaning of a word by breaking it down into its component parts, i.e. prefix, root (or stem) and ending. Roots can only be learned by constant exposure to Russian. There is only a limited number of prefixes, and a knowledge of these will help you in understanding Russian. Here are some of them with their approximate meanings:

Prefix	Meaning	Example
без- бес-	*without*	беспла́тно *free, i.e. without paying*
в-	*into (en-)*	вход *entrance*
вз- вс- вос-	*upwards*	взлёт *take-off*
вы-	*out of (ex-)*	вы́ход *exit*
до-	*up to (the end)*	до́читать *to read to the end*
за-	*for (purpose)*	заходи́те *come and see us!*
из- ис-	*from*	и́здали *from a long way away*
на-	*onto*	напра́во *to the right*
не- ни-	*not, un-*	негра́мотность *illiteracy*
о- об-	*about*	описа́ть *to describe*
от-	*from*	отходи́ть *to depart*
пере-	*across, trans-*	перехо́д *crossing*
по-	*a little*	почита́ть *to read a little*
при-	*towards*	прие́зд *arrival*
про-	*through*	проходи́ть *to go through*
раз- рас-	*separation*	ра́зный *different*
с- со-	*with, together from*	съезд *meeting* сходи́ть *to alight*
у-	*away from*	уходи́ть, *to go away*

Suffixes are the part of a word that appears after the root, and they too can tell you something about the meaning of the word itself. **-ция** can often be the equivalent of the English *-tion*, as can **-ость**. Words ending in **-ость** are always feminine. They are often the equivalent of the English *-ence* or *-ness*: **незави́симый** (*independent*), **незави́симость** (*independence*). Other common suffixes are **-тель** (often *-er*) as in **чита́тель** (*reader*), and **-ник**, as in **спу́тник** (**с** + **пут** + **ник**): *fellow-traveller, companion,* or, of course, *satellite.* The feminine of words ending in **-ник** ends in **-ница**, which is also added to the **-тель** words: **учи́тельница** (*woman teacher*). Other suffixes are the endings listed in the rest of the grammar section. These give you information about whether the word is a verb, a noun, etc., and about its number, gender, case or person.

Recording scripts

Included here are all dialogues
not printed in the Units.

Unit 1

EXERCISE 8
– Здра́вствуйте. Это вы хоти́те
такси́?
– А такси́! Ма́ма, такси́.
– Хорошо́, я сейча́с.
– Куда́ вы е́дете?
– В Большо́й теа́тр, пожа́луйста.
– Хорошо́.
– Вот Большо́й теа́тр.
– Спаси́бо.
  (pays)
– Спаси́бо, и до свида́ния.
– До свида́ния.

Unit 2

EXERCISE 7
– Здра́вствуйте!
– Здра́вствуйте!
– А Ва́ня до́ма?
– Да до́ма. Ва́ня! Извини́те, как
вас зову́т?
– Ви́ктор Тру́шин.
– Ма́ма, кто э́то?
– Ва́ня, э́то Ви́ктор Тру́шин.
– А, хорошо́. Познако́мьтесь.
Это Ви́ктор, э́то ма́ма.
– О́чень ра́да.
– О́чень рад.
– Скажи́те, Ви́ктор, как ва́ша
ма́ма?
– Ничего́, спаси́бо. Она́ сейча́с
до́ма.

Unit 3

EXERCISE 5
1
– Скажи́те, пожа́луйста, где
метро́?
– Иди́те напра́во, пото́м нале́во
и пря́мо.
– Это далеко́?
– Да нет, то́лько оди́н киломе́тр.

2
– Извини́те, пожа́луйста, где
кино́?
– Кино́? Иди́те пря́мо, напра́во,
нале́во и пря́мо.
– Это далеко́?
– Да, далеко́, три киломе́тра.

3
– Прости́те, пожа́луйста, где
стадио́н?
– Стадио́н? Напра́во, напра́во и
пря́мо.
– Это далеко́?
– Да, нет! Здесь ря́дом.

4
– Прости́те, пожа́луйста, где
здесь рестора́н?
– Рестора́н? Иди́те нале́во,
напра́во и опя́ть напра́во.
– Это далеко́?
– Да, но мо́жно взять такси́.
– Спаси́бо вам большо́е.
– Пожа́луйста.

5
– Извини́те, пожа́луйста, где
здесь стоя́нка такси́?
– Такси́? Иди́те напра́во, напра́во,
нале́во и пря́мо. Там стоя́нка.
– Это далеко́?
– Нет, два киломе́тра. Это не
так далеко́.
– Спаси́бо.
– Пожа́луйста.

EXERCISE 8
1
– Прости́те, где здесь рестора́н?
– Вот там, напра́во.
– Он откры́т?
– Нет, сейча́с закры́т. Кафе́
сейча́с откры́то.

2
– Прости́те, вы не зна́ете, где
здесь кино́?
– Вот здесь нале́во, но сего́дня
кинотеа́тр закры́т.
– Он за́втра бу́дет откры́т?
– Да.

3
– Извини́те, где кафе́?
– Кафе́? Пря́мо по коридо́ру.
– Оно́ откры́то?
– Да, кафе́ всегда́ откры́то.

4
– Прости́те, пожа́луйста, где
здесь буфе́т?
– Вот напра́во, но сего́дня
закры́т на ремо́нт.

5
– А, вот и кафе́.
– Вот и меню́. Есть пи́во, вино́
и во́дка.

Unit 4

EXERCISE 6
– Алло́, э́то О́льга?
– Нет, Ната́ша.
– А, Ната́ша, здра́вствуй! Это
И́горь. Как дела́?
– Ничего́, а как ты?
– То́же ничего́. Ната́ша, О́льгу
мо́жно?
– Да. О́льга!
– Алло́, И́горь?
– О́ля, слу́шай. У меня́ биле́ты в
теа́тр. Пойдём, да?
– Когда́?
– Сего́дня.
– Нет, сего́дня я занята́. А
за́втра мо́жно?
– Хорошо́, пойдём за́втра.

Unit 5

EXERCISE 4
– Что идёт в па́рке?
– Ну, в па́рке идёт конце́рт.

– Что идёт в кино́?
– Ну, в кино́ идёт фильм
«Клеопа́тра».

– Что идёт в Большо́м теа́тре?
– В Большо́м теа́тре идёт о́пера
«Князь И́горь».

– Что идёт в университе́те?
– В университе́те ле́кция о
ко́смосе.

Unit 6

EXERCISE 2
1
– Де́вушка, скажи́те,
пожа́луйста, у вас есть ма́рки?
– Есть. Ско́лько вам?
– Да́йте, пожа́луйста, шесть.
– Вот, пожа́луйста, шесть ма́рок.
– Спаси́бо.

2
– Де́вушка, скажи́те, пожа́луйста,
у вас есть биле́ты?
– Есть. Ско́лько вам?
– Да́йте, пожа́луйста, два.
– Вот вам два биле́та.
– Спаси́бо.

3
– Де́вушка, скажи́те,
пожа́луйста, у вас есть
откры́тки?

– Есть. Ско́лько вам?
– Да́йте, пожа́луйста, пять.
– Вот вам пять откры́ток.
– Спаси́бо.

4
– Де́вушка, скажи́те, пожа́луйста, у вас есть пи́во?
– Есть. Ско́лько вам?
– Да́йте, пожа́луйста, три буты́лки.
– Вот вам три буты́лки.
– Спаси́бо.

5
– Де́вушка, скажи́те, пожа́луйста, у вас есть жето́ны?
– Есть. Ско́лько вам?
– Да́йте, пожа́луйста, де́сять.
– Вот вам де́сять жето́нов.
– Спаси́бо.

EXERCISE 8
– Здра́вствуйте.
– Здра́вствуйте. Скажи́те, пожа́луйста, у вас мо́жно купи́ть биле́ты в Большо́й теа́тр?
– Нет, Большо́й теа́тр сейча́с закры́т.
– А в цирк мо́жно?
– Да, пожа́луйста, в цирк мо́жно.
– Хорошо́. Да́йте, пожа́луйста, три биле́та.
– Вот, пожа́луйста, три биле́та.

Unit 7

EXERCISE 4
– Здра́вствуй, как тебя́ зову́т?
– Ве́ра. Меня́ зову́т Ве́ра.
– Как ты пожива́ешь, Ве́ра?
– Хорошо́, спаси́бо.
– А ско́лько тебе́ лет?
– Пять. Мне пять лет.
– А что э́то у тебя́?
– Откры́тки. Это откры́тки. Вот, раз, два, три, четы́ре, пять, шесть, семь, во́семь, де́вять, де́сять откры́ток.
– А твой па́па инжене́р, да.
– Да, инжене́р. И ма́ма то́же инжене́р.

TALKING ON THE TELEPHONE
– Алло́?
– Слу́шаю вас.
– Это гости́ница Росси́я?
– Нет, не тот но́мер. Перезвони́те.

– Алло́, это гости́ница Росси́я?
– Да.
– А хорошо́. Бори́сова мо́жно к телефо́ну?

Unit 8

EXERCISE 5
Здра́вствуйте. Сего́дня в на́шей програ́мме сле́дующие переда́чи:
В 14 часо́в футбо́л. Игра́ют Локомоти́в Москва́ и Че́лси, А́нглия.
В 17 часо́в 10 мину́т Две судьбы́. 5-я се́рия.
В 18 часо́в Но́вости.
В 18 часо́в 15 мину́т Конце́рт По́ла Макка́ртни на Кра́сной пло́щади.
В 20 часо́в 20 мину́т Криминальная Россия
В 21 час Вре́мя.
В 21 час 30 мину́т Премье́ра Пирс Бро́снан в фи́льме «Эвели́н».
В 23 часа́ 10 мину́т Софи́ Лоре́н, Марче́лло Мастроя́нни в коме́дии «Вчера́, сего́дня, за́втра».
Передаём после́дние изве́стия.

EXERCISE 9
– Са́ша, почему́ вы всё смо́трите телеви́зор? Почему́ вы не гуля́ете, не игра́ете в те́ннис, не чита́ете кни́гу?
– Потому́ что не люблю́ гуля́ть, не люблю́ игра́ть в те́ннис.
– Мы все лю́бим смотре́ть по телеви́зору фи́льмы и спорт. Но нельзя́ же сиде́ть весь день. Ни́на, ты до́ктор. Скажи́ ему́, что э́то нехорошо́.
– Да, э́то нехорошо́, Са́ша. А́нна лю́бит гуля́ть, Ви́ктор игра́ет в футбо́л, да, Ви́ктор? И ваш брат игра́ет.
– Мой брат сейча́с не игра́ет. Он говори́т, что не лю́бит футбо́л.
– Ви́ктор, пойдём в парк, погуля́ем.
– Нет, спаси́бо. Прости́те, я хочу́ смотре́ть хокке́й по телеви́зору. Я о́чень люблю́ смотре́ть хокке́й.

Unit 9

EXERCISE 2
– Свобо́дно?
– Пожа́луйста. Сади́тесь.
– *(to himself)* Ну, здесь о́чень хоро́ший рестора́н.

– Де́вушка!
– Слу́шаю вас!
– Сейча́с мо́жно у́жинать?
– Мо́жно, уже́ семь часо́в.

– Да́йте, пожа́луйста, меню́.
– Вот, пожа́луйста, меню́.
– Посмо́трим, кака́я там ры́ба.
– Что вы хоти́те?
– Мне, пожа́луйста, икру́ и шампа́нское.
– У нас то́лько кра́сная икра́.
– Хорошо́.

– И пото́м?
– У вас есть борщ? И суда́к?
– Есть.
– Хорошо́. Да́йте, пожа́луйста, и борщ и судака́. А пото́м ко́фе и конья́к.
– Хорошо́.

– Вот, пожа́луйста, икра́ и шампа́нское. Прия́тного аппети́та!
– Спаси́бо.
– Пожа́луйста.
– Ой, как я люблю́ ру́сское шампа́нское.

– Де́вушка, да́йте мне, пожа́луйста, счёт.
– Вот он.
– Ой-ой-ой!

EXERCISE 4
– Сади́тесь, пожа́луйста, сади́тесь!
– Мо́жно здесь?
– Мо́жно, пожа́луйста. Вот хлеб и заку́ски. Типи́чные ру́сские заку́ски. Вот чёрная икра́, помидо́ры, колбаса́, ветчина́, огурцы́ и смета́на. Прия́тного аппети́та! Ку́шайте на здоро́вье!
– А извини́те, кака́я там ры́ба?
– Это осетри́на, ру́сская осетри́на. А пото́м суп, а второ́е блю́до ку́рица с карто́шкой.

Unit 10

EXERCISE 5
1 Скажи́те, пожа́луйста, где здесь Большо́й теа́тр?
2 Ми́ла, здра́вствуй, как ты пожива́ешь?
3 Ми́ша, хоти́те во́дку?
4 О́ля, пойдём со мной в теа́тр.
5 Скажи́те, рестора́н в теа́тре откры́т?
6 И́горь, э́то ва́ша газе́та?

7 А вам, Ни́на, чай и́ли ко́фе?
  То́же ко́фе?
8 Ю́рий Ива́нович, это мой
  оте́ц.
9 Алло́, Ве́ра, это О́ля.
10 Что вам, чай и́ли ко́фе?
   Чай, да?
11 Здра́вствуйте, как вы
   пожива́ете?

Unit 11

EXERCISE 4
– Здра́вствуйте, дороги́е друзья́.
  Я ваш экскурсово́д. Меня́
  зову́т Дми́трий Никола́евич
  Пу́хов – Ди́ма. Сего́дня у́жин
  в 8 часо́в. За́втра, зна́чит,
  в суббо́ту, с 8.00 до 9.10
  за́втрак.
– Когда́ бу́дет экску́рсия по
  Москве́?
– Экску́рсия бу́дет с 9.30 до
  12.00 часо́в.
– Что бу́дет в 14.30?
– В 14.30 мы бу́дем в зоопа́рке.
  Пото́м в 19 часо́в - Большо́й
  теа́тр и в 23.00 часа́ у́жин.
– В воскресе́нье, 9-ого ию́ля с
  8.00 до 9.00 - за́втрак. По́сле
  за́втрака в 10 часо́в экску́рсия
  по Кремлю́. В 13 часо́в - обе́д.

Unit 13

EXERCISE 6

1
– Скажи́те, пожа́луйста, как
  мне дое́хать до Петродворца́?
– Мо́жно на электри́чке с
  Балти́йского вокза́ла до
  ста́нции «Но́вый Петерго́ф».
– Ско́лько мину́т идёт
  электри́чка?
– Три́дцать пять.
– А пото́м мо́жно пешко́м?
– Лу́чше на авто́бусе но́мер
  три́ста пятьдеся́т и́ли три́ста
  пятьдеся́т оди́н.
– Спаси́бо.
– Пожа́луйста.

2
– Скажи́те, пожа́луйста, как
  мне дое́хать до Па́вловска?
– Мо́жно на электри́чке с
  Ви́тебского вокза́ла до
  ста́нции «Па́вловск».
– Ско́лько мину́т идёт
  электри́чка?
– Три́дцать пять.

– А пото́м мо́жно пешко́м?
– Мо́жно че́рез парк, мо́жно
  та́кже на авто́бусе но́мер
  три́ста се́мьдесят и́ли три́ста
  во́семьдесят три.
– Спаси́бо.
– Пожа́луйста.

3
– Скажи́те, пожа́луйста, как
  мне дое́хать до Ца́рского
  Села́?
– Мо́жно на электри́чке с
  Ви́тебского вокза́ла до
  ста́нции «Де́тское Село́».
– Ско́лько мину́т идёт
  электри́чка?
– Два́дцать пять.
– А пото́м мо́жно пешко́м?
– Лу́чше на авто́бусе но́мер
  три́ста се́мьдесят оди́н и́ли
  три́ста во́семьдесят два.
– Спаси́бо.
– Пожа́луйста.

4
– Скажи́те, пожа́луйста, как
  мне дое́хать до Ломоно́сова?
– Мо́жно на электри́чке с
  Балти́йского вокза́ла до
  ста́нции «Ораниенба́ум ».
– Ско́лько мину́т идёт
  электри́чка?
– Пятьдеся́т пять.
– А пото́м мо́жно пешко́м?
– Мо́жно.
– Спаси́бо.
– Пожа́луйста.

Unit 15

EXERCISE 7
1 В 1917 г. Октя́брьская
  револю́ция.
2 В 1924 г. у́мер Влади́мир
  Ильи́ч Ле́нин.
3 В 1945 г. ко́нчилась Вели́кая
  Оте́чественная война́.
4 В 1953 г. у́мер Ио́сиф
  Виссарио́нович Ста́лин.
5 В 1991 г. распа́лся Сове́тский
  Сою́з.

Unit 18

EXERCISE 3

1
– Мне, пожа́луйста, Воло́дину,
  Ната́лью Петро́вну.
– Она́ сейча́с рабо́тает в
  поликли́нике но́мер два́дцать
  два.

– А вы не зна́ете телефо́н?
– Две́сти девяно́сто во́семь
  шестьдеся́т шесть три́дцать
  во́семь.
– Спаси́бо.
– Пожа́луйста.

2
– Мне, пожа́луйста, Воло́дину,
  Ната́лью Петро́вну.
– Она́ сейча́с рабо́тает
  в поликли́нике но́мер
  шестьдеся́т семь.
– А вы не зна́ете телефо́н?
– Четы́реста се́мьдесят
  два́дцать оди́н се́мьдесят
  оди́н.
– Спаси́бо.
– Пожа́луйста.

3
– Мне, пожа́луйста, Воло́дину,
  Ната́лью Петро́вну.
– Она́ сейча́с рабо́тает в
  поликли́нике но́мер девяно́сто
  три.
– А вы не зна́ете телефо́н?
– Сто три́дцать два со́рок
  четы́ре шестьдеся́т семь.
– Спаси́бо.
– Пожа́луйста.

4
– Мне, пожа́луйста, Воло́дину,
  Ната́лью Петро́вну.
– Она́ сейча́с рабо́тает
  в поликли́нике но́мер
  во́семьдесят оди́н.
– А вы не зна́ете телефо́н?
– Три́ста пятна́дцать два́дцать
  пять де́сять.
– Спаси́бо.
– Пожа́луйста.

5
– Мне, пожа́луйста, Воло́дину,
  Ната́лью Петро́вну.
– Она́ сейча́с рабо́тает в
  поликли́нике но́мер пятьдеся́т
  четы́ре.
– А вы не зна́ете телефо́н?
– Пятьсо́т со́рок два девяно́сто
  два́дцать пять.
– Спаси́бо.
– Пожа́луйста.

6
– Мне, пожа́луйста, Воло́дину,
  Ната́лью Петро́вну.
– Да, это я.

Key to the exercises

Unit 1

EXERCISE 2
1 pay
2 an airmail letter
3 traffic stops
4 Nevsky Prospekt
5 такси
6 tea

EXERCISE 3
1 Éто такси.
2 Éто ресторáн.
3 Éто теáтр.
4 Éто парк.
5 Éто метрó.
6 Éто винó.
7 Éто пáпа.
8 Éто мáма.
9 Éто пианúст.
10 Éто оркéстр.

EXERCISE 5
1 Нет, éто не пáпа, éто тáкси.
2 Нет, éто не пианúст, éто ресторáн.
3 Нет, éто не парк, éто теáтр.
4 Нет, éто не винó, éто парк.
5 Нет, éто не оркéстр, éто метрó.
6 Нет, éто не такси, éто винó.
7 Нет, éто не мáма, éто пáпа.
8 Нет, éто не теáтр, éто мáма.
9 Нет, éто не ресторáн, éто пианúст.
10 Нет, éто не метрó, éто оркéстр.

EXERCISE 6
1 7   6 1
2 9   7 8
3 4   8 3
4 6   9 2
5 10   10 5

EXERCISE 7
1 оркéстр 10   6 парк 4
2 винó 6   7 мáма 8
3 пáпа 7   8 метрó 5
4 такси 1   9 пианúст 9
5 ресторáн 2 10 теáтр 3

EXERCISE 8
The Bolshoi Theatre

EXERCISE 9
1 Films
2 Beer
3 City Bank
4 Кáнторов
5 taxi and underground

PLAYING WITH WORDS
1 спорт   4 нет
2 теáтр   5 такси
3 ресторáн

Unit 2

EXERCISE 2
1 7   6 1
2 8   7 14
3 4   8 3
4 6   9 2
5 10   10 5

EXERCISE 3
1 3   6 12
2 5   7 13
3 9   8 2
4 10   9 1
5 11   10 6

EXERCISE 4
1 Вот он. (orchestra)
2 Вот он. (father)
3 Вот онá. (mother)
4 Вот он. (pianist)
5 Вот он. (table)
6 Вот онá. (vodka)
7 Вот онá. (water)
8 Вот онó. (wine)
9 Вот онó. (beer)

EXERCISE 6
Toronto is in Canada.
The Dynamo stadium is in Moscow.
Ivan is in London.
Madrid is in Spain.
Nina is in the Caucasus.
Kiev is in the Ukraine.

EXERCISE 7
Dialogue:
Мáма, éто Víktor.
Zdrástvuyte, Óchen' ráda.
Zdrástvuyte, Óchen' rad.
Pápa, éto Víktor.
Zdrástvuyte. Óchen' rad.
Zdrástvuyte. Óchen' rad.

Expressions from the table:
Как вас зовýт?
Spasíbo
Nichevó.
Как мáма?

WORD SQUARE 1
1 КАВКАЗ
2 ЗООПАРК
3 КИНО
4 ОПЕРА
5 АППАРАТ
6 ТЕАТР
7 РЕСТОРАН
8 НОМЕР

WORD SQUARE 2
КАКАО
ВИСКИ
КВАС
СУП
ЛИМОНАД
ПИВО
ВИНО
ВОДА
ВОДКА

Unit 3

EXERCISE 2
1 11   6 27
2 4   7 20
3 5   8 16
4 9   9 7
5 15   10 2

EXERCISE 3
1 15   6 26
2 6   7 17
3 20   8 10
4 8   9 14
5 7   10 22

EXERCISE 4
1 ←   5 →
2 →   6 ←
3 ←   7 ←
4 →   8 →

EXERCISE 5

1	→	←	↑		
2	↑	→	←	↑	✓
3	→	→	↑		
4	←	→	→		✓
5	→	→	←	↑	

EXERCISE 6
1 4   4 3
2 5   5 1
3 5

EXERCISE 7
1 VSEGDÁ   4 SEYCHÁS
2 зáвтра   5 VSEGDÁ
3 SEVÓDNYA

EXERCISE 8
1 No
2 Tomorrow
3 Always
4 Repairs
5 Beer, wine and vodka

ALPHABET GAME
1 ФУТБОЛ   4 БЮРО
2 КАФЕ   5 ВХОД
3 ФОТО

JUMBLED WORDS
1 МЕНЮ
2 ДИНАМО
3 ПЕРЕХОД
4 ТЕЛЕФОН
5 УНИВЕРСИТЕТ

Unit 4

EXERCISE 2
1 15   6 17
2 11   7 22
3 18   8 13
4 6   9 4
5 2   10 9

EXERCISE 3
1 17   6 10
2 8   7 2
3 15   8 6
4 21   9 13
5 16   10 5

EXERCISE 4

1 Don't walk on the grass!
2 No entry!
3 Don't take photographs!
4 No exit!
5 No smoking here!
6 No crossing!
7 No smoking!

EXERCISE 5

1 – Биле́т мо́zнно?
 – Pozhа́lsta. Вот он.
 –Спаси́бо.
2 – Во́дку мо́zнно?
 – Pozhа́lsta. Вот она́.
 – Спаси́бо.
3 – Грибы́ мо́zнно?
 – Pozhа́lsta. Вот они́.
 – Спаси́бо.
4 – Ма́рку мо́zнно?
 – Pozhа́lsta. Вот она́.
 – Спаси́бо.
5 – Стака́н мо́zнно?
 – Pozhа́lsta. Вот он.
 – Спаси́бо.
6 – Телефо́н мо́zнно?
 – Pozhа́lsta. Вот он.
 – Спаси́бо.

EXERCISE 6

1 Natasha (Ната́ша)
2 Yes (Да)
3 Igor (И́горь)
4 To go to the theatre (Идти́ в теа́тр)
5 She is busy (Она́ занята́)
6 Tomorrow (За́втра)

JUMBLED WORDS 1

1 ГРИБЫ
2 ПРОГРАММА
3 ЭНЕРГИЯ
4 АЭРОФЛОТ
5 ВЫХОД
Hidden word:ГОРОД

JUMBLED WORDS 2

1 ГАЗЕТА
2 АВТОБУС
3 ЭКСПРЕСС
4 РОССИЯ
5 ЭКСКУРСИЯ
6 ИЗВЕСТИЯ
Hidden word: ТУРИСТ

MATCHING SYMBOLS

1 САМОЛЁТ
2 БИЛЕТ
3 РОССИЯ
4 ВЫХОД
5 НЕДЕЛЯ

Unit 5

EXERCISE 2

1 4	6 10
2 12	7 26
3 22	8 6
4 19	9 3
5 5	10 16

EXERCISE 3

1 16	6 20
2 6	7 22
3 15	8 17
4 21	9 25
5 12	10 7

EXERCISE 4

В па́рке идёт конце́рт.
В кино́ идёт фильм.
В Большо́м теа́тре идёт о́пера.
В университе́те идёт ле́кция.

EXERCISE 5

1 agency
2 piracy
3 hooliganism
4 administration
5 mobilisation
6 concentration
7 confederation
8 revolution

EXERCISE 6

Он в рестора́не.
Он в теа́тре.
Она́ в па́рке.
Они́ в па́рке.
Она́ в Москве́.
Он в зоопа́рке.
Она́ в апте́ке.
Он в рестора́не.
Он в кварти́ре.
Он в автома́те.

EXERCISE 7

1 в Росси́и
2 в це́нтре Москвы́
3 входи́ть
4 входи́ть
5 вхо́да
6 матч

EXERCISE 8

автобусы 4
туале́т(м) 8
ка́сса 1
вы́ход 3
метро́ 6
не кури́ть 10
такси́ 5
Ни́на 2
туале́т(ж) 9
телефо́н-автома́т 7

JUMBLED WORDS 1

1 МОЖНО
2 ПОЧТА
3 ЧЕХОВ
4 ЦИРК
5 МУЖЧИНА
6 ОПЕРА

JUMBLED WORDS 2

1 ЧАЙКА
2 ШОССЕ
3 ИНФОРМАЦИЯ
4 ЦЕНТР
5 ЖЕНЩИНА
6 ХОРОШО
7 МАТЧ
8 КОНЦЕРТ

Unit 6

EXERCISE 2

биле́ты 2	ма́рки 6
пи́во 3	жето́ны 10
откры́тки 5	

EXERCISE 3

восемна́дцать 18
двена́дцать 12
девятна́дцать 19
оди́ннадцать 11
пятна́дцать 15
семна́дцать 17
трина́дцать 13
четы́рнадцать 14
шестна́дцать 16

EXERCISE 4

во́семьдесят 80
два́дцать 20
девяно́сто 90
пятьдеся́т 50
се́мьдесят 70
три́дцать 30
шестьдеся́т 60
со́рок 40

EXERCISE 5

две́сти 200
пятьсо́т 500
семьсо́т 700
три́ста 300
восемьсо́т 800
четы́реста 400
девятьсо́т 900
шестьсо́т 600
сто 100

EXERCISE 6

1 in		6	into
2 in/at		7	at
3 to		8	to
4 to		9	into/onto
5 in		10	in

EXERCISE 7

Покажи́те, пожа́луйста
Да́йте, пожа́луйста

1 во́дку и вино́
2 ма́рку и откры́тку
3 кни́гу и газе́ту
4 стака́н и ча́шку
5 самова́р и чай

EXERCISE 8

1 Tickets to the Bolshoi Theatre (Биле́ты в Большо́й теа́тр)
2 It's closed just now (Сейча́с закры́т)
3 The circus (Цирк)
4 Yes, it's possible (Да, мо́жно)
5 Three tickets (Три биле́та)

Crossword

Across

1 де́вять
5 нет
6 я
8 три
10 да
11 бале́т
13 во
14 ша́пка
17 эта́ж
19 автома́т
21 щи
22 он
23 но́мер
25 буфе́т
26 дом
27 тасс
29 Оде́сса
30 стоп
31 бу́тсы
32 она́

Down

1 де́вушка
2 вот
3 три
4 кафе́
7 оно́
9 рок
12 а́том
13 вы
15 плане́та
16 авто́бус
17 э́тот
18 Дина́мо
20 анекдо́т
24 ра́да
27 тот
28 суп

PUT THINGS IN THEIR PLACE
Де́вушка в Оде́ссе
Ша́пка на де́вушке
Бу́тсы в авто́бусе
Она́ в но́мере (hotel room)

FIND THE CLUE
но́мер шесть
но́мер оди́н
но́мер во́семь
но́мер два
но́мер де́вять
но́мер пять
но́мер три (во́семь)
но́мер де́сять
но́мер четы́ре and но́мер семь are missing.

Unit 7

EXERCISE 1
1 Ле́нин (Lenin)
2 Ста́лин (Stalin)
3 Хрущёв (Khrushchev)
4 Горбачёв (Gorbachev)
5 Е́льцин (Yeltsin)
6 Пу́тин (Putin)

EXERCISE 2
1 Алексе́й Бори́сович
2 Ни́на Алексе́евна
3 Серге́й Па́влович
4 Ива́н Никола́евич
5 А́нна Ива́новна

EXERCISE 3
1 здра́вствуй
2 здра́вствуйте
3 здра́вствуйте
4 здра́вствуй
5 здра́вствуйте
6 здра́вствуй
7 здра́вствуйте

EXERCISE 4
1 Vera
2 Five
3 Postcards
4 Ten
5 He's an engineer
6 She's an engineer as well
They are on 'ты' terms

EXERCISE 5
1 Росси́я больша́я страна́
2 Оли́мпус япо́нский фотоаппара́т
3 Де́вушка, у вас есть кра́сное вино́?
4 Москва́ росси́йская столи́ца

5 На столе́ францу́зское шампа́нское
6 Дина́мовцы хоро́шие футболи́сты
7 Нью-Йорк Таймс америка́нская газе́та
8 Бори́с Годуно́в ру́сский царь
9 Оде́сса украи́нский порт
10 Ма́нчестер англи́йский го́род
(Other combinations may be possible, but make sure they all fit in!)

EXERCISE 6
1 Russia   5 Ukraine
2 England   6 Poland
3 USA   7 Canada
4 Germany 8 France

Reading handwriting
СУВЕНИРЫ
ФОТОГРАФИЯ
СТОЛИЧНАЯ ВОДКА

Unit 8

EXERCISE 1
1 Мне хо́лодно. +1
2 Мне хо́лодно. -2
3 Мне тепло́. +7
4 Мне тепло́. +16
5 Мне хо́лодно. -22
6 Мне жа́рко. +23
(You may not agree: some people feel colder, or hotter, than others!)

EXERCISE 2
1 18.20   6 15.25
2 21.05   7 17.03
3 22.10   8 13.35
4 19.15   9 02.49
5 12.22   10 10.55

EXERCISE 3
1 09.00 часо́в
2 15.00 часо́в
3 02.00 часа́
4 22.00 часа́
5 15.00 часо́в
6 12.00 часо́в
7 07.00 часо́в
8 20.00 часо́в
9 04.00 часа́

EXERCISE 4
1 18.00 News
2 21.00 Vremya – the main news programme
3 19.50 Who Wants to be a Millionaire?

4 23.00 Thriller *Mr Frost*
5 14.00 Football Russian Championship Dinamo, Spartak live broadcast
6 16.00 Gala Concert
7 18.30 Serial: *Mistress of Fate*, part 33

EXERCISE 5
1 14.00: Lokomotiv Moscow and Chelsea
2 23.10
3 Paul McCartney in Red Square
4 17.10
5 20.20
6 21.30
7 18.00 and 21.00

EXERCISE 6
1 Я игра́ю в футбо́л.
2 Он/она́ лю́бит игра́ть на гита́ре.
3 Вы гуля́ете в па́рке.
4 Они́ говоря́т по-ру́сски.
5 Он/она́ говори́т по-англи́йски.
6 Ты смо́тришь телеви́зор.
7 Мы не зна́ем.

EXERCISE 7
1 Потому́ что идёт ремо́нт.
2 Потому́ что там хорошо́.
3 Потому́ что хорошо́ игра́ю.
4 Потому́ что она́ краси́вая.
5 Потому́ что сего́дня ми́нус 20 гра́дусов.
6 Потому́ что он о́чень краси́вый го́род.

EXERCISE 8
1 video-camera (camcorder)
2 distributor
3 investor
4 yoghurt
5 college
6 computer
7 printer
8 radiator
9 safe
10 supermarket
11 charter
12 shop-tour (shopping trip, usually abroad)

EXERCISE 9
1 Doctor

2 Walking
3 Watches TV
4 Films and sport
5 Ice-hockey

Reading handwriting
The advertisement in your office
British tea in Russia
'Fiat' car repairs
ШЕКСПИР
ЧАСЫ

WORD SQUARE
ФАКС
ДИЛЕР
ДИСК
КСЕРОКС
МАНГО
КОТТЕДЖ
КЛИЕНТ
КОД
ОФИС
ДОК

Unit 9

EXERCISE 1
Miss Benson 37/2/9/17/21/28
Mr Brown 24/4/8/16/20/25
Mr Smith 35/11/13/22/33/27
Mr Hart 34/7/12/23/31/26

EXERCISE 2
1 Yes
2 7 o'clock
3 Fish
4 Black caviar
5 Coffee and brandy
6 He loves Russian champagne
7 Very hefty!

EXERCISE 3
чёрная икра́ 7
шампа́нское 8
ку́рица 11
фру́кты 9
ры́ба 6
вода́ 1
сала́т 4
шашлы́к 12
ко́фе 3
моро́женое 5
грибы́ 2
во́дка 10

EXERCISE 4
Black caviar, tomatoes, sausage, ham, cucumbers and smetana (sour

cream), sturgeon.
The main course is
chicken and potatoes

EXERCISE 5
1 mushrooms
2 bill
3 newspaper
4 ticket
5 flowers
6 chicken
7 bread
8 samovar
9 beer

PLAYING WITH WORDS
КАРП
ЗАКУСКИ
ПЛОВ
СОК
СУП
ЯИЧНИЦА
САЛАТ
КОТЛЕТ
ЛИМОН
ИКРА

MISSING LETTERS
1 Шампа́нское ру́сское (полусухо́е)
2 Сарди́ны в ма́сле
3 Сала́т из помидо́ров
4 Сок тома́тный
5 Бифште́кс натура́льный
6 Икра́ (кра́сная)
7 Вода́ минера́льная
8 Чай с лимо́ном
9 Хлеб с ма́слом

Reading handwriting
ЭКСПРЕСС
КАФЕ

Unit 10

EXERCISE 1
1 В   4 А
2 Г   5 Б
3 Б   6 Б

EXERCISE 2
1 столе́
2 смо́трит
3 чита́ет
4 идёт
5 по

EXERCISE 3
1 c   5 e
2 b   6 g
3 a   7 f
4 d

EXERCISE 4
1 Good books on Russian cathedrals and monasteries
2 Books on Moscow cathedrals, and those in Vladimir and Suzdal
3 Are they in English or only in Russian?
4 A beautiful book about Rublyov
5 He has to rush off

EXERCISE 5
Хорошо́, а вы? 11
Нет, сейча́с закры́т. 5
Иди́те пря́мо, пото́м нале́во. 1
Нет, то́лько лимона́д. 3
Ничего́, а ты? 2
Здра́вствуйте, о́чень рад. 8
Нет, да́йте, пожа́луйста, ко́фе. 10
Нет, не хочу́. Я сего́дня занята́. 4
Нет, не моя́. 6
Нет, да́йте, пожа́луйста, чай. 7
Оля, приве́т! Как дела́? 9

EXERCISE 6
1 9 ✓ Fisherman's
2 5 Black Stream
3 6 ✓ Ladoga (lake)
4 10 Academic
5 4 ✓ Alexander Nevsky Sq (Russian prince)
6 5 Moscow
7 2 Nevsky Prospect
8 2 Narva (battle of Peter the Great)
9 9 Polytechnic
10 4 ✓ Seaside
11 6 ✓ Lomonosov (Great Russian scholar)
12 2 Dostoyevsky

Crossword
Across
1 простите
7 и
10 мне
12 ага
14 стоит
16 пунш
17 этот
19 но
20 арест
22 но
23 АН
24 Риге
25 от
27 ничего
29 так
33 по
35 нравится
37 Дон
38 не
39 Оля
41 ГУМ
42 на
43 гулять
45 любят
51 бар
52 хор
53 за
54 том
55 часов
Down
1 пив
2 ресторане
3 ост
4 смотрю
5 татарин
6 МГУ
7 и
8 не
9 десять
11 Нина
13 АН
15 тонна
16 при
18 они
21 сегодня
22 нота
26 девять
28 час
30 кроль
31 да
32 оян
33 по
34 она
36 Тула
40 ля
43 газ
44 ура
46 Юра
47 бис
48 то
49 Ира
50 по
51 Бр

Unit 11

EXERCISE 1
Fri 16 June
Tues 10 November
Mon 25 April
Sat 1 July
Wed 30 December
Sun 13 October
Thurs 29 January

EXERCISE 2
1 суббо́ту
2 понеде́льник

3 воскресе́нье
4 сре́ду
5 пя́тницу
6 четве́рг
7 вто́рник

EXERCISE 3
1 часо́в   8 часа́
2 за́втрака   9 обе́да
3 Москве́   10 часо́в
4 це́нтре   11 у́жина
5 го́рода   12 ку́хне
6 обе́да   13 футбо́ле
7 па́рке

EXERCISE 4
1 9.30–12   4 23.00
2 зоопа́рк   5 10.00
3 19.00   6 обе́д

EXERCISE 5
1 a 8.30–19.30
  b 10.00–18.00
  c 14.00–15.00
2 a 10.00–22.00
  b 10.00–22.00
3 a Tuesday, Thursday Saturday
  b 17.00–20.00 (Tuesday and Thursday),10.00–15.00 (Saturday)
4 a Monday to Friday
  b 20.00
  c 13.00–14.00

EXERCISE 6
1 Hong Kong
2 Hitler
3 Holland
4 Hamlet
5 Copenhagen

EXERCISE 7
Ива́н (зимо́й) goes to the stadium to watch ice-hockey; (ле́том) works at the dacha on Saturdays and watches football every evening.
Ири́на (зимо́й) goes to concerts in the Conservatoire; (ле́том) works with her husband at the dacha and reads novels in the evenings.
Бо́ря (зимо́й) plays chess; (ле́том) plays chess.
Ма́ша (зимо́й) listens to rock music; (ле́том) sunbathes at the dacha.

EXERCISE 8

1 **a** Bolshoi Theatre
b *Evgeniy (Eugene) Onegin*
c 7.30
2 **a** *Resurrection*
b Tolstoy
c 7.30
3 *Jesus Christ Superstar* and *Hamlet*
4 **a** *Coppelia*
b Saturday
c Delibes
5 **a** *Seagull*
b Friday
6 Nothing, it's closed!

Unit 12

EXERCISE 1

1 1113–25
2 1147
3 1223
4 1227
5 1240–1480
6 Ivan IV became tsar
7 Boris Godunov
8 Peter went to Holland and Britain
9 Founding of St Petersburg
10 War with Napoleon
11 1861
12 1917
13 1924
14 1953
15 1991

EXERCISE 2

1 The past tense after я ends in -л
2 Each time a **я** form (first person singular) occurs, add **-а** to the end of the verb

EXERCISE 3

1 была́   4 была́
2 был/-а́   5 был
3 бы́ли   6 бы́ли

EXERCISE 4

1 Coffee and egg
2 Read a newspaper in the library
3 Watched a film; she enjoyed the film
4 Physics
5 Mushrooms
6 In a bank

EXERCISE 5

1 бу́дем обе́дать
2 чита́л/а
3 бу́дет смотре́ть
4 гуля́ли
5 игра́ла
6 бу́дете игра́ть
7 сдала́
8 рабо́тает

EXERCISE 6

1
a рома́н «Война́ и мир»
b стихи́ «Я вас люби́л»
c рома́н «Отцы́ и де́ти»
d пье́су «Ревизо́р»
e рома́н «Преступле́ние и наказа́ние»
f пье́су «Три сестры́»
2
a Никола́й
b Серге́й
c Серге́й
d Васи́лий
e Михаи́л
f Па́вел
3
a Пу́шкин
b Го́голь
c Достое́вский
d Турге́нев
e Толсто́й
f Евге́ний Оне́гин
g Ревизо́р
h Отцы́ и де́ти
i Преступле́ние и наказа́ние, Идио́т, Бра́тья Карама́зовы
j Ча́йка, Три сестры́, Дя́дя Ва́ня, Вишнёвый сад

Unit 13

EXERCISE 1

a Kiev   **b** Moscow
Smolensk   Finland
Kursk   Baltic
Yaroslavl   Warsaw

EXERCISE 2

1 The ticket office
2 St Petersburg
3 In the big hall on the left

EXERCISE 3

1 Today
2 Sleeper in a compartment
3 No 6 at 23.10 or No 2 at 23.55
4 No 2 'Red Arrow'
5 Platform 1

EXERCISE 4

1 48   5 14 or 28
2 48   6 28
3 160   7 6
4 160   8 2

EXERCISE 5

1 **a** Tambov
b Yes
c 92
2 **a** Murmansk
b No
c 186
3 Novgorod
4 Underground
5 Exit to the town or Metro

EXERCISE 6

1 Петродворе́ц, Балти́йский; Но́вый Петерго́ф; 35; 350/1
2 Па́вловск; Ви́тебский; Па́вловск; 35; 370/383 or on foot
3 Ца́рское Село́; Ви́тебский; Де́тское село́; 25; 371/382
4 Ломоно́сов; Балти́йский; Ораниенба́ум; 55; on foot

EXERCISE 7

1 се́вере   4 се́вере
2 восто́ке   5 за́паде
3 се́вере   6 се́вере

EXERCISE 8

1 to go away (on foot)
2 to go away (by vehicle)
3 to depart (of a train, etc.)
4 departure (vehicle)
5 departure (on foot)
6 departure (of train, etc.)

EXERCISE 9

1 to go out (on foot) **из**
2 to drive (a vehicle) out **из**
3 entrance (pedestrian) **в**
4 exit (pedestrian) **из**
5 entry (vehicle) **в**
6 exit (vehicle) **из**

Reading

Moscow

1 About ten million
2 Books, records, cassettes and CDs

St Petersburg

1 They are straight and wide
2 It is a very large museum and art gallery, where there are paintings by Western artists
3 Nevsky Prospekt; the River Neva

Yaroslavl

1 By train; five hours
2 **a** Sixteenth century
b 1010

Unit 14

EXERCISE 1

1 Moscow University (MGU)
2 20th June, 2005
3 3 months (90 days)
4 Alan Smith
5 London
6 20

EXERCISE 2

1 Julia Thomas (single-entry), James Morgan (multi-entry)
2 Tourism
3 Domodedovo, Moscow
4 Cultural links
5 St Petersburg

EXERCISE 3

1 On the left in the corner
2 He doesn't like queues
3 Twenty minutes
4 No
5 In dollars
6 Two dollars

EXERCISE 4

1 ✓ books
2 Saturdays and Sundays

EXERCISE 5

1 false, she wants to buy for her parents as well
2 true, a son and daughter
3 true, he is six, she is eight
4 false, she wants typical Russian ones
5 true, it is an old street with lots of character
6 true, they sell lots of souvenirs
7 false, there is a minibus
8 true, she bought a book about architecture
9 false, the book is in English
10 false, New Arbat is better for books and CDs

EXERCISE 6
1 ма́ленькая су́мка
  моско́вский аэропо́рт
  но́вые теле́жки
2 де́тская игру́шка
  кра́сный кана́л
  университе́тское
  приглаше́ние
3 хоро́шие но́вости
  чёрная икра́
  прия́тный тамо́женник

EXERCISE 7
1 Он хоте́л бы пойти́, но
  рестора́н сего́дня
  закры́т.
2 Они́ хоте́ли бы пойти́,
  но библиоте́ка сего́дня
  закры́та.
3 Он хоте́л бы пойти́, но
  кино́ сего́дня закры́то.
4 Она́ хоте́ла бы пойти́,
  но стадио́н сего́дня
  закры́т.
5 Он хоте́л бы пойти́, но
  кафе́ сего́дня закры́то.

EXERCISE 8
1 In the university in
  St Petersburg
2 Stroll along the Nevsky
  Prospekt and drink juice
  in a small cafe
3 Her father was giving
  lectures at London
  University
4 In a large comfortable
  hotel
5 Trafalgar Square and
  Downing Street
6 Washington and New
  York
7 Visit the White House
  and the Empire State
  Building, and go up to
  the 102nd floor

EXERCISE 9
1 atomic energy
2 bookshop
3 entry visa
4 Nevsky Prospekt
5 'beer bar'
6 Cathedral square
7 telephone conversation
8 library day

Unit 15

EXERCISE 1
1 Moscow State University
2 State Universal Shop
  (store)
3 Department of Visas
  and the Registration of
  Foreign Citizens
4 Moscow Arts
  (Academic) Theatre

EXERCISE 2
1 Moscow city transport
2 Ministry of Finance
3 State insurance company
4 Industrial Construction
  Bank
5 Russian Telecom

EXERCISE 3
1 N.V. Gogol
2 P.I. Tchaikovsky
3 M.V. Lomonosov
4 A.S. Pushkin
5 D.D. Shostakovich
6 N.A. Rimsky-Korsakov
7 Peter the Great

EXERCISE 4
1 1223   5 1861
2 1547   6 1941
3 1605   7 1999
4 1703

EXERCISE 5
1 Genghis Khan and the
  Mongol army defeated
  the Slavs
  Чингисха́н и
  монго́льская а́рмия
  разби́ли славя́нскую
  а́рмию
2 Ivan IV became tsar
  Ива́н IV стал царём
3 Boris Godunov died
  Бори́с Годуно́в у́мер
4 Founding of
  St Petersburg
  Основа́ние Санкт-
  Петербу́рга
5 Peasant reform
  Крестья́нская рефо́рма
6 Second world war
  Вели́кая Оте́чественная
  война́ (literally the
  Great Patriotic War)
7 Yeltsin resigned

EXERCISE 6
1 В 1227 г. у́мер
  Чингисха́н.
2 В 1914 г. начала́сь
  пе́рвая мирова́я война́.

3 В 1697 г. Пётр
  Вели́кий пое́хал в
  Голла́ндию.
4 В 1945 г. ко́нчилась
  Вели́кая
  Оте́чественная война́.
5 В 1480 г. ко́нчилось
  тата́рское и́го.
6 В 1796 г. умерла́
  Екатери́на II.

EXERCISE 7
1 **1917**: October
  revolution
2 **1924**: Lenin died
3 **1945**: end of the
  Second World War
4 **1953**: death of Stalin
5 **1991**: The end of the
  Soviet Union

EXERCISE 8
1
1 j   7 g
2 b   8 f
3 h   9 i
4 d   10 l
5 a   11 c
6 k   12 e
2
a В сентябре́
b Бори́сов, Ива́н
  Никола́евич
c Во вто́рник
d В лаборато́рии и в
  библиоте́ке
e Нет, америка́нский
f В Санкт-Петербу́рге

EXERCISE 9
Лёвин: **9.35**
Алексе́ева: **15.32**
Сега́ль: **20.50**
Моро́зова: **24.00**
Есе́нин: **03.55**
Петро́ва: **17.59**

Unit 16

EXERCISE 1
1 Watches
2 10.00–19.00
3 Flats and dachas
4 a guarantee and credit

EXERCISE 2
1 Clothes
2 Charm (Sharm)

EXERCISE 3
a International Language
  Centre 'English for All'
b Trip to England to
  study at a Scarborough
  language school
c Three weeks

EXERCISE 4
Some of the items sold by
Savar Electronics are:
computers, printers, laser
printers, fax machines,
telephones, mobile phones,
televisions, video players,
camcorders, false banknote
detectors, ultraviolet lamps,
calculators, and as the ad
says, 'much more'!
Fax number: 165-16-83

EXERCISE 5
1 бо́льше лю́бят ви́ски,
  чем во́дку.
2 бо́льше лю́бят вино́,
  чем пи́во.
3 ме́ньше лю́бят чай с
  лимо́ном, чем с
  мо́локом.
4 ме́ньше лю́бят хлеб,
  чем рис.
5 бо́льше лю́бят
  бейсбо́л, чем кри́кет.
6 бо́льше икры́, чем в
  Ита́лии.

EXERCISE 6
1 ху́же. (англича́нин)
2 меньше. (америка́нец)
3 бо́льше. (ру́сский)
4 бо́льше. (шотла́ндец)

EXERCISE 7
1 бо́льше нра́вится
2 пое́дем на
  тролле́йбусе
3 пойти́ в четве́рг
4 хоте́л(а) бы
5 бо́льше нра́вится

EXERCISE 8
1 Edinburgh
2 Wine, champagne,
  beer, cocktails, brandy
3 He thinks Russian
  women drink less
4 Because they are not
  wearing the kilt
5 That it is a national
  costume worn by
  soldiers and men on
  special days
6 The theatre

183

Unit 17

EXERCISE 1
1 Thailand and Malaysia
2 Spain (Costa Brava, Costa Dorada, Costa del Sol, Costa Blanca)
3 from 7839 roubles
4 from 17869 roubles
5 Salzburg and Vienna
6 Maldives, Seychelles, Mauritius
7 Spain, Italy, France, England

EXERCISE 2
1 Seaside holidays
2 Comfortable hotels, prestige resorts, excursions, magnificent relaxation and entertainment
3 Spain, Turkey, Italy, Israel, Greece, Cyprus, Bulgaria, Malta, Egypt, Majorca
4 Reasonable, child discounts
5 in comfort, without any problems

EXERCISE 3
1 New Year
2 Wedding day
3 Congratulations!
4 Christmas
5 New Year

EXERCISE 4
1 Before exams
2 Before a meal
3 On a birthday
4 Any time (success)
5 On a birthday (long life)
6 At night
7 Before bed

EXERCISE 5
1 New Year's greeting
2 Success, health and more trips to St Petersburg

EXERCISE 6
1 Нóвым гóдом
2 днём рождéния
3 горя́чий привéт
4 Поздравля́ю
5 Целýю и обнима́ю
6 Всегó хорóшего (дóброго/лýчшего)

EXERCISE 7
1 dramatise
2 emigrate
3 register
4 plan
5 regulate
6 pack

EXERCISE 8
1 Around the whole of Europe
2 By car
3 It was very beautiful with elegant houses
4 His surname is Italian
5 It was as expensive as Paris; petrol was very expensive

EXERCISE 9
1 Junior chess championship of the world
2 Graz, Austria
3 He is also a Russian, a former champion, and he came second, half a point behind.
4 Fries-Nilsen
5 France
6 Sergey Sukhoruchenkov; 42 h 26 min 28 sec.
7 Ramazan Galyaletdinov from Samara, Sergey Morozov from Moscow and Alexander Averin from Samara

CROSSWORD
Across
1 новым годом
10 во
11 она
12 боа
13 опера
15 по
17 май
18 ли
19 сети
20 обо
21 парк
22 за
23 Елена
25 днём рождения
30 рту
32 ие
33 чек
34 мода
35 а
36 Динамо
38 им
39 вне
40 газ
41 стол
42 Лене
43 Йорк
45 Отто
48 вид
50 тройка
51 он
52 юбка
53 самолёт

Down
1 но
2 он
3 вам
4 мой
5 гала
6 ОВИР
7 до
8 опера
9 метро
10 в Риме
12 бал
14 аллея
15 поздравляю
16 об Антоне
21 скидка
24 ночи
26 милые
27 жена
28 но
29 Идиот
31 ученик
37 о / т
40 гора
41 сок
44 ром
46 та
47 они
49 да
51 от

Unit 18

EXERCISE 1
1 I have got a sore throat
2 My arm hurts
3 My nose hurts
4 I have got a pain in my leg
5 I have toothache

EXERCISE 2
1 The service desk
2 The medical unit in the hotel
3 High temperature, sore throat, slight headache, no appetite
4 Orders tea with lemon
5 Looks at his throat and takes his temperature; writes out a prescription
6 Not very high
7 Tablets three times a day; rest in bed

EXERCISE 3
1 22 298 66 38
2 67 470 21 71
3 93 132 44 67
4 81 315 25 10
5 54 542 90 25

She works in health centre no. 54.

EXERCISE 4
1 2   6 8
2 1   7 6
3 7   8 3
4 9   9 4
5 5

EXERCISE 5
1 Емý хорошó
2 Тебé жáрко
3 Вам теплó
4 Нам плóхо
5 Мне хóлодно
6 Вам скýчно
7 Ей лýчше
8 Емý хýже
9 Им сты́дно

EXERCISE 6
1 b
2 c
3 a

EXERCISE 7
1 d   6 a
2 g   7 h
3 e   8 j
4 c   9 i
5 f   10 b

EXERCISE 8
1 Тáня должнá читáть э́ту кни́гу.
2 Ивáн дóлжен читáть э́ту кни́гу.
3 Тóля и Ира должны́ читáть э́ту кни́гу.
4 Ни́на Николáевна должнá читáть э́ту кни́гу.
5 Студéнт дóлжен читáть э́ту кни́гу.
6 Учени́ца должнá читáть э́ту кни́гу.
7 Вáня дóлжен читáть э́ту кни́гу.
8 Англичáнин дóлжен читáть э́ту кни́гу.
9 Мы должны́ читáть э́ту кни́гу.

10 Она́ должна́ чита́ть
   э́ту кни́гу.
11 Он до́лжен чита́ть
   э́ту кни́гу.
12 Вы должны́ чита́ть
   э́ту кни́гу.

Unit 19

EXERCISE 1
1 186 73 87
2 133 44 22 or 133 44 26
3 124 59 17 or 124 79 17
4 495 40 50
5 491 88 58
6 397 47 61
7 128 29 50 or 128 99 34

EXERCISE 3
1 927 84 03
2 Borshch
3 Natasha
4 Vodka
5 Go to Novgorod and the
  theatre
6 About 7

EXERCISE 4
1 Hotel 'Na Sadovoy'
2 319 96 91
3 Take the underground
  to Kupchino (last station)
  and then catch a
  trolleybus
4 She doesn't
5 Twenty to twenty-five
  minutes

EXERCISE 5
1 There are nine
  occurrences – входи́
  (twice), снима́й,
  проходи́ (four times),
  сади́сь and вы́пьем
2 It's raining outside
3 In the kitchen
4 It's so full of books it
  looks more like a library
5 To Sarah's visit (arrival),
  her husband, brothers,
  sisters and all his
  Scottish and American
  friends
6 To Volodya and
  Natasha

EXERCISE 6
1 За мои́х ру́сских
  друзе́й!
2 За Ва́ню!
3 За Са́шу!
4 За ва́ше (твоё)
  здоро́вье!

5 За хозя́йку!
6 За сча́стье!
7 За ваш (твой) день
  рожде́ния!

EXERCISE 7
1 Tomorrow
2 On Saturday
3 At Christmas
4 At Easter
5 In the morning
6 In the New Year
7 On Wednesday

Unit 20

EXERCISE 1
1
Дороги́е мои́! Вот мы с
ма́мой в Ло́ндоне! Здесь
о́чень интере́сно, но
пого́да не така́я хоро́шая,
как у вас в Москве́. Мы
бы́ли во мно́гих
интере́сных места́х.
Здесь о́чень мно́го
хоро́ших теа́тров. Вчера́
мы смотре́ли пье́су «Дя́дя
Ва́ня» — по-англи́йски!
Актёры о́чень хорошо́
игра́ли. Пото́м мы пошли́
в кита́йский рестора́н. Я
съел суп из кра́бов, а
пото́м креве́тки с гриба́ми
и с ри́сом. Все там пи́ли
кита́йский чай. Ма́ме там
бы́ло хорошо́, а мне не́
было. Я люблю́ на́ши
ру́сские блю́да! Хоте́ли
пообе́дать в типи́чном
англи́йском рестора́не, но
ка́жется там все
рестора́ны и́ли кита́йские,
и́ли францу́зские, и́ли
италья́нские!

Авто́бусы здесь кра́сные,
двухэта́жные, и их о́чень
мно́го. Здесь о́чень
мно́го такси́. Они́
больши́е, чёрные.

Ну, нам пора́! Бу́дьте
здоро́вы! Целу́ем!
Па́па и ма́ма

2 Moscow
3 It was a famous
  Russian play
4 To a Chinese restaurant
5 They didn't see one
6 Taxis and red double-
  decker buses

EXERCISE 2
2 краси́вые   7 бо́льше
3 нра́вится   8 бо́льше
4 столи́ца   9 ме́ньше
5 люблю́   10 ху́же
6 бо́льше   11 ду́маю

EXERCISE 3
1 Moscow
2 The one from
  St Petersburg
3 The palaces are beautiful
4 They are equal to the
  Moscow ones

EXERCISE 4
Фами́лия   4
И́мя   6
О́тчество   5
Да́та рожде́ния   9
Ме́сто рожде́ния 3
А́дрес   1
И́мя отца́   2
О́тчество отца́   7
Национа́льность 10
Профе́ссия   8

EXERCISE 5
С Но́вым го́дом!   5
С днём рожде́ния!   3
С пра́здником!   1
Прия́тного аппети́та! 2
Поздравля́ю!   4

EXERCISE 6
1 До́брое у́тро
  Здра́вствуйте/
  пожива́ете
2 Прия́тного аппети́та!
  Спаси́бо
3 всего́
  Всего́ хоро́шего/
  до́брого/лу́чшего
4 Споко́йной но́чи

EXERCISE 7
1 пло́хо
2 неё
3 хо́лодно
4 апте́ку
5 лека́рство

EXERCISE 8
1 День рожде́ния
  сестры́ в суббо́ту
  (It's his sister's
  birthday on Saturday)
2 Вино́ и во́дку (Wine
  and vodka)
3 Сто (A hundred)
4 Кот ду Рон (Cotes du
  Rhone)

5 Четы́реста пятьдеся́т
  рубле́й (450 roubles)
6 Двена́дцать. Даю́т
  ски́дку на двена́дцать
  (Twelve, because he
  gets a discount)
7 Столи́чная, Ру́сский
  станда́рт, и́мпортная
  (Stolichnaya, Russian
  Standard, imported)
8 И́мпортная Абсолю́т
  (imported Absolut)
9 четы́реста девяно́сто
  рубле́й (490 roubles)
10 В пя́тницу в
   оди́ннадцать часо́в
   утра́ (At 11am on
   Friday)

185

Russian–English vocabulary

The unit where each word first occurs, or is discussed in detail, is given after each word.

The gender for nouns is given, where not obvious from the ending. Foreign nouns, whose endings never change, are marked *indec* (indeclinable).

Verbs are given in the imperfective form first: покупáть*(imperfective)/*купи́ть *(perfective)* читáть/про- indicates that читáть is imperfective and прочитáть is perfective.

Abbreviations

+A + accusative case
+D + dative case
+G + genitive case
+I + instrumental case
+P + prepositional case
adj adjective
dim diminutive
f feminine
gen genitive
indec indeclinable
m masculine
n neuter
perf perfective
pl plural

A

a 2 *and, but*
абонемéнт 11 *season ticket*
áвгуст 11 *August*
áвиа 1 *airmail*
австри́йский 17 *Austrian*
автóбус 3 *bus*
автомáт 5 *vending machine*
автомоби́ль *m* 8 *car*
агá 11 *aha*
агéнтство 5 *agency*
администрáтор 3 *manager*
администрáция 5 *administration*
áдрес 10 *address*
академи́ческий 11 *academic*
актёр 20 *actor*
актри́са 10 *actress*
Алексáндр 7 *Alexander*
Алексáндра 7 *Alexandra*
Алексéй 7 *Alexei*
Алёша 7 *Alyosha (dim of* Алексéй)

аллó 7 *hello (on phone)*
Амéрика 5 *America*
америкáнец 7 *American m*
америкáнка 7 *American f*
америкáнский 7 *American adj*
англи́йский 7 *English adj*
англичáнин *pl* англичáне 7 *Englishman*
англичáнка 7 *Englishwoman*
Áнглия 5 *England*
анкéта 14 *form*
Áнна 2 *Anna*
Антóн 2 *Anton*
антропологи́я 15 *anthropology*
Áня 7 *Anya (dim of* Áнна)
аппарáт 1 *camera, apparatus*
аппети́т 18 *appetite*
апрéль *m* 11 *April*
аптéка 2 *chemist*
Арбáт 6 *Arbat (street in Moscow)*
áрмия 14 *army*
архитектýра 12 *architecture*
ассорти́ *indec* 9 *assortment*
áтом 1 *atom*
áтомный 14 *atomic*
аэропóрт 14 *airport*
Аэрофлóт 4 *Aeroflot*

Б

бáбушка 5 *old woman, grandmother*
багáж 14 *luggage*
балалáйка 8 *balalaika*
балéт 5 *ballet*
балкóн 4 *balcony*
баллáда 8 *ballad*
банк 3 *bank*
банкомáт 14 *cash machine*
бáня 11 *bath house*
бар 3 *bar*
бежáть/по- 10 *to run*
без + G 11 *without*
бейсбóл 16 *baseball*
бéлый 9 *white*
бельё 13 *bed-linen*
бензи́н 17 *petrol*
бесплáтно 20 *free (of charge)*
бефстрóганов 9 *beef Stroganoff*
библиотéка 12 *library*
библиотéчный 14 *library adj*
бизнесмéн 8 *businessman*
билéт 4 *ticket*
бифштéкс 5 *rissole, steak*
бланк 4 *form*
блины́ 9 *pancakes*
блюдо 9 *dish*
Бог 10 *God*

Бóже 10 *God (form of address)*
болéзнь *f* 18 *illness*
бóлен, больнá, больны́ 18 *ill*
болéть (боли́т) 18 *to hurt*
больни́ца 18 *hospital*
больнóй, больнáя 18 *patient*
бóльше 16 *bigger, more*
бóльше ничегó 18 *nothing else*
большóе спаси́бо 9 *thanks very much*
большóй 3 *big*
Большóй теáтр 3 *Bolshoi Theatre*
Бори́с 7 *Boris*
Бори́с Годунóв 12 *Boris Godunov (Russian tsar)*
борщ 9 *borshch*
Бóря 7 *Borya (dim of* Бори́с)
боя́рин *pl* боя́ре 12 *boyar*
брат *pl* брáтья 12 *brother*
бýдý, бýдешь ... 11 *I will, you will ...*
бýдь(те) 17 *be*
бульóн 3 *clear soup*
бýтсы 4 *football boots*
буты́лка 6 *bottle*
буфéт 3 *snack bar*
бы: хотéл бы 14 *would: I would like*
быть 12 *to be*
бюрó *indec* 3 *office*
бюрó обслýживания 6 *service bureau*

В

в (во) + P 2 *in*
в (во) + A 6 *into, to*
в котóром часý 19 *at what time*
вагóн 13 *carriage*
вагóн-ресторáн 13 *restaurant car*
валли́ец 7 *Welshman*
валли́йка 7 *Welsh woman*
валли́йский 7 *Welsh adj*
валю́та 14 *currency*
вам 8 *you (dative of* вы)
вáнная 11 *bathroom*
Вáня 7 *Vanya (dim of* Ивáн)
варéнье 11 *jam*
ваш, -а, -е, -и 2 *your*
век 12 *century*
вели́кий 12 *great*
великолéпный 15 *magnificent*
Великобритáния 16 *Great Britain*
велосипéд 17 *bicycle*
Верхоя́нск 8 *Verkhoyansk (town in Siberia)*
веснá 11 *spring*

вéсти 8 *news*
весь 9 *all*
ветчинá 9 *ham*
вéчер 5 *evening*
вечери́нка 20 *party*
вид 15 *type, kind*
видеокáмера 8 *camcorder*
ви́деть (я ви́жу)/у- 16 *to see*
ви́за 14 *visa*
ви́зовая анкéта 14 *visa form*
Ви́ктор 2 *Viktor*
ви́нный 16 *wine adj*
винó 1 *wine*
висéть 13 *to hang*
ви́ски *indec* 9 *whisky*
Ви́тя 7 *Vitya (dim of* Ви́ктор)
Вишнёвый сад 12 *The Cherry Orchard*
ви́шня 16 *cherry*
вкус 16 *taste*
вкýсный 7 *tasty*
Владивостóк 8 *Vladivostok*
Влади́мир 10 *Vladimir (town near Moscow)*
Влади́мир 2 *Vladimir (man's name)*
вмéсте 14 *together*
внe + G 15 *outside*
водá 2 *water*
води́тель *m* 6 *driver*
вóдка 2 *vodka*
возьмý 10 *(I) will take*
войнá 12 *war*
Войнá и мир 2 *War and Peace*
вокзáл (на вокзáле) 13 *station (main) (in the station)*
Вóлга 5 *Volga (river and car)*
Волгогрáд 8 *Volgograd*
волейбóл 15 *volleyball*
Волóдя 7 *Volodya (dim of* Влади́мир)
вон там 14 *over there*
восемнáдцать 6 *eighteen*
вóсемь 6 *eight*
восемьдесят 6 *eighty*
восемьсóт 6 *eight hundred*
воскресéние 11 *resurrection*
воскресéнье 11 *Sunday*
востóк (на востóке) 13 *east (in the east)*
восьмёрка 15 *eight*
восьмóй 11 *eighth*
вот 2 *here (is)*
врач 12 *doctor*
врéмя *n* 8 *time*
все 12 *everyone*
всё 14 *everything, all the time*
всегдá 3 *always*
Всегó дóброго/ хорóшего/ лýчшего! 17 *All the best*

встава́ть/встать 12 *to get up*
встре́ча 19 *meeting*
встреча́ться/встре́титься 17 *to meet (each other)*
вто́рник 11 *Tuesday*
второ́й 9 *second*
вуз 15 *higher educational institution*
вход 3 *entrance*
входи́ть/войти́ 5 *to go in*
вчера́ 12 *yesterday*
въезд 13 *entrance (vehicle)*
въездна́я ви́за 14 *entry visa*
вы 7 *you (formal)*
Вы не туда́ попа́ли 7 *wrong number*
Вы сейча́с выхо́дите? 6 *Are you getting off?*
вы́езд 13 *exit (vehicle)*
выезжа́ть/вы́ехать 13 *to go out (by vehicle)*
выздора́вливать/вы́здороветь 17 *to recover (health)*
выпи́сывать/вы́писать 18 *to write out*
высо́кий 18 *high; tall*
высо́тное зда́ние 20 *skyscraper*
вы́сший 15 *higher*
вы́ход 4 *exit*
выходи́ть/вы́йти 4 *to exit, go out (on foot)*
выходно́й день 11 *day off*

Г

газ 19 *gas*
газе́та 4 *newspaper*
газо́н 4 *lawn*
галере́я 13 *gallery*
Гали́на 7 *Galina*
гало́ши 11 *overshoes, galoshes*
Га́ля 7 *Galya (dim of Гали́на)*
га́мбургер 15 *hamburger*
Га́млет 5 *Hamlet*
гардеро́б 11 *cloakroom*
гармо́ния 15 *harmony*
где 2 *where*
Герма́ния 7 *Germany*
гимна́зия 15 *high school*
гита́ра 8 *guitar*
Ги́тлер 11 *Hitler*
гла́вный 10 *main*
глаз *pl* глаза́ 18 *eye (eyes)*
Гли́нка 18 *Glinka (Russian composer)*
говори́ть/сказа́ть 7 *to speak*
говори́ть/поговори́ть 19 *to have a talk*
говя́дина 9 *beef*
Го́голь *m* 10 *Gogol*
год (в про́шлом году́) 4 *year (last year)*
годовщи́на 17 *anniversary*
Голла́ндия 11 *Holland*
голова́ 18 *head*
го́нки 17 *race*
Гонко́нг 11 *Hong Kong*

Горбачёв 12 *Gorbachev*
горизо́нт 11 *horizon*
го́рло 18 *throat*
го́род 4 *town, city*
городско́й 14 *municipal, town adj*
горя́чий 17 *hot, warmest (greetings)*
гости́ная 19 *living room*
гости́ница 10 *hotel*
гость *m* (в гостя́х) 16 *visitor (visiting)*
госуда́рственный 11 *state adj*
госуда́рство 15 *state*
гото́в, -а, -ы 9 *ready*
гото́вить/пригото́вить 19 *to cook*
гра́дус 8 *degree*
граждани́н 14 *citizen*
гражда́нская война́ 12 *civil war*
грани́ца (за грани́цу) 17 *border (abroad)*
гриб 4 *mushroom*
грибно́й 9 *mushroom (adj)*
грипп 18 *flu*
гро́зный 12 *threatening, 'terrible'*
грузи́нский 9 *Georgian*
гуля́ть 8 *to walk*
ГУМ 3 *GUM*

Д

да 1 *yes*
Дава́й вы́пьем 19 *Let us drink*
Дава́йте на ты! 7 *Let's say 'ты'*
дава́ть (даю́, даёшь)/дать 16 *to give*
да́же 16 *even*
Да́йте, пожа́луйста ... 6 *Give (me) please*
далеко́ 3 *far*
Да́льний восто́к 13 *Far East (also of Russia)*
да́льше 16 *further*
да́ма 5 *lady*
Да́ма с соба́чкой 12 *The Lady with the Little Dog*
да́та 2 *date*
датча́нин 17 *Dane*
да́ча 11 *dacha, country cottage*
да́чник 13 да́ча *owner*
два 2 *two*
два́дцать 6 *twenty*
двена́дцать 6 *twelve*
две́ри закрыва́ются 6 *doors are closing*
дверь *f* 6 *door*
две́сти 6 *two hundred*
дво́е 14 *two*
дво́йка 15 *two*
двор 5 *courtyard*
дворе́ц 20 *palace*
двухко́мнатная кварти́ра 19 *two-roomed flat*

двухэта́жный дом 19 *two-storeyed building*
де́вочка 6 *girl (little)*
де́вушка 6 *girl (form of address in shop)*
девяно́сто 6 *ninety*
девятиэта́жный дом 19 *nine-storeyed building*
девя́тка 15 *nine*
девятна́дцать 6 *nineteen*
девя́тый 11 *ninth*
де́вять 6 *nine*
девятьсо́т 6 *nine hundred*
дежу́рная 18 *woman on duty (floor supervisor)*
декабри́ст 12 *Decembrist*
дека́брь *m* 11 *December*
деклара́ция 14 *declaration*
де́лать/с- (де́лать переса́дку) 6 *to do, make (to change trains)*
де́ло в том, что 16 *the fact is that*
де́ло вку́са 16 *matter of taste*
демонстра́ция 5 *demonstration*
день *m* 11 *day*
день рожде́ния 17 *birthday*
де́ньги *pl* 14 *money*
дере́вня 20 *village*
деся́тка 15 *ten*
деся́тый 11 *tenth*
де́сять 6 *ten*
де́ти 12 *children*
де́тский 14 *children's*
деше́вле 16 *cheaper*
дешёвый 16 *cheap*
джинто́ник 17 *gin and tonic*
дива́н 19 *settee*
ди́лер 8 *dealer*
Дина́мо 2 *Dynamo*
дина́мовец 7 *Dynamo player*
дире́ктор 20 *director*
диск 8 *disc*
дистрибью́тер 8 *distributor*
для + G 14 *for*
до + G 9 *until, before, up to*
до свида́ния 1 *goodbye*
до́брое у́тро 17 *good morning*
до́брый ве́чер 5 *good evening*
до́брый день 17 *good afternoon*
договори́лись 19 *agreed*
доезжа́ть/дое́хать до + G 13 *to get to*
дождь *m* (идёт дождь) 13 *rain (it is raining)*
док 8 *dock (maritime)*
до́ктор 18 *doctor*
до́лгий 17 *long (time)*
до́лжен, -жна́, -жны́ 18 *should*
до́ллар 15 *dollar*
дом 2 *house*
до́ма 2 *at home*
допла́та 19 *extra payment*
доро́га 17 *road*
дорого́й 10 *expensive*
доро́же 16 *more expensive*

досту́пный 17 *reasonably priced; affordable*
до́чка 14 *daughter*
драмати́ческий 15 *dramatic*
друг (*plural* друзья́) 19 *friend*
ду́мать 13 *to think*
душа́ 12 *soul*
Дя́дя Ва́ня 12 *Uncle Vanya*

Е

Евге́ний 7 *Eugene*
Евге́ния 7 *Eugenia*
Евро́па 17 *Europe*
его́ 14 *his*
еди́нство 17 *unity*
еди́ный биле́т 6 *season ticket*
её 14 *her*
е́здить 17 *to go (by vehicle)*
Екатери́на 12 *Catherine*
Еле́на 7 *Yelena, Helen*
Е́льцин 7 *Yeltsin*
е́сли 16 *if*
есть/съесть- 9 *to eat*
есть 6 *there is, are, (I) have*
е́хать/по- 13 *to go (by vehicle)*
ещё 13 *still, another*

Ж

жа́реный 9 *roast, fried*
жа́рко 8 *hot*
жела́ть 17 *to wish*
желе́зная доро́га 13 *railway*
жена́ 9 *wife*
же́нщина 5 *woman*
Же́ня 7 *Zhenya (dim of Евге́ний and Евге́ния)*
жёсткий 13 *hard, second-class (train)*
жето́н 6 *token (on underground)*
живо́т 18 *stomach*
Жигули́ 5 *Zhiguli (car)*
жизнь *f* 12 *life*
жило́й дом 20 *apartment block*
жира́ф 3 *giraffe*
жить 12 *to live*
жура́вль *m* 16 *crane*

З

за + A (За ва́ше здоро́вье!) 9 *for (Your health!)*
заболева́ть/заболе́ть 18 *to fall ill*
заведе́ние 15 *institution*
за́втра 3 *tomorrow*
за́втрак 9 *breakfast*
за́втракать/по- 9 *to have breakfast*
загора́ть 11 *to sunbathe*
Заго́рск 10 *Zagorsk (now Се́ргиев поса́д)*
заходи́ть/зайти́ 10 *call in*
зака́зывать/заказа́ть 18 *to order, book*
закры́т, -а, -ы 3 *closed*
закрыва́ть(ся)/закры́ть (ся)(закро́йте) 6 *to close (Close imperative)*
заку́ски 9 *hors d'oeuvre*
зал 13 *hall*

187

занима́ть/заня́ть 17 to occupy
занима́ться + I 15 to do, study, play
за́нят, -á, -ы 9 occupied
за́пад (на за́паде) 13 west (in the west)
заходи́ть/зайти́ (к+ D) 14 to call in (to see)
защи́тник 17 defender
звезда́ 11 star
звони́ть/по- 18 to ring
зда́ние 13 building
здесь 2 here
здоро́вый 17 healthy
здоро́вье 9 health
здра́вствуй(те) 1 hello
зелёный 14 green
Зени́т 3 Zenit (sports team)
зима́ 11 winter
знать 8 to know
зна́чит 10 it means
Золото́е кольцо́ 10 Golden Ring
зо́на 13 zone
зоопа́рк 2 zoo
зуб 18 tooth
зубно́й врач 18 dentist

И

и 2 and
Ива́н 2 Ivan
Ива́н гро́зный 12 Ivan the Terrible
игра́ть (в футбо́л) (на балала́йке) 8 to play (football) (the balalaika)
игру́шка 14 toy
идио́т 12 idiot
идти́/пойти́ 5 to go (on foot), be on (theatre, etc.)
из + G 9 from
изба́ 20 wooden house
изве́стия pl 4 news
изве́стный 12 famous
извеще́ние 14 declaration
извини́(те) 3 excuse me
ико́на 10 icon
иконоста́с 10 iconostasis
икра́ 9 caviar
и́ли 9 or
иллюстра́ция 10 illustration
и́мени 15 named after, in the name of
имени́ны 17 name day
и́мпортный 20 imported
и́мя n 7 first name
инве́стор 8 investor
и́ндекс 19 post code
иногда́ 16 sometimes
иностра́нный 14 foreign
институ́т 10 institute
интере́с 14 interest
интере́сный 12 interesting
Интури́ст 17 Intourist (travel company)
информа́ция 5 information
И́ра 7 Ira (dim of Ири́на)
Ири́на 7 Irina

Ирку́тск 8 Irkutsk (town in Siberia)
ирла́ндец 7 Irishman
Ирла́ндия 7 Ireland
ирла́ндка 7 Irish woman
ирла́ндский 7 Irish adj
Испа́ния 2 Spain
истори́ческий 14 historical
исто́рия 12 history, story
Ита́лия 7 Italy
италья́нский 20 Italian adj
их 14 their
ию́ль m 11 July
ию́нь m 11 June
йогу́рт 8 yoghurt

К

к + D 13 towards, to (see)
к сожале́нию 16 unfortunately
Кавка́з (на Кавка́зе) 2 Caucasus (in the Caucasus)
ка́ждый 11 each
ка́жется (мне ка́жется) 16 it seems (I think)
как 2 how, as, like
Как вас зову́т? 2 What's your name?
Как вы пожива́ете/ты пожива́ешь? 7 How are you?
Как дела́? 2 How are you?
Как мне прое́хать 6 How do I get to (by vehicle)
Как мне пройти́ 6 How do I get to (on foot)
Как по-ру́сски ...? 2 What's the Russian for ...?
Как тебя́/вас зову́т? 7 What is your name?
Како́е сего́дня число́? 11 What's the date today?
како́й 12 which (kind of)
Како́й сего́дня день? 11 What day is it?
Кана́да 2 Canada
кана́дец 7 Canadian m
кана́дка 7 Canadian f
кана́дский 7 Canadian adj
кана́л 8 channel, canal
кани́кулы 17 holidays (student)
капитали́зм 2 capitalism
карти́на 13 picture
карти́нная галере́я 13 art gallery
ка́рточка 14 card
карто́шка 9 potatoes
ка́сса 1 box office, cash desk
кассе́та 13 cassette
ката́ние на конька́х 3 skating
ката́ние на лы́жах 3 skiing
ката́ться на конька́х 11 to go skating
ката́ться на лы́жах 11 to go skiing

ката́ться на саня́х 11 to go tobogganing
кафе́ indec 3 cafe
кварти́ра 6 flat
квас 2 kvas
кефи́р 9 yoghurt
Ки́ев 2 Kiev
кило́ indec 2 kilo
киломе́тр 2 kilometre
кино́ indec 2 cinema
кинотеа́тр 20 cinema (building)
кио́ск 2 kiosk
Кипр 17 Cyprus
Кита́й 16 China
кита́йский 20 Chinese adj
класс 8 class
клие́нт 8 client
кли́мат 3 climate
клуб 3 club
кни́га 6 book
кни́жный магази́н 14 book shop
князь m 12 prince
когда́ 3 when
код 8 code
Ко́ка ко́ла 2 Coca-Cola
кокте́йль m 16 cocktail
колбаса́ 9 sausage (continental)
коле́но 18 knee
колле́дж 8 college
кольцева́я ли́ния 6 Circle Line
коме́та 1 comet
коми́ссия 14 commission
комме́рческий 15 commercial
коммуни́зм 2 communism
ко́мната 10 room
компа́кт-диск 13 compact disc
компо́стер 6 ticket machine
компью́тер 8 computer
кому́ (dative of кто) 19 who to
комфорта́бельный 14 comfortable
коне́ц 12 end
коне́чно 10 of course
коне́чный 19 last
консервато́рия 11 Conservatoire
конститу́ция 5 constitution
контролёр 6 inspector
конфедера́ция 5 confederation
концентра́ция 5 concentration
конце́рт 5 concert, concerto
конце́ртный зал 11 concert hall
конча́ть(ся)/ко́нчить(ся) 12 to end
конья́к 6 brandy
кооперати́в 19 co-operative
Копенга́ген 11 Copenhagen
коридо́р 8 corridor
ко́рпус 19 block
корреспонде́нт 13 correspondent
ко́смос 9 space

костю́м 3 suit, costume
котте́дж 8 cottage
ко́фе m indec 6 coffee
краб 20 crab
краси́вый 5 beautiful
Кра́сная пло́щадь 5 Red Square
Кра́сная стрела́ 13 Red Arrow
Краснода́р 8 Krasnodar (town in S. Russia)
кра́сный 5 red
креве́тки 9 prawns
креди́тная ка́рточка 14 credit card
Кремль m 3 Kremlin
крепостно́й 12 serf
кре́пость f 12 fortress
крестья́нин 12 peasant adj
крестья́нский 12 peasant
кри́кет 16 cricket
крокоди́л 2 crocodile
кроссво́рд 6 crossword
Крым (в Крыму́) 12 Crimea (in the Crimea)
ксе́рокс 8 photocopier
кто 1 who
куда́ 13 where (to)
купа́ться 11 to swim
купе́ indec 13 compartment
купе́йный 13 with compartments
купи́ть 12 buy perf of покупа́ть
кури́тельная ко́мната 4 smoking room
кури́ть 4 to smoke
ку́рица 9 chicken
куро́рт 17 resort
курс 15 course
ку́хня 9 kitchen, cuisine
ку́шать (Ку́шайте!) 9 to eat (colloq. Tuck in!)

Л

лаборато́рия 15 laboratory
ла́вра 10 monastery (large)
Ла́да 5 Lada (car)
ла́дно 16 OK
лапша́ 9 noodles
лежа́ть 11 to lie
лека́рство 18 medicine
ле́кция 5 lecture
Ле́на 7 Lena (dim of Еле́на)
Ле́нин 7 Lenin
Ленингра́д 12 Leningrad
лет gen pl of год 12 years
ле́то 11 summer
лётчик 14 pilot
Ли́за 2 Lisa
лимо́н 9 lemon
лимона́д 2 lemonade
ли́ния 6 line
литерату́рный 4 literary
литр 2 litre
лице́й 15 high school
лицо́ 18 face
ли́шний 12 superfluous, extra
ло́био 9 beans (Georgian)

лови́ть ры́бу 11 *to go fishing*
ло́жа 4 *box (in theatre)*
Локомоти́в 3 *Lokomotiv*
Ло́ндон 2 *London*
лосо́сь *m* 9 *salmon*
лу́чше 6 *better*
льго́ты 16 *concessions*
люби́мый 19 *favourite*
люби́ть 8 *to like, love*
любо́вь *f* 12 *love*
лю́ди *pl of* челове́к 14 *people*

М

Магада́н 8 *Magadan*
магази́н 11 *shop*
Мадри́д 2 *Madrid*
май 4 *May*
ма́ленький 14 *small*
ма́льчик 8 *boy*
малы́ш 8 *child*
ма́ма 1 *mother, mum*
ма́нго *indec* 8 *mango*
Мари́инский теа́тр 6
  Mariinsky Theatre
ма́рка 1 *stamp, model
  (of camera, etc.)*
Марс 2 *Mars*
март 11 *March*
маршру́тка 6 *minibus*
матрёшка 14 *nested dolls*
матч 5 *match (sports)*
маши́на 5 *car*
МГУ 4 *Moscow University*
Ме́дный вса́дник 12
  Bronze Horseman
медпу́нкт 18 *medical unit*
междунаро́дный 17
  international
ме́ньше 16 *smaller, less*
меню́ *indec* 3 *menu*
Меня́ зову́т ... 2 *My name is ...*
меня́ть (на + *A*) 19
  to exchange for
Мёртвые ду́ши 12
  Dead Souls
ме́сто 4 *place, seat*
ме́сяц 15 *month*
Метео́р 13 *hydrofoil (make of)*
метр 19 *metre*
метро́ *indec* 1 *underground*
миграцио́нная ка́рта 14
  migration card
Ми́ла 17 *Mila
  (dim of* Людми́ла)
милиционе́р 16 *policeman*
миллио́н 13 *million*
миллионе́р 8 *millionaire*
ми́лый 17 *dear*
ми́мо + *G* 19 *past*
минера́льная вода́ 9
  mineral water
министе́рство 15 *ministry*
ми́нус 6 *minus*
мину́та 8 *minute*
мир 17 *world*
мирово́й 12 *world*
мисс 9 *Miss*
ми́ссис *indec* 9 *Mrs*
ми́стер 9 *Mr*
Михаи́л 7 *Mikhail, Michael*

Ми́ша 7 *Misha (dim of* Михаи́л)
мне 8 *me (dative of* я)
Мне ... лет. 7 *I am ... years
  old*
мне, пожа́луйста, ... 9
  Can I please have ...
мно́го + *gen* 12 *many*
мобилиза́ция 5 *mobilisation*
мо́жет быть 16 *perhaps*
мо́жно 4 *possible*
Мо́жно на ты? 7 *Can I call
  you* ты?
мой, моя́, моё, мои́ 14 *my*
моли́ться 10 *to pray*
молоко́ 16 *milk*
монасты́рь *m* 10 *monastery,
  convent*
монго́льский 12 *Mongol*
мо́ре 12 *sea*
морж 11 *walrus*
моро́женое 9 *ice-cream*
Москва́ 1 *Moscow*
москви́ч 5 *Muscovite
  (and make of car)*
моско́вский 8 *Moscow adj*
моско́вское вре́мя 8
  Moscow time
мост 12 *bridge*
му́дрый 13 *wise*
муж 11 *husband*
мужчи́на 5 *man*
музе́й 10 *museum, art gallery*
му́зыка 8 *music*
мультфи́льм 8 *cartoon*
Му́рманск 8 *Murmansk*
Му́соргский 11 *Mussorgsky*
МХАТ 11 *Moscow Arts Theatre*
мы 8 *we*
мя́гкий 13 *soft*
мясно́й 9 *meat adj*
мя́со 9 *meat*

Н

на + *P* 2 *on*
на + *A* 6 *onto, for*
набира́ть/набра́ть 18 *to dial,
  amass*
на́до 10 *necessary*
надо́лго 19 *for a long time*
наза́д 12 *ago*
называ́ться/назва́ться 13
  to be called
нале́во 3 *to the left, on the
  left*
напи́ток 9 *drink*
напиши́те 6 *write*
напра́во 3 *to the right, on the
  right*
наприме́р 12 *for example*
напро́тив 6 *opposite*
наро́дный 17 *national*
наступа́ющий 17 *coming*
Ната́лья 7 *Natalya*
Ната́ша 7 *Natasha
  (dim of* Ната́лья)
натура́льный 9 *natural*
находи́ться 13 *to be situated*
национа́льность *f* 20
  nationality
национа́льный 16 *national*

нача́ло 12 *beginning*
начина́ть(ся)/нача́ть(ся)
  12 *to begin*
наш, -а, -е, -и 14 *our*
не 1 *not*
Не зна́ю. 7 *I don't know*
не пра́вда ли 17 *isn't this so?*
Не тот но́мер 7
  wrong number
не́бо 16 *sky*
Нева́ 12 *Neva
  (river in St Petersburg)*
Не́вский проспе́кт 3 *Nevsky
  Prospekt*
недалеко́ от 3 *not far from*
неде́ля 4 *week*
незави́симость *f* 17
  independence
незави́симый 8 *independent*
нельзя́ 4 *impossible*
не́мец 7 *German m*
неме́цкий 7 *German adj*
не́мка 7 *German f*
немно́жко 13 *little*
не́сколько 12 *several, a few*
нет 1 *no*
неудовлетвори́тельно
  15 *unsatisfactory*
ни́зкий 16 *low*
Ники́та 7 *Nikita*
никогда́ 16 *never*
Ни́на 2 *Nina*
ничего́ 2 *OK*
но 10 *but*
Но́вгород 19 *Novgorod*
Новосиби́рск 8 *Novosibirsk*
но́вости 8 *news*
но́вый 5 *new*
нога́ 18 *leg, foot*
но́мер 1 *number, hotel room*
нос 18 *nose*
носи́ть 11 *to wear*
ночь *f* 5 *night*
ноя́брь *m* 11 *November*
нра́вится (мне нра́вится)
  8 *like (I like)*
ну 16 *well*
ну́жно 10 *must, necessary*

О

о (об) 10 *about*
обе́д 9 *dinner*
обе́дать/по- 9 *to have dinner*
обме́н 14 *change (money)*
обме́нивать/обменя́ть 14
  to change (money)
обме́нный пункт 14
  exchange point
обнима́ть/обня́ть 17
  to embrace
ОВИ́Р 14 *OVIR (visa
  registration office)*
огуре́ц 9 *cucumber*
оде́жда 14 *clothes*
оди́н 1 *one*
оди́ннадцать 6 *eleven*
одна́жды 12 *once*
однокомнатная кварти́ра
  19 *one-room flat*

одноэта́жный дом 19
  *bungalow, single-storeyed
  house*
о́коло + *G* 13 *about, near*
октя́брь *m* 11 *October*
октя́брьский 12 *October*
О́льга 4 *Olga*
О́ля 7 *Olya (dim of* О́льга)
Омск 8 *Omsk*
он, она́, оно́, они́ 2 *he, she,
  it, they*
о́пера 1 *opera*
о́перная сту́дия 15 *opera
  studio*
опя́ть 18 *again*
организова́ть 17 *to organise*
орке́стр 1 *orchestra*
Оруже́йная пала́та 10
  Armoury museum
освобожде́ние 12 *liberation*
о́сень *f* 11 *autumn*
осетри́на 9 *sturgeon*
основа́ние 12 *foundation*
осно́вывать/основа́ть 13
  to found
остано́вка 6 *stop*
осторо́жно 6 *be careful*
от + *G* 13 *from*
отбыва́ть/отбы́ть 13 *to depart*
отбы́тие 13 *departure*
отде́л 14 *department*
о́тдых 17 *relaxation*
отдыха́ть/отдохну́ть 18
  to relax
оте́ц 7 *father*
оте́чественная война́ 12
  *'patriotic' war (on Russian
  territory)*
Вели́кая оте́чественная
  война́ 12 *Second World
  War*
оте́чество 17 *fatherland*
открыва́ть/откры́ть
  (откро́йте) 14 *to open
  (Open imperative)*
откры́т, -а, -ы 3 *open*
откры́тка 5 *(post)card*
отку́да 16 *where from*
отли́чный 15 *excellent*
отопле́ние 19 *heating*
отправи́тель *m* 19 *sender*
отправле́ние 13 *sending,
  departure*
отправля́ться/отпра́виться
  13 *to depart*
о́тпуск 17 *holiday*
отсю́да 13 *from here*
о́тчество 7 *patronymic*
отъе́зд 13 *departure
  (by vehicle)*
о́фис 3 *office*
о́чень 2 *very*
О́чень прия́тно! 7
  Pleased to meet you!
о́чередь *f* 14 *queue*
очко́ 17 *point*

П

Па́вел 7 *Pavel, Paul*
Па́влова 7 *Pavlova*

пальто́ *indec* 11 *overcoat*
па́па *m* 1 *father, dad*
Пари́ж 8 *Paris*
парк 1 *park*
парте́р 4 *stalls*
па́спорт 1 *passport*
пасса́ж 11 *shopping centre*
Па́сха 17 *Easter*
па́уза 18 *pause*
педагоги́ческий 15
  pedagogical
пе́йте (*from* пить) 18 *drink!*
пельме́ни 9 *pelmeny*
  (*Siberian dumplings*)
Пе́пси *indec* 2 *Pepsi*
пе́рвенство 17 *championship*
пе́рвый 7 *first*
передава́ть/переда́ть 17
  to pass on, broadcast
Передаём после́дние
  изве́стия 8 *Here is the*
  latest news
переда́ча 8 *broadcast*
Перезвони́те 7 *Ring again*
переса́дка 6 *change*
  (*trains etc.*)
переу́лок 19 *side street*
перехо́д 3 *crossing*
переходи́ть/перейти́ 5
  to cross
Петропа́вловская кре́пость
  12 *St Peter and Paul Fortress*
Пётр 7 *Pyotr*
Пётр вели́кий 12
  Peter the Great
Пе́тя 7 *Petya (dim of* Пётр*)*
пешко́м 13 *on foot*
пиани́ст 1 *pianist*
пивно́й 14 *beer adj*
пи́во 1 *beer*
пира́тство 5 *piracy*
писа́тель *m* 12 *writer*
писа́ть (пишу́, пи́шешь)/на-
  10 *to write*
пистоле́т 14 *pistol*
письмо́ 12 *letter*
пить/вы́- 9 *to drink*
пла́вленный сыр 16
  processed cheese
план 6 *map*
пласти́нка 13 *record*
плати́ть/за- 14 *to pay (for)*
платфо́рма 13 *platform*
плацка́ртный 13
  open carriage
плечо́ 18 *shoulder*
плов 9 *pillau*
пло́хо 2 *badly, ill*
плохо́й 16 *bad*
пло́щадь *f* 5 *square*
плюс 6 *plus*
по + *D* 8 *along, on, around*
по-англи́йски 8 *in English*
по-ва́шему 8 *in your opinion*
по-италья́нски 17 *in Italian*
по-мо́ему 8 *in my opinion*
по-ру́сски 2 *in Russian*
по-тво́ему 8 *in your opinion*
побе́да 17 *victory*
победи́тель *m* 17 *winner*

по́весть *f* 12 *story (long)*
пого́да 8 *weather*
пограни́чник 14 *border guard*
пода́рок 14 *gift*
Подмоско́вье 20
  Moscow region
поднима́ться/подня́ться
  14 *to go up, ascend*
подру́га 11 *friend (girl)*
подъе́зд 5 *entrance*
  (*to a block of flats*)
по́езд *pl* поезда́ 13 *train*
поезда́ да́льнего сле́дования
  13 *long distance trains*
пое́здка 17 *journey*
пое́хали 18 *let's go!*
пожа́луй 10 *perhaps,*
  very likely
пожа́луйста 1 *please*
по́здно 16 *late*
поздравля́ть/поздра́вить
  17 *to congratulate*
(поздравля́ю вас с + *I*)
  (*I congratulate you on*)
Познако́мьтесь 7
  Introduce yourselves!
Пойдём 4 *Let's go*
Покажи́те, пожа́луйста...
  6 *Show me please*
пока́зывать/показа́ть 10
  to show
покупа́ть/купи́ть 11 *to buy*
поку́пка 14 *a purchase*
поликли́ника 18 *health centre*
поли́тика 14 *politics*
полити́чный 14 *political*
полусухо́й 9 *medium dry*
получа́ть/получи́ть 17
  to get, obtain
полчаса́ 18 *half an hour*
по́лька 7 *Polish woman*
по́льский 7 *Polish adj*
По́льша 7 *Poland*
поля́к 7 *Polish man*
помидо́р 9 *tomato*
помога́ть/помо́чь 18 *to help*
поня́тно 18 *understood*
популя́рный 18 *popular*
пора́ 20 (*it is*) *time to*
порт 7 *port*
портве́йн 9 *port (wine)*
посеща́ть/посети́ть 14
  to visit
по́сле + *G* 11 *after*
посмотре́ть 10 *to look (perf*
  of смотре́ть*)*
посмо́трим 18 *Let's have a*
  look!
постро́енный 13 *built*
пото́м 6 *then, next*
потому́ что 8 *because*
почему́ 8 *why*
по́чта 5 *post-office*
пошли́ 18 *let's go!*
поэ́т 12 *poet*
поясно́е вре́мя 15 *zone time*
пра́вда 2 *truth, Is it true?*
правосла́вие 10
  Orthodox church

пра́здник 16 *holiday*
предлага́ть/предложи́ть
  19 *to propose*
премье́р-мини́стр 14
  prime minister
премье́ра 8 *premiere*
преподава́тель *m* 15
  teacher, lecturer m
преподава́тельница 15
  teacher, lecturer f
Преступле́ние и наказа́ние
  12 *Crime and Punishment*
при + *P* 13 *in the time of*
прибыва́ть/прибы́ть 13
  to arrive
прибы́тие 13 *arrival*
приве́т 7 *hello, greetings*
приглаше́ние 14 *invitation*
при́городные поезда́ 13
  local trains
прие́зд 13 *arrival (by vehicle)*
приезжа́ть/прие́хать 13
  to arrive (by vehicle)
прилета́ть/прилете́ть 14
  to arrive (by plane)
принима́ть/приня́ть 18 *to take*
при́нтер 8 *printer*
приро́да 12 *nature*
прихо́д 13 *arrival (on foot)*
приходи́ть/прийти́ 5
  to arrive, come (on foot)
прия́тно 2 *pleasant*
Прия́тного аппети́та! 9
  Have a good meal. 'Bon
  appetit'.
прия́тный 14 *pleasant*
проводни́к 13 *attendant*
  (*on train*)
програ́мма 4 *programme*
продава́ть/прода́ть 14 *to sell*
прода́жа 14 *sale*
проду́кты 15 *groceries*
проездно́й биле́т 6
  season ticket
промы́шленность *f* 15
  industry
про́пуск 4 *pass*
проспе́кт 3 (*main*) *road*
прости́те 3 *excuse me*
просту́да 18 *cold*
профе́ссия 20 *profession*
профе́ссор 15 *professor*
профитро́ли 9 *profiteroles*
проходи́ть/пройти́ 14
  to go through
про́шлый (в про́шлом году́)
  12 *last, past (last year)*
пря́мо 3 *straight ahead*
прямо́й 13 *straight*
прямо́й эфи́р 8 *live broadcast*
Псков 12 *Pskov*
Пу́лково 14 *Pulkovo*
  (*St Petersburg's airport*)
пункт 14 *point*
пункт назначе́ния 15
  destination
путёвка 17 *package tour*
путеше́ствовать 17 *to travel*
путч 12 *putsch*
путь *m* 17 *journey*

Пу́шкин 5 *Pushkin*
пье́са 8 *play*
пятёрка 15 *five*
пятиэта́жный дом 19
  five-storeyed building
пятна́дцать 6 *fifteen*
пя́тница 11 *Friday*
пя́тый 11 *fifth*
пять 5 *five*
пятьдеся́т 6 *fifty*
пятьсо́т 6 *five hundred*

Р

рабо́тать 11 *to work*
рад, ра́да 2 *pleased*
радиа́тор 8 *radiator*
ра́дио *indec* 8 *radio*
раз 6 *once, one (counting);*
  time, occasion
разбива́ть/разби́ть 12
  to smash
развлече́ние 17
  entertainment
разгово́р 14 *conversation*
райо́н 15 *district*
ра́но 13 *early*
ра́ньше 17 *previously, earlier*
распада́ться/распа́сться 12
  disintegrate
расписа́ние 13 *timetable*
расска́з 12 *story*
расска́зывать/рассказа́ть
  16 *to tell*
Ревизо́р 12 *The Government*
  Inspector
револю́ция 5 *revolution*
регистра́ция 14 *registration*
резиде́нция 14 *residence*
река́ 13 *river*
рекла́ма 8 *advert*
рекомендова́ть 20
  to recommend
рекордсме́нка 2 *record*
  holder f
ремо́нт 3 *repair*
репети́тор 15 *coach*
рестора́н 1 *restaurant*
рефо́рма 12 *reform*
реце́пт 18 *prescription*
реша́ть/реши́ть 19 *to decide*
рис 9 *rice*
роди́ть 12 *to give birth*
роди́ться 12 *to be born*
рожде́ние 17 *birth*
Рождество́ 17 *Christmas*
рок-му́зыка 11 *rock music*
роль *f* 10 *part, role*
рома́н 8 *novel*
росси́йский 2 *Russian*
Росси́я 4 *Russia*
рубль *m* 14 *rouble*
рука́ 18 *hand, arm*
ру́сская 7 *Russian woman*
ру́сский 2 *Russian adj,*
  Russian man
Русь *f* 12 *Rus'*
  (*early Russian state*)
ры́ба 9 *fish*
рыбно́й 9 *fish adj*

рынок (на рынке) 12 *market (in the market)*
рюмка 19 *glass (small)*
ряд 4 *row*

С

с + G 9 *from*
с + I 9 *with*
с приветом 10 *best wishes*
сад (детский сад) 15 *garden (kindergarten)*
садитесь 9 *sit down*
садиться/сесть 11 *to sit down, get on (bus etc)*
салат 9 *salad*
самовар 1 *samovar*
самолёт 4 *aeroplane*
самый 12 *most*
санитарный 11 *cleaning*
Санкт-Петербург 4 *St Petersburg*
сациви 9 *satsivi (Georgian dish)*
Саша 7 *Sasha (dim of Александр and Александра)*
Сбербанк 11 *Savings Bank*
свадьба 17 *wedding*
свинина 9 *pork*
свободно 9 *free*
свободный 13 *free*
сворачивать/свернуть 19 *to turn off*
сдавать/сдать 12 *to take/pass (exams)*
сдавать/сдать 19 *to rent out*
север (на севере) 13 *north (in the north)*
северный 20 *northern*
сегодня 3 *today*
седьмой 11 *seventh*
сейф 8 *safe*
сейчас 3 *now*
семёрка 15 *seven*
семинар 15 *seminar*
семнадцать 6 *seventeen*
семь 6 *seven*
семьдесят 6 *seventy*
семьсот 6 *seven hundred*
сентябрь m 11 *September*
Сергей 7 *Sergei*
Сергиев Посад 10 *Sergiyev Posad (formerly Загорск)*
сердце 18 *heart*
серебряный 17 *silver*
Серёжа 7 *Seryozha (dim of Сергей)*
серия 8 *part (in a series)*
сестра 2 *sister*
сидеть 16 *to sit*
симфония 11 *symphony*
синица 16 *tit, blue tit*
скажи(те) 7 *tell (me)*
сказать 17 *to say (perf of говорить)*
скидка 16 *discount*
сколько 6 *how many*
Сколько сейчас времени? 8 *What's the time?*

Сколько стоит ...? 6 *How much does ... cost?*
Сколько тебе/вам лет? 7 *How old are you?*
скоро 19 *soon*
скорый 13 *fast*
скучно 18 *bored*
славянский 12 *Slavonic*
Славянский базар 9 *(restaurant in Moscow)*
сладкий 9 *sweet*
сладкое 9 *dessert*
следующий 6 *next*
случаться/случиться 15 *happen*
слушать/по- 11 *to listen*
слушаю вас 7 *hello (on phone), yes (waiter in restaurant)*
смерть f 12 *death*
сметана 9 *smetana, sour cream*
смотреть/по- (телевизор) 8 *to watch (television)*
смотреть/по- на + A 10 *to look at*
Смутное время 12 *The Time of Troubles*
снег 13 *snow*
снимать/снять (сниму, снимешь) 19 *to let (flat); to take off (clothes)*
собор 10 *cathedral*
соборный 14 *cathedral adj*
Советский Союз 12 *Soviet Union*
совсем 17 *completely, quite*
согласен, -сна, -сны 16 *agree*
сок 9 *juice*
солдат 8 *soldier*
солёный 9 *salted*
солнце (на солнце) 11 *sun (in the sun)*
соль f 9 *salt*
сон 17 *sleep*
сорок 6 *forty*
соус 16 *sauce*
спальный вагон 13 *sleeping carriage*
спальня 19 *bedroom*
Спартак 3 *Spartak*
спасибо 1 *thank you*
спаситель m 10 *saviour*
спина 18 *back*
спокойной ночи 5 *good night*
спорт 1 *sport*
спортсмен 2 *sportsman*
спортсменка 2 *sportswoman*
среда 11 *Wednesday*
средний 11 *middle*
стадион 2 *stadium*
стакан 1 *glass*
Сталин 12 *Stalin*
Станиславский 10 *Stanislavsky*
станция 6 *station*
старше чем 13 *older than*
старый 5 *old*

стать (*perf of* становиться) 12 *to become*
стихи 12 *poetry*
сто 6 *hundred*
стоить 6 *to cost*
стойте 6 *stop*
стол 2 *table*
столица 7 *capital*
Столичная 9 *(type of vodka – from the capital)*
столовая 12 *canteen*
стоп 6 *stop*
стоять 13 *to stand*
страна 7 *country*
страховка 18 *insurance*
Стрельцы 12 *streltsy (Peter the Great's bodyguard)*
строить/по- 15 *to build*
студент 2 *student m*
студентка 2 *student f*
студенческий 15 *student adj*
студия 15 *studio*
стыдно 18 *ashamed*
суббота 11 *Saturday*
сувенир 14 *souvenir*
судак 9 *zander*
судьба 8 *fate*
Суздаль m 10 *Suzdal*
сумка 14 *bag*
суп 9 *soup*
супермаркет 8 *supermarket*
сухой 9 *dry*
счастливый 17 *happy*
счастье 17 *happiness, luck*
счёт 9 *bill*
США 7 *USA*
съесть 20 *to eat perf of есть*
сын 14 *son*
сыр 9 *cheese*

Т

таблетка 18 *tablet*
так 13 *so*
также 11 *also*
такой 20 *so, such*
такси indec 1 *taxi*
таксист 1 *taxi driver*
талон 6 *ticket (on bus), coupon*
там 6 *there*
Тамара 7 *Tamara*
таможенная декларация 14 *customs declaration*
таможенник 14 *customs official*
таможня 14 *customs*
танцевать/по- 12 *to dance*
тапочки 11 *slippers*
татарин 12 *Tartar*
Татарское иго 12 *Tartar Yoke*
Тверь f 12 *Tver'*
твой, твоя, твоё, твои 14 *your (familiar)*
творог 9 *curd cheese*
театр 1 *theatre*
тебе 8 *you (dative of ты)*
телевидение 8 *television*
телевизор 8 *television (set)*
телеграмма 4 *telegram*
тележка 14 *trolley*

телефон 3 *telephone*
телефон-автомат 5 *telephone box*
телефонный 14 *telephone adj*
температура 18 *temperature*
теннис 8 *tennis*
тепло 8 *warm*
теплоход 13 *motor vessel, boat*
тёплый 11 *warm*
термометр 18 *thermometer*
технологический 10 *technological*
типичный 14 *typical*
тише 16 *quieter*
то есть 16 *that is*
то же самое 16 *same*
товары pl 16 *goods*
тогда 19 *then (at that time)*
тоже 11 *also*
Толстой 2 *Tolstoy*
только 10 *only*
томатный 9 *tomato adj*
торговать 15 *to trade*
Торпедо 3 *Torpedo*
торт 9 *gateau*
тост 9 *toast*
трамвай 6 *tram*
транспорт 15 *transport*
третий 10 *third*
Третьяковская галерея 6 *Tretyakov Gallery*
трёхкомнатная квартира 19 *three room flat*
трёхэтажный 19 *three storeyed*
три 3 *three*
тридцать 6 *thirty*
триллер 8 *thriller*
тринадцать 6 *thirteen*
триста 6 *three hundred*
Троица 10 *Trinity*
Троице-Сериева лавра 10 *Trinity-St Sergius Monastery*
тройка 15 *three*
троллейбус 6 *trolley bus*
труд 17 *labour*
туалет 3 *toilet*
туда 14 *there (motion)*
турагентство 17 *travel agency*
турист 4 *tourist*
Турция 17 *Turkey*
туфли pl 19 *shoes*
ты 7 *you (informal)*
тысяча 6 *thousand*

У

У вас есть ...? 6 *Do you have ...?*
У меня/нас есть 6 *I/We have*
У тебя/вас есть 6 *You have*
уважаемый 17 *respected, dear*
уважение 17 *respect*
угол (в углу) 14 *corner (in the corner)*
удобный 19 *convenient*
удовлетворительно 15 *satisfactory*

уезжа́ть/уе́хать 13 *to leave (by vehicle)*
уже́ 16 *already*
у́жин 9 *supper*
у́жинать/по- 9 *to have supper*
узбе́к 3 *Uzbek man*
Узбекиста́н 3 *Uzbekistan*
Украи́на (на Украи́не) 2 *Ukraine (in Ukraine)*
украи́нец 7 *Ukrainian man*
украи́нка 7 *Ukrainian woman*
украи́нский 7 *Ukrainian adj*
у́лица 8 *street*
умира́ть/умере́ть (*past* у́мер, умерла́...) 12 *to die*
университе́т 2 *university*
университе́тский 14 *university adj*
усло́вные едини́цы 6 *conditional units*
Успе́нский собо́р 10 *Assumption Cathedral*
успе́х 17 *success*
у́тро 11 *morning*
у́хо (*pl* у́ши) 18 *ear (ears)*
ухо́д 13 *departure (on foot)*
уходи́ть/уйти́ 13 *to leave (on foot)*
уча́сток 11 *plot of land*
уче́бный 15 *educational*
учени́к 15 *pupil m*
учени́ца 15 *pupil f*
учи́тель *m* 15 *teacher m*
учи́тельница 15 *teacher f*
учи́ть/на- 12 *to teach*
учи́ться 12 *to study*
уша́нка 11 *hat with ear flaps*
Уэ́льс 7 *Wales*

Ф
факс 8 *fax*
фами́лия 7 *surname*
февра́ль *m* 11 *February*
федера́ция 7 *federation*
фи́зика 12 *physics*
филармо́ния 15 *philharmonic*
филе́ *indec* 9 *fillet*
фильм 3 *film*
фи́рма 8 *firm*
флот 4 *fleet*
форе́ль *f* 9 *trout*
фо́то *indec* 3 *photograph*
фотоаппара́т 7 *camera*

фотографи́ровать 4 *to photograph*
фотогра́фия 10 *photograph*
Фра́нция 7 *France*
францу́женка 7 *French woman*
францу́з 7 *French man*
францу́зский 7 *French adj*
фрукто́вый 9 *fruit adj*
фру́кты 9 *fruit*
фунт 14 *pound (money and weight)*
футбо́л 3 *football*
футболи́ст 7 *footballer*
футбо́льный 10 *football adj*

Х
Хва́тит! 19 *Enough!*
хлеб 9 *bread*
ходи́ть 4 *to go (on foot)*
хозя́ин 13 *host, landlord*
хозя́йка 8 *hostess, landlady*
хокке́й 3 *ice-hockey*
хо́лодно 8 *cold*
хоро́ший 7 *good*
хорошо́ 1 *fine, good*
хоте́ть 9 *to want*
храм 10 *church, cathedral*
Храм Васи́лия Блаже́нного 10 *St Basil's Cathedral*
Христо́с (Христо́с воскре́с!) 10 *Christ (Christ has risen!)*
Хрущёв 10 *Khrushchev*
худо́жественный 8 *artistic*
худо́жник 13 *artist*
ху́же 16 *worse*
хулига́нство 5 *hooliganism*

Ц
царь *m* 7 *tsar*
цветы́ 5 *flowers*
целова́ть/по- 17 *to kiss*
цена́ 16 *price*
центр 5 *centre*
центра́льный 11 *central*
це́рковь *f* 10 *church*
цирк 5 *circus*

Ч
чай 6 *tea*
ча́йка 5 *seagull*
Чайко́вский 5 *Tchaikovsky*
ча́ртер 8 *charter*
час 8 *hour, o'clock*
ча́сто 12 *often*

часы́ 10 *watch, clock*
ча́шка 6 *cup*
чек 6 *receipt (from* ка́сса)
челове́к 12 *person*
чем 16 *than*
чемода́н 14 *suitcase*
чемпио́н 17 *champion*
че́рез + *A* 14 *in (time), through, across*
Чёрное мо́ре 17 *Black Sea*
чёрный 9 *black*
четве́рг 11 *Thursday*
четвёрка 15 *four*
четвёртый 10 *fourth*
четы́ре 4 *four*
четы́реста 6 *four hundred*
четы́рнадцать 6 *fourteen*
Че́хов 5 *Chekhov*
Чингисха́н 12 *Genghis Khan*
чита́ть/про- 8 *to read*
что 1 *what*
что ли 16 *well*
что случи́лось 15 *What happened*
что-нибу́дь 18 *something*
чу́вствовать себя́ 18 *to feel*

Ш
шампа́нское 6 *champagne*
ша́пка 7 *hat*
ша́хматы 11 *chess*
шашлы́к 5 *kebab*
шашлы́чная 5 *kebab restaurant*
шве́дский стол 9 *smorgasbord, buffet*
Шекспи́р 11 *Shakespeare*
Шереме́тьево 14 *Sheremetevo (Moscow's international airport)*
шестёрка 15 *six*
шестна́дцатый 13 *sixteenth*
шестна́дцать 6 *sixteen*
шесто́й 15 *sixth*
шесть 6 *six*
шестьдеся́т 6 *sixty*
шестьсо́т 6 *six hundred*
ше́я 18 *neck*
Шине́ль *f* 12 *The Overcoat*
широ́кий 13 *wide*
шко́ла 15 *school*
шоп-тур 8 *shopping tour*
шоссе́ *indec* 5 *highway*
Шостако́вич 11 *Shostakovich*
шотла́ндец 7 *Scotsman*

Шотла́ндия 7 *Scotland*
шотла́ндка 7 *Scotswoman*
шотла́ндский 7 *Scottish adj*
шпро́ты 9 *sprats*

Щ
щи 5 *cabbage soup*
щипцы́ 5 *pincers*
щу́ка 9 *pike*

Э
Эдинбу́рг 16 *Edinburgh*
экза́мен 12 *examination*
экску́рсия 4 *excursion*
экспре́сс 4 *express*
элега́нтный 17 *elegant*
электри́чество 5 *electricity*
электри́чка 13 *local train*
эне́ргия 4 *energy*
Эрмита́ж 3 *Hermitage*
эскала́тор 6 *escalator*
эта́ж 5 *floor, storey*
этногра́фия 15 *ethnography*
э́то 1 *this, it*
э́тот, э́та. э́то, э́ти 8 *this*

Ю
ю́бка 16 *skirt*
юг (на ю́ге) 13 *south (in the south)*
ю́мор 3 *humour*
юмористи́ческий 12 *humorous*
ю́ный 17 *young*
Ю́ра 7 *Yura (dim of* Ю́рий)
Ю́рий 7 *Yuriy*
Ю́рий Долгору́кий 12 *Yuriy 'Longhand'*

Я
я 1 *I*
язы́к 10 *language, tongue*
яи́чница 9 *fried egg*
яйцо́ 9 *egg*
Я́лта 12 *Yalta*
янва́рь *m* 11 *January*
Япо́ния 16 *Japan*
япо́нский 7 *Japanese adj*
Яросла́вль *m* 13 *Yaroslavl*
я́рус 4 *'Gods' (theatre)*
я́сли *pl* 15 *nursery school*
Я́сная Поля́на 12 *(Tolstoy's estate)*

Acknowledgements

We thank Natalya Levina, of Moscow State Pedagogical University, and Sue Purcell, who has made many suggestions for improving the text.

Thanks also to Terry Doyle for his brilliantly innovative TV series, to Alan Wilding for producing the original audio recordings, and to the many people who helped with the previous two editions of the book. We are especially grateful to Julia Bivon and Jo Mullis for their patience and help.